GW01458260

CAMBRIDGE ENGLISH for schools

Teacher's Book Two

ANDREW LITTLEJOHN & DIANA HICKS

CAMBRIDGE
UNIVERSITY PRESS

PUBLISHED BY THE PRESS SYNDICATE OF THE UNIVERSITY OF CAMBRIDGE
The Pitt Building, Trumpington Street, Cambridge, United Kingdom

CAMBRIDGE UNIVERSITY PRESS
The Edinburgh Building, Cambridge CB2 2RU, UK
40 West 20th Street, New York, NY 10011–4211, USA
10 Stamford Road, Oakleigh, VIC 3166, Australia
Ruiz de Alarcón 13, 28014 Madrid, Spain
Dock House, The Waterfront, Cape Town 8001, South Africa

http://www.cambridge.org

© Cambridge University Press 1998

First published 1996
Fifth printing 2001

Printed in the United Kingdom at the University Press, Cambridge

ISBN 0 521 42178 0 Teacher's Book
ISBN 0 521 42170 5 Student's Book
ISBN 0 521 42174 8 Workbook
ISBN 0 521 42182 9 Class Cassette Set
ISBN 0 521 42131 4 Workbook Cassette

Copyright
The pages in this book marked 'Language worksheets, © Cambridge
University Press 1996, Photocopiable', or 'Say it clearly! worksheets,
© Cambridge University Press 1996, Photocopiable' may be photocopied
free of charge for classroom use by the purchasing individual or institution.
This permission to copy does not extend to branches or additional schools of
an institution. All other copying is subject to permission from the publisher.

Contents

Map of *Cambridge English for Schools 2*

Introduction

Who is the course for?

Cambridge English for Schools (*CES*) is a four-level course aimed at young students. Level 2 is for students who have done approximately one year of English before, or who have used *CES* Level 1.

For what type of teaching situations is it intended?

CES has been designed with a variety of possible situations in mind – from small classes with flexible furniture arrangements to fairly large classes with furniture fixed to the ground, from schools with considerable resources to schools with limited funds. The realities of many classes – with learners of varying abilities and varying levels of motivation and cooperation – have been given serious consideration and have shaped the approach and philosophy of the course (see *Rationale*, page 7).

What does it aim to do?

CES contains four different syllabuses.

1 At the centre of the course is the *language syllabus*. Through it, students develop their knowledge of English and their abilities to use English in various ways.

2 Complementing this, the course has an *education syllabus*. The materials aim to broaden the students' knowledge of the world and to build on what they are learning in other areas of their school life. Topics presented in *CES*, therefore, contain *curriculum links* with History, Science, Geography and so on. The materials also aim to develop *cross-curriculum* attitudes and abilities, such as working independently, caring for the environment, working with others and so on. In addition, the materials focus on *cross-cultural* topics, aiming to develop the students' knowledge of English-speaking societies and, through them, learn about their own society.

3 At the same time, a *learner involvement syllabus* aims to help the learners to take more responsibility for their own learning and to feel that their classes are 'their own'.

4 In addition to these aims for the learners, *CES* also aims to offer *support for teachers* in a number of ways:

- Detailed, practical suggestions in an easy-to-use *A to Z of methodology*. (See page 111.)
- Easy-to-use Unit notes. (See page 22.)
- Additional Unit notes on teaching classes with mixed abilities. (See any *Topic* or *Language focus* Unit.)
- Photocopiable *Language* and *Say it clearly!* worksheets. (See page 156.)
- Advice on how the course may be lengthened or shortened. (See page 17.)
- Suggestions for investigating classroom language learning. (See any *Topic* or *Language focus* Unit.)
- A list of useful classroom phrases. (See page 175.)

How long does the course take?

Each level (except the Starter) of *CES* is intended for approximately 80–100 hours of classroom work. However, the course has a flexible design enabling it to be made either shorter or longer. (See pages 17–18, for more details.)

What does the course consist of?

Level 2 has six components:

A Student's Book	A Teacher's Book
A Workbook	A Class Cassette Set
A Workbook Cassette	A Classroom Video

See *CES 2 at a glance*, page 13, for more details of each component.

This Teacher's Book contains:

- A detailed rationale for the course. (See page 7.)
- *CES 2 at a glance*: a visual overview of the course. (See page 13.)
- Some introductory notes on using the course. (See page 17.)
- A special note on 'A Parcel of English'. (See page 19.)
- Guidance on using the Units and planning lessons. (See page 22 onwards.)
- An A–Z of practical suggestions for teaching. (See page 111.)
- Supplementary photocopiable *Language* and *Say it clearly!* worksheets. (See page 156.)

Please turn to the section which interests you most!

Rationale

Summary

Cambridge English for Schools has been based on a reconsideration of the possibilities of English language teaching with secondary age students and the part that teaching materials can play. It offers a new approach in which wider educational goals, student involvement, and support for teachers combine to provide a significant step forward in English language teaching. This introduction describes the *aims*, *syllabus*, and *methodology* of the course and the role of evaluation.

English, language learning and education

For many teachers, the teaching of young adolescents poses some of the greatest and most rewarding challenges. For the students, a new school, new circles of friends, new interests and new experiences can all combine to make the period both exciting and demanding. It is also a time when the basis of their approach to learning, perhaps for the rest of their lives, is formed. This is especially true in the learning of foreign languages, where their first experiences define, for them, what language learning is all about and if it is something at which they can succeed.

In many classrooms all over the world, the initial experience of learning English is one of tremendous energy and imagination, in which the students feel that a whole new world is opening up for them as they learn to express themselves in another language. It is, however, also a sad fact that for other students it is sometimes a time of failure and disappointment in which they gradually feel left behind, often resorting to misbehaviour in the classroom and a gradual rejection of the work that the teacher is doing for them. It is thus important for everybody involved in teaching adolescents to try to determine the routes to success. In the pages which follow in this introduction, we have set out what we believe in our experience is the basis for success in teaching and learning English and the basis on which *Cambridge English for Schools* is built. We will describe this under four main headings:

1 **Aims**, which describes the purposes of the course.
2 **Syllabus**, which describes what the students will be learning about.
3 **Methodology**, which describes the types of activities included.
4 **Evaluation**, which describes how learning and learning activities will be assessed.

1 AIMS

Summary

The main aims of *CES* are:
- to develop the students' abilities to use and understand English.
- to broaden the students' understanding and knowledge of the world.
- to involve the students and to develop their abilities to manage their own learning.
- to support teachers in developing their own teaching abilities and their own understanding of language learning.

1.1 Learning English and learning about the world

At the centre of the course is the aim of developing the students' abilities to use and understand English. For the vast majority of students, however, whether of secondary or adult age, language itself *is simply not interesting enough* to command their continual attention. Many courses have thus drawn on what are seen as exciting teenage topics (pop music, fashion, discos, fast food and so on) in order to try to motivate the students. It is our view, however, that there is a much greater potential for language teaching. For secondary age students, this period in their lives is one when they have a great hunger for knowledge, want to learn about the world and want to learn to be able to do different things for themselves. As a subject without a clearly defined 'body of knowledge' (apart from grammar, words, etc.), learning English thus presents a unique opportunity to meet this eagerness to learn by offering both a broader *educational* approach to teaching the language and a rich variety of topics from which the students can learn. It is precisely this which *CES* aims to provide.

Example: The *Topic* Units and the Themes in the Student's Book.

1.2 Student involvement

One of the keys to successful learning, however, is *involvement*. Whilst interesting topics and richer, meaningful content are very important, the vital element in learning anything is that the students feel that the learning is *theirs*, and that they feel they are a part of what goes on in the classroom. Without this, it is very difficult for the students to sustain any motivation they may have or which the teacher or course materials may try to bring. All too often, we see the results of a lack of involvement: bored, seemingly tired students, some of whom resort to misbehaviour and make teaching an uphill struggle. In *Cambridge English for Schools*, we have thus given careful thought to ways of involving the students. Throughout the course, there are points at which they can make decisions, think about what they have just done, and gradually take more responsibility for their own learning.

Examples: Unit 3, Exs. 5 and 8; Unit 4, Ex. 5; Unit 5, Ex. 6; Supplementary Unit B; Workbook Units 6, 11, 16, 21, 26 and 31.

1.3 Support for teachers

English language teaching, however, offers opportunities not only for the students to learn, but for teachers to develop their own teaching. Through the course, therefore, we aim to provide both clear guidance in using the materials and support in understanding and thinking about some key areas in language teaching. Our purpose in doing this is to assist teachers in understanding why particular ways of working in *their* classes appear to succeed or fail and to thus make their teaching a more rewarding experience for both the students and themselves.

Examples: The *A to Z of methodology*; notes on mixed-ability classes in the *Topic* and *Language focus* Units; the 'overview' sections before each Theme and Unit, and the subsequent detailed Teaching Notes.

---

2 SYLLABUS

Summary

CES contains four principal syllabuses: i) a language syllabus, mainly of structure, vocabulary, reading and writing; ii) an educational syllabus of educational topics and abilities; iii) a learner-involvement syllabus which requires students to make decisions about learning; iv) a teacher support syllabus which provides ideas for teaching and for classroom research.

From the outline of the aims of the course, one can see that four different syllabuses underlie the structure of *CES*. They are: i) a language development syllabus; ii) an educational syllabus; iii) a learner involvement syllabus; and iv) a teacher support syllabus.

2.1 The language development syllabus

At the heart of the language syllabus in *CES* lies a **structural progression**. The course moves, in the familiar way, from the present tenses, through to the past tenses, future tenses and so on. All of this is made explicit to the students in the *Language focus* Units, with students either being presented with explanations or being encouraged to work out their own rules for forming and using language. We have chosen to use a structural language syllabus for a number of reasons. In our view, it provides a systematic 'mapping out' which enables students to generate an infinite number of new utterances and eventually use language to express what they wish to say. It is also a familiar means of organising language which allows teachers and learners either to come to

CES from other courses or to go on to other work. The language syllabus, however, is not a narrow 'step by step' one. Our aim is not that students master each new structure the first time it appears but that they *notice* it, since the course returns to each language point several times with numerous opportunities to learn.

At the same time, however, the course stresses **vocabulary development** right from the start, continually recycling vocabulary items through new texts, exercises and record pages. At the end of each *Topic* Unit, the students can draw together the vocabulary they have learnt and record the meanings on a *Language Record* page. In addition, the Workbook contains further work on vocabulary and a *picture dictionary*.

In terms of the '**four skills**', *CES* draws on each of the skills in as natural a way as possible. Writing, for example, may be used as a means of preparing for a spoken task; listening and reading as a basis for sharing reactions and ideas. Writing, in particular, features quite a lot in *CES* since, in our experience, used appropriately, writing can give students the chance to plan, to reflect and to ask for help. Spoken, 'social English', however is also highlighted in special '*Out and about*' sections and drawn together in a short phrase book section in the *Language Records*.

In Level 1 of the course, listening is mainly treated as a means of consolidating language already presented to students, rather than as 'listening comprehension' in the traditional sense. We have approached it in this way as, in our experience, the circumstances under which many teachers teach (with classroom and outside noise, and limited audio facilities) frequently make listening work very difficult to undertake when students are not familiar with the basic sounds of English. In Level 2, however, listening work is presented for comprehension. We have, however, avoided the traditional listening text followed by comprehension questions, since we wish to encourage more engagement with the text that the students hear. Normally, therefore, students are asked to formulate their own ideas before they listen, and then to compare them with what they hear on the recording. This, in our experience, promotes a much more active and personalised approach to listening.

Examples: The *Map of CES 2*, pages 4–5; *Language Record* pages 49 and 55; *Out and about*, page 53; Workbook page 23; Listening work, Unit 8, Ex. 7.

2.2 The educational syllabus

In addition to the language aims of the course, *CES* also aims to make a direct contribution to the students' general educational development. The course therefore also has an *educational syllabus* which has three main aspects: *curriculum links* with other subject areas; *cross curriculum* abilities and attitudes and *cross-cultural* topics.

In terms of *curriculum links*, the topics in *CES* have direct connections with the work the students will do in other school subjects, but in a fresh, innovative way. These links mean that students are given the opportunity to broaden their knowledge and understanding of the world and to contribute what they already know. There is therefore a natural, real reason for communicating and for working with the language.

Examples: Topics in Themes A–F in the Student's Book.

In connection with *cross-curriculum* abilities and attitudes, the course contributes in a number of different ways. Through the presentation of different kinds of texts (such as graphs, maps, diagrams, poems and newspaper style articles) the students become familiar with understanding and presenting ideas in a variety of modes. The course also shows students how they can gather, develop and organise their own ideas through, for example, 'brainstorming' aspects of a topic. The ability to work independently is supported through practical advice on how they can help themselves learn. Broader concerns, such as health education, the rainforest, and the global economy, also feature as topics for language work.

Examples: Text presentation: Unit 3, Ex. 4; Unit 10, Ex. 4; Unit 28, Ex. 4. Brainstorming: Unit 5, Ex. 1; Unit 10, Ex. 1; Unit 18, Ex. 1. 'Help yourself' Units: Workbook Units 6, 11, 16, 21, 26, 31. Broader issues: Units 3, 8 and 23.

The third element in the educational syllabus is *cross-cultural* awareness. The *Culture matters* Units in the Student's Book aim to develop the students' understanding of life in Britain and the United States and how this compares with their own country. In addition, numerous tasks within other Units ask the students to compare across cultures, for example, in connection with school life and climate. A further feature is the *Parcel of English* scheme, which is intended to bring students in different parts of the world into contact with each other.

Examples: *Culture matters*: Units 6, 11, 16, 21, 26 and 31; Unit 18, Exs. 3 and 5. A *Parcel of English*: Supplementary Unit A and Notes on page 19.

2.3 The learner involvement syllabus

In *CES*, the direct, personal involvement of the learners plays a very important part. An important element of the course is the involvement of the students in **decisions** over *what* they will work on and *how* they will work. The intention with this, as explained earlier, is to give the students a greater sense of ownership in language learning, such that they feel that what they learn is 'theirs'.

Recognising, however, that students may not have experience in thinking about such things, the course approaches this very gradually. In each of the Topic Units, two *Decide* tasks ask the students to make a choice over what they will do next. The first *Decide* task provides a choice of three exercises. The second *Decide* task provides two exercises and the option for the students themselves to decide what they would like to do, perhaps making use of the *Ideas list* at the back of the book. In each of the *Language focus* Units, a *Do it yourself!* task gives the students a chance to decide and plan what they would like to do as part of a later lesson. (See *Do it yourself* in the *A to Z of methodology*.) Students also become involved in making their own exercises (and in building up an *Exercise Box* for the class) and, later in devising their own tests. In addition, evaluation tasks recur at various points in the course, asking the students to consider what they did in particular tasks (see section 4 below).

A further aspect of the course is that topics have been chosen which give the possibility for students to contribute their own **personal ideas** and **experience**. The 'cross-curriculum' aspect of this is important, as we have said, but further examples are in relation to family life, personal memories, writing poems, and so on.

Examples: Unit 3, Exs. 5 and 8; Unit 4, Ex. 5; Unit 5, Ex. 6; Supplementary Unit B.

2.4 The teacher support syllabus

As was mentioned in 1.3 above, an important aim of the course is to support teachers in working with a particular class and in developing their teaching abilities. To a certain extent, any coursebook will help teachers learn more about teaching by introducing them to types of exercises and ways of approaching classroom work which they have perhaps not met before. In *CES*, however, this is taken one step further.

At the back of this Teacher's Book, there is an *A to Z of methodology*, outlining some of the main aspects of teaching and giving practical classroom suggestions. Cross references to this *A to Z* are given in the Teaching Notes for each Unit, but we hope that teachers will consult the *A to Z* at their leisure as a means of refreshing or developing their knowledge of teaching. In addition, at the beginning of the *Language focus* Units, there are some questions to stimulate your thinking about aspects of teaching. These are followed up in the relevant *A to Z* entry with notes on *Researching the classroom*.

Additional support is also given for teaching classes of mixed-ability students. In the Teaching Notes for the *Topic* and *Language focus* Units, there are ideas for how to give more support for particular exercises or how to make them more demanding. For students who require further practice, there are supplementary worksheets which you may photocopy.

Examples: The *A to Z of methodology*, pages 111–140; mixed-ability notes, Unit 8, Ex. 3; '*What happened with Units …?*', Unit 3; *Researching the classroom*, Unit 4; photocopiable worksheets, pages 157–174.

3 METHODOLOGY

Summary

Tasks in *CES* aim to encourage the students to use English creatively, not only reproductively, and to contribute their own ideas and experiences. The instructions in the Student's Book provide clear indications for both the teacher and the students. In general, 'larger' tasks are included in order to give the students more 'space' and more control over their work. Tasks allow students with different levels of ability to work on the same topic and additional support is also provided for classes with mixed abilities. Initially, an active role for the mother tongue is also suggested.

A number of aspects of *CES* come under the general heading of 'methodology' which we will briefly describe here. They are: i) a creative approach to language learning; ii) personalisation; iii) transparency; iv) learning centredness; v) catering for classes with mixed abilities; and vi) use of the mother tongue.

It would probably be fair to say that language teaching generally emphasises what we would call '*reproductive*' approaches to language learning. These include various forms of repetition (choral, substitution, reading aloud, and so on) and other tasks where students are expected to *reproduce* the information and language presented to them (for example, traditional comprehension questions) as in the traditional 'Presentation–Practice–Production' model of teaching. There is no doubt reproductive tasks are an important part of classroom language learning. We believe, however, that if we want students to develop the ability to express what they wish to say in English, then we also need to provide tasks which encourage the students to use the language **creatively** and not simply reproductively. This means that classroom tasks need to provide opportunities for the students to contribute their

own ideas, share experiences and reactions. In *CES*, therefore, we have included tasks throughout the course which aim to do this, for example, by encouraging them to give their personal opinions or ideas about something, to write short texts for other students to read, and to design their own practice exercises, without following a tightly controlled model.

Examples: *Activity* Units: 5, 10, 15, 20, 25, 30.

Creativity as an aspect of methodology is also closely related to personalisation. By **personalisation** we mean the process of bringing about 'ownership' which we referred to earlier. This happens in two main ways in *CES*. Firstly, wherever possible, students are asked to contribute their own ideas and content (for example, accounts of personal experiences, photos, and so on). Secondly, as the course progresses, the students are brought further and further into making decisions about their learning, within the clear constraints laid down by the teacher and the coursebook. This, as we mentioned earlier, includes the various 'evaluation' tasks in the course which ask the students to think back over what they have done and how they can improve it next time, and the tasks where the students have to decide what they wish to do next.

Examples: Unit 1, Ex. 1; Unit 3, Ex. 1; Unit 4, Ex. 5; Unit 7, Exs. 1, 6 and 7.

A third aspect of the course in terms of methodology is what we call **transparency**. This means that it should be clear to everyone (teacher and students) what the materials are suggesting. This, we believe, is particularly important for the students, since greater learner involvement depends on understanding what is going on in the classroom. In addition, experience tells us that it is difficult – if not impossible – for many students to maintain 100% concentration 100% of the time. For this reason, the Student's Book includes full instructions for each task, such that both the teacher and the students have the same information. Initially, of course, the students' language level may mean that they are not always able to benefit from this, but as the course develops we hope that this enables them to have a clearer understanding of what they are doing and why.

Examples: the instructions for tasks in the Student's Book.

In general, *CES* includes few of the conventional 'paced' oral activities, such as drills and choral repetition, that one often finds in course materials. In contrast, the tasks in the course centre on '**learning**' (rather than 'teaching'). In addition, they are generally 'larger', in which, for example, students have to write something, read something or share ideas with a neighbour, before being called upon to produce language to the whole class. Our purpose in designing such tasks is to allow students more time to think, plan and ask questions, and thus approach language learning in a more relaxed fashion.

Examples: Unit 1, Ex. 1; Unit 28, Ex. 1; and the *Activity* Units.

Larger tasks also make it easier for students to respond at their own level of ability. In addition, however, *CES* includes further support for classes with **mixed levels of ability**. Some students may require further practice exercises than the ones in the Student's Book and Workbook, and for these students additional **Supplementary language worksheets** are given at the back of this Teacher's Book. We recognise, however, that using one particular unit of materials in the same way with an entire class may not always be appropriate and for this reason, the Teaching Notes for the *Topic* and *Language focus* Units include suggestions for how more support can be given to students or how the tasks can be made more

demanding. The *Time to spare?* and the *Revision Box* sections also offer further support for students.

Examples: Language worksheets, pages 157–171; Teaching Notes, Units 3 and 4; *Time to spare?* Units 3 and 4; *Revision Box*, Unit 4.

A final aspect of methodology is the **use of mother tongue**. In *CES* the mother tongue plays an important role in two main ways. Firstly, a number of tasks, particularly in the *Language focus* Units, ask the students to think about the structure of their language and to compare it with English. Secondly, as the Teaching Notes make clear, we anticipate that some of the more complex planning tasks and evaluation stages may take place in the mother tongue, particularly in the early stages of the course. There are a number of reasons why we have designed the course in this way.

When people are learning they always try to make sense of 'what is new' by comparing it with what they already know. This means that, whatever the teacher or the coursebook says, students *will* translate the foreign language into their own language. It is therefore best if this is done explicitly so that misconceptions can be avoided. In addition, we believe that many students feel completely powerless and lost in language classes, especially in the initial stages, and thus the use of the mother tongue can ease them into language learning. Use of the mother tongue also gives the students an opportunity to participate more fully in making decisions over their own learning.

Examples: Unit 4, Ex. 3.1; Unit 9, Exs. 4.1 and Ex. 6; the *Language Record* pages after the *Topic* Units.

4 EVALUATION

Summary

Evaluation of the students' learning takes the form of tests in the Workbook and student-produced tests. Evaluation also focuses on how the students are working, in the form of brief discussion tasks set out in the Student's Book.

As we have already suggested, evaluation plays an important part in *CES*. There are two main ways in which it does so: evaluation of how much language the students have learnt, and evaluation of the actual process of learning.

In terms of **evaluation of language**, the Student's Book includes an initial test in Unit 2 and a number of self-tests in the Workbook. The Student's Book also includes some simple tests which are intended as examples for students to write their own tests. We have included student-

designed tests since we feel that self-assessment is a vital part of successful language learning. Too often students view tests as a very negative experience in which someone else makes judgements over them. Making tests available to the students and involving them in designing their own class tests is intended to reduce this fear and encourage them to view tests as a potentially useful part of their learning.

Examples: Student's Book Units 12, 22 and 32; Workbook Units 7, 17 and 27.

In terms of **evaluation** of *how* the students are learning, the course includes tasks (particularly at the end of a Theme and a large *Activity*) which ask the students to think about how well they worked, the problems they had, and how they might do it better next time. As suggested earlier, the purpose of doing this is to raise the students' awareness of how they are learning and to make them feel more involved in their language course and able to participate in making decisions over both what they need and would like to do.

Examples: the last exercises in the *Revision and evaluation* Units and in *Activity* Units.

We hope that you enjoy using *Cambridge English for Schools* and that both you and your students find it a rewarding course to work with. We welcome any comments on the materials – whether negative or positive. Please write to us:

Andrew Littlejohn and Diana Hicks
c/o English Language Teaching
Cambridge University Press
The Edinburgh Building
Shaftesbury Road
Cambridge CB2 2RU
England

You can also send a fax to: ++44 1223 325984

Or you can send an e-mail message to: Andrew Littlejohn and Diana Hicks: aldh@cup.cam.ac.uk

There is also a World Wide Web Site where you can get continuing information on the course:

http://www.uk.cambridge.org/elt/ces

Cambridge English for Schools 2 at a glance

THE STUDENT'S BOOK

The course contains six Themes.

THEME A	THEME B	THEME C	THEME D	THEME E	THEME F
A good life	Life on Earth	Back in time	Below the clouds	Across borders	Energy in our lives

Each Theme contains five Units, with approximately the following number of lessons:

TOPIC UNIT	LANGUAGE FOCUS UNIT	ACTIVITY	CULTURE MATTERS	REVISION
3 lessons	2–3 lessons	1 lesson	1 lesson in total	1–2 lessons

In each Theme, there is a TOPIC Unit which focuses on different aspects of the Theme. Students read, write, listen and talk about the topic. There is particular emphasis on vocabulary.

There are notes which show you the topic in the Unit and its links with other school subjects.

3 Topic Sports for everybody

Sports and health; curriculum links with Sports and Health Education

1 Sports and you

Discuss these questions with your class.

Do you do any sports?
How often do you do them?
Which sports do you like doing?

Discussion
Extra practice • WB Ex. 3

Following each *Topic* Unit, there is a LANGUAGE FOCUS Unit. Here the students focus on grammar, functions, social English and classroom language.

3 'Quickly', 'suddenly' and 'quietly'

3.1 What do you say?

How do you say these sentences in your language?

4 Out and about with English

4.1 What can you say?

What can you say in your English lesson in these sit

a You don't understand a word.   c You want a dicti
b You can't hear.   d You don't know

4.2 In class

Listen. Alison and Will are in a Mathematics l

4 Language focus

Verb + -ing: adverbs; classroom phrases

1 Susan Spencer, the swimmer

Reading and listening
Extra practice • WB Ex. 1

Peter Black talked to Susan Spencer about her training.
Read (and listen) to what she said.

Interview with Susan Spencer

At the end of the *Topic* and *Language focus* Units there is a LANGUAGE RECORD. Here, the students can note down the meanings of the words and phrases they have learned and complete some examples of the grammar points.

Language Record

Write the meaning of the words in your language.

ample
imming makes you very flexible.
rts are good for your health.
an does her homework at school.
w many sports do you do?
w much energy do you need for football?
tball is a very popular sport.
an's life is probably different from your life.
football, you run quickly.

Language Record

Your own phrase book! CLASSROOM PHRASES

Add more phrases. Write the meaning in your language.

How do you pronounce this word?
Can you check this?
Sorry, I don't understand.
Can you repeat that?

After the *Language focus* Unit, there is an ACTIVITY Unit. This involves the students in using the language they have learnt and in working with other students to share their ideas for a larger piece of work.

> ## 5 Activity A good life
> Making a poster
> *Extra practice · WB Unit 5*
>
> You will need: some large pieces of paper, pens, glue, scissors and pictures.
>
> Before your lesson: planning and collecting pictures for your poster
>
> **1 What do you need for a good life?**
>
> Work with your class. Brainstorm the things that you need for 'a good life'. Make an idea map on the board.

> ## 6 Culture matters At school in the United States
> School in the United States and in your country
> WB Unit 6:
> *Help yourself with vocabulary*
>
> **1 Your school day**
> *Discussion*
>
> What time do you begin and finish school each day?
> How does your school day begin? Do you eat anything at school? What? When?
> How many lessons do you have each day?
>
> **2 Lee's school**
> *Reading*

Each Theme also contains a CULTURE MATTERS Unit. This teaches the students about life in Britain and the United States and encourages them to compare it with life in their own country.

The last Unit in each Theme is REVISION AND EVALUATION. This asks the students to think about how much they have learnt and revises the language they have covered. In some *Revision and evaluation* Units they can also make a test for themselves. The last part of the Unit asks the students to think about *how* they are learning.

> ## 7 Revision and evaluation
> Revision of Units 3–6
> *Extra practice · WB Unit 7*
> *Test yourself*
>
> **1 How well do you know it?**
> *Self-assessment*
>
> How well do you think you know the English you learnt in Units 3–6? Put a tick (√) in the table.
>
> | | very well | OK | a little |
> |---|---|---|---|
> | Talk about your day | | | |
> | Talk about your likes and dislikes | | | |
> | Describe how somebody does something | | | |

> **6 Looking back at Units 3–6**
>
> **6.1 Group discussion**
>
> Form groups of three or four students.
> Decide, with your class, which groups will lo
>
> Unit 3 *or* Unit 4 *or* Units 5 and 6.
>
> In your group, decide who will report back t
> Look through the Units you chose and talk a

> **7 Learning vocabulary**
>
> Work by yourself.
> Answer the questions with a tick (√).
>
> 1 Do you forget n
> 2 Do you have pro
> 3 Do you have pro
> 4 Do you make m
> 5 Do you practise
>
> Compare your answers with your neighbour and other people in your

At the back of the Student's Book, there are also two SUPPLEMENTARY UNITS. These should be done as soon as possible so that students can make use of them throughout their course.

The first *Supplementary Unit* is A PARCEL OF ENGLISH. A *Parcel of English* is a package of work which the students produce and which describes their school, their class, where they live and so on. You can exchange parcels with another school or class and so continue to use English for genuine communication. Cambridge University Press offers a registration scheme to link *CES* classes in different countries. (See page 19 in the Teacher's Book.)

> ## Supplementary Unit A A Parcel of English
>
> **WHAT IS A PARCEL OF ENGLISH?**
> A Parcel of English is something you can make to describe your school and where you live. You can include photographs, postcards, maps, recipes – almost anything. You can send your parcel to another class and receive a parcel from them. Cambridge University Press can link you to another school.
>
> Before you do this Unit
>
> **1 Pictures of you and your town**
>
> Draw a small picture of yourself (5 cm × 5 cm)

The second *Supplementary Unit* is MAKING AN EXERCISE BOX. An *Exercise Box* is a collection of exercises that students can devise themselves and build for the whole class to use for homework, extra classwork or when they have time to spare. At the back of the Student's Book is a list of ideas to help them design their own practice exercises.

> ## Supplementary Unit B Making an Exercise Box
>
> Writing exercises helps you learn English. In this Unit you can make a box of exercises for other students to do. You can also use the box when you have time to spare.
> Writing your own exercises

> ### Ideas list
>
> Here are some ideas to help you make your own exercises. (R name on the back of your card.)
>
> **Idea 1 Word halves**
> Choose some words and cut them in half.
> swimming
> sport
> lungs
> strong

THE TEACHER'S BOOK

The Teacher's Book contains a RATIONALE for the course. This explains why the course is the way it is, the aims, the content and the methodology of the course and the way in which evaluation is treated.

Some notes on the course are included in USING *CES 2*. This also explains how the course can be lengthened or shortened.

Rationale

Summary
Cambridge English for Schools has been based on a reconsideration of the possibilities of English

In many classrooms all over the world, the initial experience of learning English is one of tremendous energy and imagination, in which the students feel that a whole new world is opening up for them as they learn to express themselves in another language. It is, however, also a sad fact that for other students it is sometimes a time of failure and disappointment in which they gradually feel left behind, often resorting to misbehaviour in the classroom and a gradual rejection of the work that the teacher is doing for them. It is thus important for everybody involved in teaching adolescents to try to

Using *Cambridge English for Schools 2*

This section gives an overview of what the different Units do and some ways in which the course can be shortened or extended.

What do the different Units do?

As the 'at a glance' section shows, there are five types of Units in the Student's Book: *Topic* Units, *Language focus* Units, *Activity* Units, *Culture matters* Units and *Revision and evaluation* Units.

Topic Units

such as some writing, a booklet, or a poster. We anticipate these Units taking approximately one fifty-minute lesson each in total, though this may be split up over a number of lessons and may be extended. These Units are important for three main reasons:

• Firstly, they provide an opportunity for the students to say what they wish to say, and thus develop the ability to express *themselves* in English.
• Secondly, extended work in small groups gives the students time to learn from each other and to ask each other questions without feeling embarrassed

There are also SPECIAL NOTES ON THE SUPPLEMENTARY UNITS, including the PARCEL OF ENGLISH registration scheme.
These link to the Teaching Notes at the back of the book.

Special note on 'A Parcel of English' registration scheme and the Supplementary Units

SUPPLEMENTARY UNIT A   A PARCEL OF ENGLISH

...l of English allows teachers to register their ...h Cambridge University Press and receive ...ur class has completed the *Parcel of English* ...entary Unit A), you can exchange your class's ...h a 'twin' class. The *Parcel of English* scheme is ...o bring English alive as a means of international

different countries to make contact with each other and to develop continuing links.

Full Teaching Notes for the *Parcel of English* are on page 141. These also explain what to do if you have used the *Parcel of English* scheme previously.

Supplementary Unit B   M

...u have done *CES 1*, please see the sections 'If you ... before, but ...' below.

...RVIEW OF MAKING AN EXERCIS

...ries Box is a box into which students can put

Supplementary Unit A   A

Note
If you have done *CES 1*, please see the sections 'If you ... below. See also 'Special note on the Supplementary U...

OVERVIEW OF THE PARCEL OF ENGL

The *Parcel of English* offers not only an opportunity for

Detailed guidance on teaching English with *CES* is provided in a handy A TO Z OF METHODOLOGY. This gives practical ideas and explanations.

An A to Z of methodology

This section contains details of some of the key areas of language teaching, particularly in relation to teaching with *CES*. You will find references to this section in the Teaching Notes for each Unit (for example: **A to Z** MOTHER TONGUE). However, it is *not* intended that you should read all of the relevant references just to prepare one lesson or that you should read the entire section all at once! This section is for *reference*: for you to read at your leisure, as and when you wish.

Cross-references to other entries in the section are also shown in small capitals, **LIKE THIS**.

A to Z AUTONOMY

What and why?   • The Workbook Cassette provides a good support for

3 Topic Sports for everybody

Sports; health; curriculum links with Sports and Health Education

1 WHAT HAPPENED WITH UNIT 1 AND UNIT 2?

Some questions to think about before you start Unit 3.

• Do you now feel you have a good idea of the amount of English that your students know? (If not, perhaps you could do some open-ended tasks about sport.

MIXED-ABILITY CLASSES.) You can use the Supplement Worksheets on page 156.
• Is it possible for you to plan time in the coming lessons for you to work with small groups of studer ...

4 Anaerobic and aerobic exercise
A to Z READING
Ask the students if they have heard of 'aerobics'. It is the name given to fitness exercises which require constant movement. (The term is also used in the promotion of types of training shoes.)

MIXED ABILITIES
More support can be given by
• going through the *Language Record* first and supplying the meanings of the words. The students can then refer to translations as they read.

For every Unit, there are detailed TEACHING NOTES, giving suggested timings and notes for the exercises. It also gives cross references to the *A–Z* section and ideas on how to use the course with mixed-ability classes.

Notes on the Workbook and Workbook answers

1 USING THE WORKBOOK

The Student's Workbook and cassette provide supplementary exercises for the work covered in the Student's Book. The unit numbers correspond to the units in the Student's Book. The contents of the Workbook units are su...
notes in th...
given with ...

There are a number of possible ways you can do this:

• before you set Workbook exercises for homework, explain clearly what the students have to do in each

Supplementary worksheets

This section includes 18 supplementary worksheets which you may photocopy for your classes. There are two types of worksheets.

LANGUAGE WORKSHEETS

The *Language worksheets* are intended to give extra support to those students who need further practice with the grammar areas presented in the *Language focus* Units. There are two worksheets for each *Language focus* Unit: one for each area of grammar covered. The worksheets

The *Language worksheets* are:

Ws. 2.1: Present simple and adjectives
Ws. 2.2: Present simple questions and pronouns
Ws. 2.3: Present continuous and comparatives
Ws. 4.1: 'special verbs' (verb '-ing')

The Teacher's Book also contains NOTES ON THE WORKBOOK AND WORKBOOK ANSWERS.

At the back of the Teacher's Book, there are SUPPLEMENTARY WORKSHEETS. These give additional practice in the main grammar points from the *Language focus* Units in the LANGUAGE WORKSHEETS and in pronunciation in the SAY IT CLEARLY! WORKSHEETS.

There is a cassette to use in the classroom.

Class Cassette Set **A**
CAMBRIDGE
ENGLISH
Level Two
for schools

THE WORKBOOK

The Workbook has the same structure as the Student's Book.

3 Topic Sports for everybody

sports; /-ing/

1 Sports for Paul

Read about Paul and the sports that he does. Can you write the correct name of the day under each bag?

Paul loves sports. He does some sport

5 _____

4 Language focus

Verb + '-ing'; expressing opinions

1 What did he say?

Reading

Steve Johnson is an international tennis player. He talked to Jane Steinberg about his work. Choose the correct reply (a-d) for each of Jane's questions.

JANE: This year is an important year for you, isn't it, Steve?

STEVE: (1)

For each Theme, there is also a HELP YOURSELF Unit which shows the students how they can get more practice.

6 Help yourself with vocabulary

Three ways to help you learn vocabulary

In Level 1, there were two ways to help you learn vocabulary. You can see them again in this Unit, and you can also see another way. Use them to learn the words in this Theme (Units 3–7).

From Level 1

1 Make a word bag

7 Test yourself

A test on Units 3–6

Here are some things you learned to do in Units 3-6. How well can you do them? Put a tick (√) in the box.

There are three TEST YOURSELF Units for students to check how much they know, and three REVISION Units. After those Units, there is a PICTURE DICTIONARY for students to record vocabulary.

12 Revision Under a volcano

Revision of Units 8–11

1 What's the word?

Read these clues. Can you find the word in the forest?

a An animal that flies.
b We take this when we are ill.
c The part of a plant under the ground.

h The Wollemi Pin
d _____
i Nobody knows t

A picture dictionary (1)

Label the picture.

body

h
h
l
a

What's the verb?

keep fit
br

At the back of the Workbook, there are the LANGUAGE SUMMARIES, containing a grammar summary and a summary of the *Out and about* section from the Student's Book.

Language summaries

Grammar summary

Units 1 and 2

PRESENT SIMPLE: POSITIVE

You can use the Present simple to talk about:
– a fact or something that happens generally:
  I live in a castle.

PRESENT SIMPLE: ALL OTHER VERBS

To make the negative with other verbs, you add 'doesn't' ('does not') or 'don't' ('do not'):

  She doesn't (does not) live in Brazil. She lives in America.
  They don't (do not) play football at school. They play

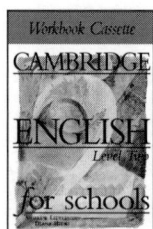

There is also a WORKBOOK CASSETTE. This contains extra listening passages, 'open dialogues' to talk to, and the songs from the Student's Book.

Workbook Cassette
CAMBRIDGE
ENGLISH
Level Two
for schools

Using *Cambridge English for Schools 2*

This section gives an overview of what the different Units do and some ways in which the course can be shortened or extended.

What do the different Units do?

As the 'at a glance' section shows, there are five types of Units in the Student's Book: *Topic* Units, *Language focus* Units, *Activity* Units, *Culture matters* Units and *Revision and evaluation* Units.

Topic Units

In the six *Topic* Units (Units 3, 8, 13, 18, 23, 28), the focus is on an aspect of the Theme, each one taking, very approximately, three fifty-minute lessons. The *Topic* Units stimulate the students' ideas and develop their understanding and knowledge of the Theme. The focus is not on language itself but on using language to understand and express ideas. While the students work on the *Topic* Units, we anticipate that they will be trying to use language they have not yet fully learnt or of which they have only a hazy idea. The teacher's role in this case would be to help the students to express their ideas (e.g. by explaining, rephrasing, supplying vocabulary as needed, translating, etc.). The *accuracy* of the student's language is thus not of vital concern here. The important point to get across to the students is that they can be 'English language users'.

Language focus Units

In the six *Language focus* Units (Units 4, 9, 14, 19, 24, 29), the focus moves from the topic to the language itself. We anticipate these Units taking approximately two to three fifty-minute lessons each. In these Units, the students have the opportunity to look closely at what they have been reading about or saying (or trying to say). The focus is thus on the student's understanding of how the language works and, as far as is possible, to 'get it right' in their own speech or writing. Although the emphasis is on accuracy in these Units, we do not expect students to learn everything first time: language learning is a slow process. However, *CES* has an open structure such that the same language will reappear in later Units. The *Language Record* page after the *Language focus* Units is designed to focus the students' understanding.

Activity Units

In the six *Activity* Units (Units 5, 10, 15, 20, 25, 30), the students work together to produce a larger piece of work such as some writing, a booklet, or a poster. We anticipate these Units taking approximately one fifty-minute lesson each in total, though this may be split up over a number of lessons and may be extended. These Units are important for three main reasons:

- Firstly, they provide an opportunity for the students to say what they wish to say, and thus develop the ability to express *themselves* in English.
- Secondly, extended work in small groups gives the students time to learn from each other and to ask each other questions without feeling embarrassed in front of the whole class.
- Thirdly, they strengthen the social element of the lesson.

The teacher's role during this work is thus likely to be one of encouraging and supporting the students by suggesting ideas, rather than fully directing them. The activities encourage the use of both accurate and fluent language. Once students have gathered together some ideas and produced a draft of their work, they can be asked to check it for spelling, grammar, and vocabulary before you look at it.

Culture matters Units

The six *Culture matters* Units (Units 6, 11, 16, 21, 26, 31) aim to present some aspects of Britain and the United States and to encourage the students to make comparisons with their own society. We anticipate these Units taking approximately one fifty-minute lesson. The aim of these Units is not accuracy in the use of language, but understanding and expressing ideas. Thus the texts in the Units are not followed by traditional 'comprehension questions', but by questions which require an understanding of the texts by asking the students what *they* think.

Revision and evaluation Units

In the six *Revision and evaluation* Units (Units 7, 12, 17, 22, 27, 32), the focus moves back to the language itself. We anticipate these Units taking one or two fifty-minute lessons, depending on how much revision the students require. Each Unit opens by asking the students to self-assess what they have learned. Three Units (7, 17 and 27) then provide revision exercises which you can either direct them to do or let them choose, depending on where you think they need further work. Returning to the self-assessment after *they* have done the revision exercises should help them to see if their own estimations are correct. The other three revision Units (12, 22 and 32) involve the students in designing part of a test for the whole class. Test-writing is a very effective way of developing the students' understanding for three main reasons:

- Firstly, it requires them to do some investigation, to focus carefully on the structure of the language, and to use it.
- Secondly, it also helps to break down the fear of tests which many students have and instead to see tests as an opportunity to find out how much they know.
- Thirdly, it helps to integrate the class, as it provides a means of students challenging each other.

The *evaluation* part of these Units gives the students an opportunity to look back at the Units in the Theme and to consider the level of difficulty of the tasks. This will provide useful feedback for you.

Supplementary Units

Two special Supplementary Units introduce the students to the *Parcel of English* idea and the *Exercise Box*. See page 141 for further notes on these Units.

Workbook and Workbook Cassette

The Workbook is similar in structure to the Student's Book. The Workbook provides additional language practice in all of the areas covered by the Student's Book, extra practice in pronunciation, ideas for helping students to help themselves, and a full language summary for reference. See page 149 for further notes on the Workbook.

How can the course be extended or shortened?

Level 2 is intended to provide material for about 80–100 classroom hours. However, the open and flexible design makes it relatively straightforward to shorten or extend the course. Each Unit is self-contained and there is no continuing story-line which forces you to do particular Units. Although the Units are placed in a logical order, it is possible to omit particular ones or to change the order for your own classes. Bearing in mind that a shorter course will not be able to take full advantage of all that *CES* contains, it is possible to *shorten* the course in the following ways:

- omit the *Extension* section of Unit 2, if the test in Unit 2 shows that the students do not need to do it. If you are short of class time, the students can do all or part of the *Extension* at home.
- omit some of the *Activity* Units.
- omit the *Revision* Units 7, 17, and 27 (or ask the students to do them at home).
- omit the *Culture matters* Units.
- omit Theme A if your students already know the language which it covers.
- omit some of the exercises in each of the *Topic* and *Language focus* Units.
- omit Theme F as the language covered there is revised in Level 3.

In terms of *extending* the course, the following components provide enormous potential for extended work:

- the *Parcel of English*
- the *Exercise Box*
- all the *Activity* Units
- student test-writing
- *Out and about* sections

In addition, the topic-based nature of the course provides an ideal basis for additional project work, supplementary reading, investigations, drama, etc. and for working with other subject teachers. The *A to Z of methodology* gives many practical suggestions in this respect.

Special note on 'A Parcel of English' registration scheme and the Supplementary Units

SUPPLEMENTARY UNIT A   A PARCEL OF ENGLISH

The *Parcel of English* allows teachers to register their classes with Cambridge University Press and receive details of another teacher and class in a different country. When your class has completed the *Parcel of English* (Supplementary Unit A), you can exchange your class's parcel with a 'twin' class. The *Parcel of English* scheme is designed to bring English alive as a means of international communication, and to give teachers the opportunity to exchange ideas and experience with each other worldwide.

To take advantage of the scheme you should register your class as soon as you begin working with *Cambridge English for Schools*. Here's what to do:

1 Complete the **registration card** at the front of this Teacher's Book.
2 Post this form to Cambridge University Press. From Cambridge, you will receive the name and address of a class in a different country which is also using *Cambridge English for Schools 2*.
3 Once your parcel is complete, you can then send a parcel to your 'twin' class. You should similarly receive a parcel from that class.

It is hoped that this will enable teachers and students in different countries to make contact with each other and to develop continuing links.

Full Teaching Notes for the *Parcel of English* are on page 141. These also explain what to do if you have used the *Parcel of English* scheme previously.

Important notes

After registering, please contact the schools directly, **not** Cambridge University Press. Unfortunately, the Press does not have sufficient staff to handle individual queries, problems, etc. **Once you have registered, please ensure that you contact the class(es) with which you are linked to avoid their disappointment**.

If your teaching situation makes it difficult to produce a *Parcel of English*, you can still participate in the link-up with other schools. In place of students' work, you can send photographs of your class and your school, postcards, and information about the place where you live.

If it is difficult for you to post a parcel abroad, you can still use the *Parcel of English* Unit and exchange your parcel with another class in your school, or with another school in your area, or simply display it in your classroom.

SUPPLEMENTARY UNIT B   MAKING AN EXERCISE BOX

The *Exercise Box* was introduced in Level 1 and continues in Level 2. Supplementary Unit B shows how students can begin to make their own exercises, using the *Ideas list* on page 150. These exercises can then be collected together (after you have checked them) and put in a box. They can then be used as homework, as extra in-class work, or when students have time to spare.

To take advantage of the *Exercise Box* idea, you should complete Supplementary Unit B *as soon as possible*. You will then be able to use it throughout your course. Full Teaching Notes for the Unit are on page 146. These also explain what to do in varying circumstances, for example, if you have previously had difficulties establishing an *Exercise Box*.

Welcome to *Cambridge English for Schools 2*

THE COVER PAGE

Each Theme in the course has a cover page to raise the students' interest and to give them an overview of what they will be learning. The first cover page, however, refers to the whole book. It aims to introduce the students to the topics covered in the Themes and to 'invite' them into learning English.

Here is a suggested procedure for using the cover page.

Suggested time: 15 minutes

1 Allow the students a few minutes to look through their book. They can do this with a neighbour.

2 Next, with the students, look through the pictures on the cover page. Tell them that these are *some* of the things they will be learning about *while* they are learning English. Ask them what they think the pictures are about.

3 Working in pairs, ask them to look through the book and to find the correct Unit for each picture. As you go through their answers, look at the relevant Unit with them.

Answers

Football:	Unit 3	Floods:	Unit 18
Parcel of English:	Supplementary Unit A	US school:	Unit 6
		Tap and water:	Unit 30
Rainforest:	Unit 8	People in street:	Unit 24
Dinosaurs:	Unit 9		
Word square:	Unit 17		

You can do 'What's in *Cambridge English for Schools 2*?', which follows the cover page, either *before* you do Unit 1, or as part of Unit 1 (Exercise 6).

What's in *Cambridge English for Schools 2*?

You can do this section either *before* you do Unit 1, or as part of Unit 1 (Exercise 6).

The activities in the '*What's in …*' section help your students get to know the Student's Book and the Workbook before you start using the course fully. (See also the '*at a glance*' section in the Teacher's Book.) The students can discover the main Themes of the books and find out about the different kinds of Units.

What you need

The Class Cassette and the Workbook Cassette for Exercise 7; the students need their Student's Book and Workbook.

Let's look at the Student's Book

1 The Themes

Allow students time to look through the Student's Book. Encourage them to look at the material at the front and the back.

> **Answers**
> Theme A: A good life. They can learn about sports, health and school life. **Theme B:** Life on Earth. They can learn about nature, trees, and dinosaurs. **Theme C:** Back in time. They can learn about life thousands of years ago. **Theme D:** Below the clouds. They can learn about climate and life in other countries. **Theme E:** Across borders. They can learn about trade between countries. **Theme F:** Energy in our lives. They can learn about energy at home and electricity.

2 The Units

> **Answers**
>
> (crossword grid)

3 At the back

> **Answers**
> a pages 157–160   b pages 152–3   c pages 150–1
> d page 149

Let's look at the Workbook

4 Inside the Workbook

Allow students some time to look through their Workbooks and to see the organisation of the book and to make comparisons with the Student's Book.

5 The Workbook Units

Workbook Units 6, 11, 16, 21, 26 and 31 are *Help Yourself* Units. Students learn about life in Britain and the United States.

6 At the back

At the back of the Workbook there is a grammar summary.

7 Listen to the page numbers

The Workbook and Class Cassettes always tell you which book and which page the recording comes from. This exercise gives the students practice in finding their way around with the cassette.

> **Answers**
> a Student's Book page 70 is Unit 14   b Student's Book page 136 is Unit 30   c Workbook page 84 is Unit 31
> d Workbook page 66 is Unit 24   e Student's Book page 40 is Unit 7   f Workbook page 30 is Unit 10

1 Welcome Back!

A SPECIAL NOTE ON UNITS 1 AND 2

Units 1 and 2 aim to provide a flexible starting-point for students, and introduce them to the course. Unit 2 consists of two parts: a test and an *Extension*. The test will help you determine how much English the students know. The *Extension* provides *optional* revision exercises for those students who need it. It is **not** intended that you work through all of the *Extension* section, unless your students are particularly weak.

The test in Unit 2 covers the Present simple (positive, negative and question forms); the use of adjectives; object and subject pronouns; the Present continuous; comparatives and superlatives; and the Past simple (some irregular and regular verbs, negatives and question forms). The *Extension* provides revision exercises covering all the aspects included in the test. See the 'Teaching notes for Unit 2' for more information.

Which parts shall I do?

Decide which of the following statements is true for you. You can then do the relevant parts.

'I am not sure how much my students know.'	→ Do Unit 1 then Unit 2. Depending on the test results, do exercises from the *Extension,* or move on to Unit 3.
'Some of my students know a little, and some of them know quite a lot.'	→ Do Unit 1 and then Unit 2 to find out who knows what! Students can then do different exercises from the *Extension* section, depending on where their problems lie. If you find that some students need to do more *Extension* exercises than others, it will probably be best to set alternative work for the better students. (See the 'Teaching Notes for Unit 2 *Extension*' for more information.)
'I am certain that my students already have a basic grasp of the language covered in the test, though not perfect.'	→ Do Unit 1, then go directly to Unit 3.

Important note: It is not expected that students have complete mastery of the items covered in the test before they move into Level 2 of the course. Themes A and B in Level 2 provide further revision work, particularly of the second half of Level 1, before the language syllabus develops much further.

TEACHING NOTES FOR UNIT 1

Note: a symbol like this: **AtoZ** means that you can find more ideas and suggestions in the *A to Z of methodology* (pages 111–140). The **AtoZ** is for you to read as you wish. You do not need to read all the sections just to prepare one lesson!

A symbol like this 📼 means that you need the cassette.

Overview of the Unit

Unit 1 aims to build a good classroom atmosphere and to introduce the students to Level 2. The open-ended exercises 1–3 will help you see how much they already know. The Unit also teaches them some classroom phrases and takes them on a guided tour of their book. (See 'What's in *CES 2*?' on page 21.)

Timing

Below are some suggested timings (in minutes). *These will vary considerably from class to class* and are only given here as a rough guide.

Important note: The timings are our estimates for *doing the exercises*. You will need to allow extra time for settling the students down to work and moving them from one exercise to another.

1	What's new?	25
2	What do you know?	10
3	What can you tell us?	25
4	Sing a song!	10
5	Are you ready?	
5.1	Some useful things	10
5.2	Some useful phrases	10
6	Find out about your book!	15

(See also **AtoZ** TIMING.)

What you need

A cassette player and the Class Cassette for Exercises 4 (song) and 6. Optionally, blank sheets of A5 (half A4) paper, if possible coloured (enough for one per student, plus some spares); and a large sheet of poster paper for Exercise 1.

Mixed-ability classes

Throughout this Teacher's Book there are additional notes on how to give more support for mixed-ability classes. Unit 1 contains many **AtoZ** OPEN-ENDED TASKS which will help you find out how much your students know.

(See also **AtoZ** MIXED ABILITIES.)

Workbook

Unit 1 in the Workbook contains the following exercises:

- Exercise 1: reading about holiday events
- Exercise 2: reading and general knowledge
- Exercise 3: writing in *The world encyclopaedia*
- Exercise 4: vocabulary in a puzzle
- Exercise 5: an open dialogue to practise speaking
- Exercise 6: a song in English

For additional notes on the use of the Workbook and Workbook answers see page 149.

Guidelines

1 What's new?

AtoZ GROUPWORK and DISPLAYING STUDENTS' WORK

The purpose of this exercise is bring the students back together again 'as a class', perhaps after a long break, and to make them the centre of classroom work right from the beginning. The task is open-ended so that you can begin to get an idea of how much they know. The writing activity will ease them back into using English again. They will naturally try to use the Past tense. This is taught in Level 1 but it is thoroughly revised in Level 2, so there is no need to insist on its absolutely correct use at this point.

You could begin with a brief class discussion before you put the students into groups. Ask a few students to tell you and the class something about themselves and what's new in their lives. Put some examples on the board of what they could write.

After the students have written about their news, you could ask them to draw a picture of themselves or add a photograph. You could then make a poster to put on the classroom wall. (See **AtoZ** POSTERS.)

- **WB Ex. 1:** reading about children's holiday news.
- **WB Ex. 5:** an open dialogue about personal news.

2 What do you know?

This can be done alone or in pairs, as a race. The puzzle draws on the students' general knowledge.

Answers

```
        3        5        8     9                              17
       i     4  e  6      m     t                              s      19
    1  2 n    c  u  m  7  o     r              12 13     16 p 18  b
       s    o  r  a  p  n    10 11           p  c  14 15 l  i  b  r
   T H E  W O R L D   E N C Y C L O P A E D I A
       o o c    p  s  a  a      s  i  a        u  l  a  i  g  e  r  z
       k t t    e  n  y      l  v        t  d  r  r  s  r  d  i
       y        t           e  e              o        i        l
       o                    s                 s
```

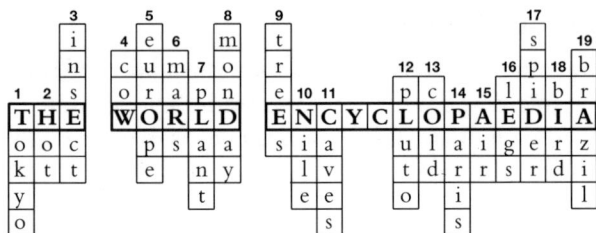

• **WB Ex. 4: a vocabulary puzzle.**

3 What can you tell us?

AtoZ INTERACTIVE WRITING, WRITING and GROUPWORK

This exercise is again open-ended so that you can get a better idea of how much the students can do. The Past simple is required for the *World of History*, so you will be able to see how well students know it. The Past is thoroughly presented and practised again later in Level 2, however. Students can write very little or a lot, depending on their level of ability and how much they are encouraged! You can encourage the better students to produce more.

Before you put the students into groups, you can ask the class for ideas about the things in the pictures and what they know about them. Read through the example text about Mexico City to show what is expected. If they can't think of anything to write about the topics in the book, they can choose another topic of their own from the *worlds of people, science, nature* or *history*. All the Topics given here come from Level 1 of the course.

Once the students are in their groups, it is important to ensure that *all* the students in the group write. This will ensure the maximum amount of discussion on the Topic and the language required ('How do you spell X?', 'What's X in English?', etc.). Each student should have his or her own copy of what they are writing.

Some ideas:

1 London: London is the capital of the United Kingdom. About seven million people live there. There are some very famous buildings there. For example, the Houses of Parliament, Buckingham Palace and 10 Downing Street, where the Prime Minister lives. London is on the River Thames.

Food: Good food has seven important elements. CARBOHYDRATES give us energy. There are carbohydrates in bread, sugar and rice. FATS make us strong and give us energy. There are fats in meat, butter, cheese and oil. FIBRE cleans the inside of our bodies. There is fibre in nuts, beans and cereals. WATER is important for our blood. It also cleans our bodies from the inside. PROTEIN helps us to grow and gives us energy. There is protein in meat, fish, and milk. MINERALS make our bones and teeth strong. There are different types of minerals in milk, vegetables, eggs, meat, cereals and many other foods. VITAMINS are important for our eyes, our skin, our bones, our hair, and for other parts of our bodies. There are vitamins in many types of food.

2 Rain: The sun shines on the rivers and lakes. Water vapour rises into the air and makes clouds. The wind blows the clouds. If a cold cloud meets a warm cloud, the warm cloud becomes water again and there is rain.

The moon: 'Our nearest neighbour'. The moon is our closest neighbour, but it is very different from Earth. Gravity on the moon is much weaker than on Earth and there isn't any air. During the day, it is very, very hot, but at night it is very, very cold. Nothing can live on the moon. Because the moon turns round at the same speed as it goes around the Earth, we always see the same side of the moon.

3 Elephants: Elephants live in Africa and Asia. The African elephant is the largest living mammal on Earth (height up to 3.8m). It has larger ears than the Asian elephant, and the female has tusks. They sleep for about four hours a day and live for about 60 years. They are vegetarians and eat fruit, leaves and grass.

The Praying Mantid: Praying Mantids are a type of insect. They live in many parts of the world, including South America and Africa. They eat small insects and spiders, but some big Mantids eat small frogs and birds. Some Mantids eat other Mantids. They start with the head first, so that they cannot get away. Some Mantids are very beautiful. The Flower Mantids from Africa look like flowers. Insects land on them to get food but, instead, the Mantids eat them!

4 Cave people: People lived in caves between about 4,000 and 6,000 years ago. They made tools from a stone called flint. They went hunting in big groups and killed mammoths, tigers, bears and other animals. They also painted elaborate pictures on the walls of their caves. About 4,000 years ago people began to move out of the caves and started farming.

Dinosaurs: Dinosaurs lived on Earth for about 75 million years. They disappeared suddenly about 65 million years ago. There were more than 800 different kinds of dinosaurs. Most of the dinosaurs were very big. Some were 30 metres long and weighed 30 tons. Some dinosaurs killed and ate other dinosaurs, but most dinosaurs ate plants. Nobody is sure why the dinosaurs disappeared but they think that an enormous meteor crashed into the Earth and the climate changed.

• **WB Ex. 2: more reading from *The world encyclopaedia*.**
• **WB Ex 3: Writing for *The world encyclopaedia*.**

4 Sing a song! All around the world 📼
AtoZ SONGS

The song is also recorded on the Workbook cassette.

5 Are you ready?
AtoZ AUTONOMY, DISCUSSION

5.1 Some useful things

This exercise aims to get the students thinking about what they will need to do in order to learn. You could ask them to make a list of things they can do with each item. If you are short of time, different pairs of students can focus on different items. That way, you can get feedback on all the items in the picture.

If the students need some help, here are some ideas. However, it is best not to overwhelm them at this stage.

Vocabulary book: make a list of words in groups/alphabetically; ask students to cover the words and to test themselves; to test each other; to read it on the bus/train/when waiting; to read it last thing at night; and to keep it in their pocket, with a dictionary, if there is a lot of English around them.

Highlighter pens: highlight words in the students' vocabulary book in different colours (blue = verb, green = adjective, etc.); and/or highlight important parts of their notes; and/or put coloured boxes around notes/exercises.

Dictionary: ask students to buy a small, bilingual dictionary and keep it with them all the time (with a vocabulary book); and/or with a friend, test each other on words they should know.

Cassette player: encourage students to listen to the Workbook cassette; to talk to themselves on the cassette (the Workbook cassette contains 'open' dialogues); to record themselves; to record a dialogue with a friend; to listen to, and repeat, the listening texts; to use the listening texts for dictation; and to write questions for another student to answer when they listen to the cassette.

Grammar book: encourage students to buy a good bilingual grammar book with a good index; to read grammar rules as they learn about them in class; and, if the book has translations, to copy out sentences in their own language and then to try to translate them, checking with the book.

Coursebooks and cassettes: ask students to do the Workbook exercises; to listen to the Workbook cassette at home; to read the Student's Book; to listen to the cassette before the lesson, and again after it; and to listen to the Workbook cassette on a personal stereo on the bus/train/when waiting, etc. (See also 'Cassette player' above.)

5.2 Some useful phrases

Before going through the list of useful phrases, give the students a few moments to write down the meanings. The phrases are very basic ones; encourage students to use them throughout the course.

6 Find out about your book!
AtoZ OVERVIEWING

See page 21 for Teaching Notes on 'What's in *Cambridge English for Schools 2?*'.

2 Test your English The world encyclopaedia

TEACHING NOTES FOR UNIT 2

Overview of the Unit

This Unit consists of a test and an *Extension* with revision exercises. The Teaching Notes here include a photocopiable Students' Answer Sheet and a Teacher's Answer Sheet. The test will give you a good idea of what English your students already know, so that you can decide whether to work on the *optional Extension* exercises or move straight to Unit 3. This allows a flexible entry into Level 2.

The test is based on sections of a 'World Encyclopaedia', covering some of the topics from Level 1 and the language syllabus. The test and the *Extension* section cover the following grammar and social language:

1 Social language
2 Present simple
3 Adjectives
4 Present tense questions
5 Pronouns
6 Present continous
7 Comparatives and superlatives
8 Past simple

Workbook

There are Workbook exercises to parallel each section of the *Extension*.

THE TEST

Timing

The test is designed to last for one lesson. However, this will depend on how much the students know and how quickly they work. Stronger students who finish before the others can be moved straight on to the first exercises in the *Extension* section. Weaker students who finish early because they cannot complete the test can be asked to write down any phrases they know in English or something about themselves (where they live, their family, how old they are, what they like/dislike, etc.).

What you need

Photocopies of the *Student's Answer Sheet* (see page 27), one per student. (Alternatively, the students can write their answers on a separate piece of paper, although this will take longer.)

Preparation

So that you can mark the test easily, make a copy of the *Answer Sheet* on page 27 for each student and ask the students to write their answers on the sheet. As the *test* in the Student's Book and the photocopiable *Student's Answer Sheet* look very different, you will first need to show the students what they have to do.

Before they start the test, show them the example answer in Section 1 so that they know how to circle their answers. Then show them the two practice sections on the Answer Sheet. While they are doing the practice questions, go round to check that they have understood what to do. When you are certain that they all understand how to circle the answers, start the test.

> **Important note:** It is important to tell the students that the test is intended to *help you and them. It is not intended as a means of evaluating the students.*

Student's Answer Sheet

Name: .... Date: ....

Class: ....

PRACTICE TEST Put a circle around a letter on the Practice Answer Sheet.
1 Most students … like tests.
2 This can help … see how much you know.
	PRACTICE ANSWER SHEET
	1 a doesn't **2 a** the cat
	  b aren't **b** you
	  c don't **c** eat

Now look at the test in your Student's Book. Put a circle around the answers on this paper.

The world of people and places

1 What are they saying?

   1 a What time is it?   **2 a** I think they're horrible.   **3 a** How far is the bus station?
     b Is it cold?   **b** I can see them.   **b** What time is the bus?
     c Do you want one?   **c** How many are there?   **c** Who is the bus driver?

2 Two Mexicos

   1 There aren't any tall buildings. A B
   2 The people don't have any cars. A B
   3 The people live in modern houses. A B

3 Skiing in Switzerland

   1 a dead **b** high **c** cheap **2 a** tall **b** ugly **c** exciting **3 a** dangerous **b** friendly **c** rainy

The world of nature

4 The fantastic world of butterflies

   1 When ....?
   2 Where ....?
   3 How long ....?

5 Animals talk!

   1 a him **b** us **c** we **2 a** our **b** them **c** their **3 a** their **b** your **c** its

The world of science

6 Make a telephone!

   1 (make) She .... a hole in the tin.
   2 (put) They .... the string in the tins.
   3 (talk) He .... to his friend and she can hear him.

7 Facts about the planets

   1 a cold **b** colder **c** the coldest **2 a** long **b** longer **c** the longest **3 a** near **b** nearer **c** the nearest

The world of history

8 Machu Picchu: the lost city of the Incas

   1 a live **b** lived **c** lives
   2 a disappear **b** is disappearing **c** disappeared
   3 a is finding **b** find **c** found
   4 a thought **b** thinks **c** is thinking
   5 a What do you see? **b** What did you see? **c** What are you seeing?

Test your English: Teacher's Answer Sheet

Total 26 marks

The world of people and places

1 What are they saying?

  1 **c** Do you want one?
  2 **a** I think they're horrible.
  3 **b** What time is the bus?

2 Two Mexicos

  1 A 2 A 3 B

3 Skiing in Switzerland

  1 **b** high
  2 **c** exciting
  3 **a** dangerous

The world of nature

4 The fantastic world of butterflies

  1 When do butterflies sleep? / When do butterflies fly?
  2 Where do butterflies live?
  3 How long do butterflies live?

5 Animals talk!

  1 c 2 c 3 c

The world of science

6 Make a telephone!

  1 She is making a hole …
  2 They are putting …
  3 He is talking …

7 Facts about the planets

  1 c 2 b 3 c

The world of history

8 Machu Picchu: the lost city of the Incas

  1 b
  2 c
  3 c
  4 a
  5 b

What to do next

To get a clearer idea of the strengths and weaknesses of the students, look at the marks gained in each section. If most of the students have gained *more than* half marks in all five sections of the test you can move directly to Unit 3, *Sports for everybody*.

If most of the students have gained *less than* half marks in some sections, move to the appropriate exercises in the *Extension* section to give the students further practice. (Alternatively, students can be put in groups to work on different sections of the *Extension* material, as required.)

The test and the *Extension* are linked directly, section to section. For example, if your students need extra practice in the language in the 'world of science' section, there are exercises in the 'world of science' section in the *Extension*.

Note: There is no *Extension* material for the 'world of history' section (Past tense) as the Past tense is taught thoroughly in Level 2 (Themes B and C). It is included in the test to give you an indication of how much students know.

Extension The world encyclopaedia

TEACHING NOTES FOR UNIT 2 EXTENSION

The *Extension* is intended to be used *selectively*, following the results of the test. It is **not** intended that you work through all of the exercises. Theme A provides more general revision work before the language syllabus develops further in Theme B. The grammar points covered in the *Extension* are as follows:

The world of people and places

Exercises 1 and 2: adjectives
Exercise 3: Present simple

The world of nature

Exercises 1–5: Present simple questions
Exercise 6: personal pronouns

The world of science

Exercises 2–4: Present continuous
Exercise 5: comparatives
Exercise 6: comparatives and superlatives

Timing

Below are some suggested timings (in minutes) for each exercise. *These will vary considerably from class to class, and from student to student.*

The world of people and places		
1	In the sun	12
2	Under the ground	15
3	Possible or impossible?	15
4	Your Language Record	5
The world of nature		
1	Animal factfile: the leopard	12
2	Read about the leopard	12
3	More animal facts	10
4	Your own questions	15
5	Summary	10
6	What's the word?	12
7	Your Language Record	5

The world of science		
1	Are we alone in the universe?	10
2	How can we find out?	20
3	They are sending radio messages into space	15
4	What's happening?	20
5	It's much bigger!	12
6	Can you complete the table?	10
7	Your Language Record	5

(See also **AtoZ** TIMING.)

What you need

Optionally, the Class Cassette and a cassette player for the following exercises:
The world of people and places (Exercise 2)
The world of nature (Exercise 2)
The world of science (Exercises 2 and 4)

Workbook

Unit 2 *Extension* in the Workbook practises the following:

The world of people and places:
• Exercise 1: adjectives
• Exercise 2: reading and Present simple
• Exercise 3: Present simple negatives

The world of nature
• Exercise 4: Present simple questions
• Exercise 5: Present simple questions
• Exercise 6: reading and Present simple questions
• Exercise 7: personal pronouns

The world of science
• Exercise 8: Present continuous
• Exercise 9: comparatives
• Exercise 10: comparatives and Present simple

Guidelines

You could divide the students into groups to work on the various sections of the *Extension*. See **AtoZ** TASKS IN GROUPS and **AtoZ** OVERVIEWING.

The world of people and places

1 In the sun
A to Z GRAMMAR

The purpose of this exercise is to practise adjectives which describe places. Allow students time to look at the picture and put the adjectives in the correct columns. Check that students understand the vocabulary, and that they know where adjectives come in sentences in English (i.e. before the noun: an **exciting** place).

- WB Ex. 1: more practice with adjectives.

> **Possible answers**
> **Words that describe the picture**: hot, boring, dry, empty, horrible, dusty, sunny, ugly, dead. **Words that don't describe the picture**: cold, exciting, expensive, happy, nice, rainy, weak, windy, beautiful, friendly.

2 Under the ground
A to Z READING, PROCESSING TIME and DISCUSSION

The full name of the place in Australia is Coober Pedy, but it is frequently known as Coober. You could ask the students to find it on a map of Australia. It is in the desert, North-West of Adelaide.

Before students read the text ask them to guess from the picture and the title what it is going to be about. Then ask them to decide what adjectives they think they will find in the text. (See Exercise 1 for ideas.)

If you feel the students will not be able to handle a text of this length, ask them initially to read only the first and last sentence of each paragraph. They can then listen to the recording and see if the text has the adjectives they predicted. Asking students to underline the words they know will also increase their self-confidence.

Students discuss their reactions to the text. This is an **A to Z OPEN TASK**, so the emphasis should be on **A to Z FLUENCY** here, rather than on accuracy.

- WB Ex. 2: more practice with the Present simple.

3 Possible or impossible?

> **Answers**
> 2 Possible. Coober has got shops. 3 Possible. Coober has got schools/teachers. 4 Impossible! Coober doesn't have a park. 5 Possible. 6 Impossible! Coober doesn't have any gardens. 7 Impossible! Coober doesn't have any roads, cars or buses. 8 Impossible! Coober is completely underground and it is in a desert.

- WB Ex. 3: more practice with Present simple negatives.

4 Your Language Record
A to Z LANGUAGE RECORD

Students should now complete the world of nature section in the *Language Record* on page 22.

The world of nature

1 Animal factfile: the leopard

> **Some possible questions:**
> Where do they live? What do they look like? What do they eat? How long do they live? How long do they sleep? Why do they have spots? How many types of leopards are there? How many teeth do they have? Do they live alone? Are they dangerous?

2 Read about the leopard
A to Z READING

Students can read silently and then say how many answers they have found.

- WB Exs. 4, 5, and 6: more Present simple questions.

3 More animal facts
A to Z PROCESSING TIME

> **Answers**
> 1 do/They eat fruit. 2 do/Because it's …. 3 does/About 136 kg of plants. 4 do/They live in Siberia. 5 do/They send out … 6 can/ Up to …

4 Your own questions
A to Z QUESTIONS

You could collect the students' questions together on a poster (see **A to Z POSTERS**) and then see how many answers they have found during the next week. Agree a day when you will discuss the poster questions with them.

5 Summary

This summary is intended to draw together the points in this section. You can read it through with the students and ask them to analyse some of their questions from Exercise 5.

6 What's the word?
A to Z PROCESSING TIME

> **Answers**
> 1 Their, They, Their 2 its 3 our, our 4 them 5 them 6 him

- WB Ex. 7: more practice with personal pronouns.

7 Your Language Record
A to Z **LANGUAGE RECORD**

The world of science

1 Are we alone in the universe?
A to Z **DISCUSSION and PROCESSING TIME**

2 How can we find out?
A to Z **READING and PROCESSING TIME**

After the students have read silently, you can play the tape before you ask for answers.

> **Answers**
> In the text, scientists are doing four different things. (Sending messages into space; listening for messages; building radio telescopes; and receiving photographs from spaceships.)

3 They are sending radio messages into space
A to Z **GRAMMAR, INDUCTIVE GRAMMAR and PROCESSING TIME**

> **Answers**
> The general rule is that the Present continuous is used for actions which are happening now, while the Present simple is used for habits, regular actions and things which are always true. The Present continuous is also used to talk about the future (e.g. I'm working tomorrow).

4 What's happening?
A to Z **PATTERN PRACTICE**

> **Answers**
> 1 She's climbing the ladder; 2 She's getting into the space rocket; 3 She's starting the rocket. 4 The rocket is leaving Earth; 5 It's flying into space. 6 It's landing on Mars; 7 She's opening the door. 8 She's getting out of the rocket; 9 She's talking to a strange creature there; 10 The creature is writing something. He is saying 'Go home Tourists!'.

- WB Ex. 8: more practice with the Present continuous.

5 It's much bigger!
A to Z **PATTERN PRACTICE and PROCESSING TIME**

This exercise revises the comparative form in English. You could ask the students to do it either before they have done Exercise 6, or afterwards.

Go through a few examples before you ask students to write down their answers using the key words given.

> **Answers**
> 1 Mars is bigger than Pluto. 2 Starship 1 is faster than Starship 2. 3 Telstar 3 is more expensive than Telstar 2. 4 Mercury is hotter than Earth.

6 Can you complete the table?
Ask the students if they remember the rule for forming the comparative and superlative:

- words of one syllable (hot, cold, long, etc.) take '-er' and '-est' (hot/hot**ter**/the hot**test**)
- words ending in 'y' take '-ier'/'-iest' (sunny/sunn**ier**/the sunn**iest**)
- other words with more than one syllable use 'more' and 'the most' (expensive/**more** expensive/**the most** expensive).

- **WB Exs. 9 and 10: more practice with comparatives.**

7 Your Language Record
A to Z **LANGUAGE RECORD**

Theme A — A good life

OVERVIEW OF THE THEME

Theme A, A good life, focuses on aspects of our life, particularly in relation to sport and free-time activities. Students learn about the contribution that sport can make to health (Unit 3), make a poster showing their ideas of what makes 'a good life' (Unit 5), and learn about life in schools in the United States (Unit 6). Grammatically, the Theme revises and consolidates the language from Level 1 and introduces 'special verbs' (e.g. I *love* listen*ing* to music) and adverbs (e.g. He drives dangerous*ly*). Student decision-making is involved through *Decide* exercises in the *Topic* Unit, and in the *Revision and evaluation* Units. Unit 4, Exercise 5 gives students a chance to plan some of their own classwork.

The Theme offers cross-curricular links with Sports, Health Education, Biology and Social/Cultural Studies.

> **Note:** As soon as possible, try to find time to do the Supplementary Units A and B. See page 19 for more details.

Using the cover page

Suggested time for the cover page: 10 minutes

The cover page visually summarises the Theme and raises the students' interest in the Units which follow. Allow time for students to look closely at the pictures. They can work alone, or in pairs, to answer the questions and write the Unit numbers in the boxes at the side.

Answers
1. Pictures: football – Unit 3; classroom – Unit 6; A good life – Unit 5; Susan Spencer – Unit 3; diagram of heart, etc. – Unit 3.
2. In Unit 3 you can learn about different types of exercise and the life of a young champion swimmer.
   In Unit 4 you can learn how to use 'special verbs' and how to form adverbs.
3. There is a puzzle on page 26, a song on page 27, and a game on page 33.
4. On page 29 there is a *Language Record*, and on page 35 there is a *Language Record* and a *Revision Box*.
5. The *Language Record*s help students to record the new language they have learned. The *Revision Boxes* revise language that has been covered before.
6. In Unit 5, students discuss what makes 'a good life' and make a poster showing their ideas.

Some additional ideas for using the cover page:

- Look through the pictures with the students. Ask them what they know about each picture.
- Discuss with the students what they can see in the pictures. Ask them what they expect to learn about in the Theme.
- After looking through the pictures, ask groups of students to find out more about one of the things in the pictures. You can then allow a few minutes at the end of some lessons in the coming weeks for them to tell the class what they have found out.
- Make a Question Poster. Put a large sheet of paper on the wall and ask the students what they would like to know about the things in the pictures. Over the next few weeks, students can try to find the answers to some of these questions (allow time at the end of some lessons for them to tell the class what they have found out). See **A to Z** POSTERS.

Topic 3 Sports for everybody

Sports; health; curriculum links with Sports and Health Education

---

1 WHAT HAPPENED WITH UNIT 1 AND UNIT 2?

Some questions to think about before you start Unit 3.

- Do you now feel you have a good idea of the amount of English that your students know? (If not, perhaps you could do some open-ended tasks about sport. See **AtoZ** OPEN-ENDED TASKS.)
- Are there many differences in level? Which students will need extra support? Which students may need to be given extra work? (See **AtoZ** TIME TO SPARE? and

MIXED-ABILITY CLASSES.) You can use the Supplementary Worksheets on page 156.
- Is it possible for you to plan time in the coming lessons for you to work with small groups of students, while the others get on with some other work?
- Look at the test results again. Which were the strongest and the weakest areas (generally) of the students? Are there any areas you would like to focus attention on in Unit 3?

---

2 TEACHING NOTES FOR UNIT 3

Important note: Some time within the next few lessons, we recommend that you plan a time to do the Supplementary Units at the back of the Student's Book. If you haven't already done so, you could also now complete the *Parcel of English* Registration Card (see page 19 for the special note on *A Parcel of English*).

Overview of the Unit

Unit 3 focuses on sport and the role it plays in keeping the body healthy. The students learn about the differences between anaerobic and aerobic exercise. The Unit includes the two *Decide* exercises where students have to decide what they will do. The first of these offers a choice between vocabulary work, guided writing and free writing. The second *Decide* exercise offers a choice between a speaking exercise, writing or *Do it yourself!* in which students can decide (in agreement with you) to do something else. The Unit also includes a song about sport.

Timing

Below are some suggested timings (in minutes) for each activity. *These will vary considerably from class to class* and are only given here as a rough guide. You can note down your anticipated lesson divisions.

Important note: These timings are estimates for *doing the exercises*. You will need to allow extra time for settling the students down and moving them from one exercise to another.

1	Sports and you	10
2	Sports that make you strong and flexible	10
3	Sports for health!	15
4	Anaerobic and aerobic exercise	15
5	Decide ...	15-20
6	Sing a song!	10
7	The life of a champion swimmer	
7.1	Susan Spencer, swimmer	5
7.2	Swimming for gold	10
8	Decide ...	15-20
9	Your Language Record	5-8

(See also **AtoZ** TIMING.)

What you need

A cassette player and the Class Cassette for Exercises 4 and 6 (song).

Mixed-ability classes and supplementary worksheets

Exercises 4, 5, 7 and 8 have additional notes for mixed-ability classes.

Say it clearly! Worksheet 1: provides practice with pronunciation of '-ing' and '-ly/ily'.

(See also **AtoZ** MIXED ABILITIES.)

Workbook

Unit 3 in the Workbook contains exercises to practise:

- Exercise 1: reading about sports
- Exercise 2: vocabulary
- Exercise 3: speaking (open dialogue)
- Exercise 4: reading about a school game
- Exercise 5: writing about daily routines
- Exercise 6: pronunciation of '-ing'
- Exercise 7: Singing a song in English

For additional notes on the use of the Workbook and Workbook answers see page 149.

Guidelines

A word with the symbol **AtoZ** shows that you can find more information in the *A to Z of methodology* (page 111). The symbol 🔲 means that you need or can use the cassette with that exercise.

1 Sports and you

AtoZ DISCUSSION

It should be possible, at this level, to conduct most of this discussion in English. As the students mention different points, you can put useful phrases and words on the board.

- **WB Ex. 3: an open dialogue about sports.**

2 Sports that make you strong and flexible

AtoZ PAIRWORK

Students discuss in pairs what they *think* the different sports do for your body: 1 to 3 for energy level, and one tick (√) to three ticks for how strong and flexible they make you.

Before you move on to the reading passage in Exercises 3 and 4, you can ask the students for their ideas. As they tell you what they have have written down in the table, you can ask them 'Why?' and encourage them to compare with the other sports in the table. For example, they may put '1' for the energy level of swimming, but 'walking' has '2' in the table.

3 Sports for health!

AtoZ READING

Ask the students to read the first part of the text (Sports for Health) silently to check their answers to Exercise 2.

Once you have checked answers with the students, you can read the passage with them to check meaning and vocabulary.

- **WB Ex. 1: extra reading.**
- **WB Ex. 2: a vocabulary puzzle.**

Answers
Football: energy 2, strong √√√, flexible √√; Running: energy 2, strong: √√√, flexible √; Squash: energy 3, strong √√, flexible √√; Swimming: energy 2, strong √√√, flexible √√√.

4 Anaerobic and aerobic exercise 🔲

AtoZ READING

Ask the students if they have heard of 'aerobics'. It is the name given to fitness exercises which require constant movement. (The term is also used in the promotion of types of training shoes.)

MIXED ABILITIES

More support can be given by

- going through the *Language Record* first and supplying the meanings of the words. The students can then refer to translations as they read.
- discussing with the students how our body works: oxygen, lungs, etc. before asking them to read. You can put key words on the blackboard as they come up.
- asking the students to underline all the words they understand and then compare with their neighbours and help each other.
- reading through the descriptions of types of exercise and then going through the list of sports with them to agree whether they are anaerobic or aerobic.

The task can be made more demanding by

- asking the students to choose another sport (perhaps one that they play) and to write a description of it similar to the descriptions in Part 1 of the article.
- giving the students a minute or two to read through the descriptions of the sports. They can then close their books, and write what they remember about one or two sports.

Answer
Swimming is better for you since it strengthens the heart and improves your blood circulation. Aerobic-type sports are: cycling, running, swimming, walking. Anaerobic-type exercises are: badminton, football, squash, table tennis. Sports which contribute relatively little are: fishing and golf (except for the walking).

5 Decide ...

AtoZ DECIDE EXERCISES, AUTONOMY and OVERVIEWING

This is the first *Decide* exercise that the students will do. Two *Decide* exercises occur in each *Topic* unit. The first one offers the students a choice of three tasks, while the second one offers them a choice of two tasks and the opportunity to do something else instead.

Before the students decide which task they want to do, go through the tasks with them so that they know what each one involves. Then let them choose a task. (See **AtoZ DECIDE EXERCISES** for more general guidelines.)

MIXED ABILITIES
Students are likely to find Exercise 5.1 easier than Exercise 5.2 and Exercise 5.2 easier than Exercise 5.3.

5.1 What's the word?

a	e	f	g	e	g	l	y	u	t	**F**	r	h		**Answers**
h	n	e	**S**	h	**L**	w	j	k	o	**L**	k	v		1 lungs
q	j	w	s	**T**	r	**E**	s	r	a	**E**	g	j		2 heart
j	o	b	h	w	**R**	r	**G**	i	u	**X**	j			3 flexible
j	y	j	a	k	o	**O**	w	**S**	t	**I**	e			4 legs
n	b	b	c	g	t	y	**N**	r	d	**B**	e	a		5 health
m	l	**B**	**O**	**D**	**Y**	i	o	**G**	s	**L**	s	**H**		6 muscles
f	s	g	e	t	e	f	h	a	s	**E**	a	**E**		7 body
j	h	s	j	j	s	**L**	**U**	**N**	**G**	**S**	a	**A**		8 excellent
E	**X**	**C**	**E**	**L**	**L**	**E**	**N**	**T**		n	a	l	t	9 strong
H	**E**	**A**	**R**	**T**		t	**M**	**U**	**S**	**C**	**L**	**E**	**S**	

Note: After students have done one of the exercises here, you could show them the next *Decide* exercise (Ex. 8). This also contains three choices, but note that the third choice is *Do it yourself!* Students can prepare to do something else related to their learning of English. (See **AtoZ DO IT YOURSELF**.)

5.2 Write about a sport

5.3 A sports team or person you like

6 Sing a song! Sports for everybody 🖭

7 The life of a champion swimmer

7.1 Susan Spencer, swimmer

AtoZ DISCUSSION

The questions here raise points which are mentioned in the text which follows. The questions are intended to encourage students to read more actively.

7.2 Swimming for gold

AtoZ READING

Allow the students some time to read silently, before you return to the questions in Exercise 7.1.

Once the students have read silently, check that they understand the meaning of particular sentences and words.

- **WB Ex. 4: reading about an English school game.**
- **WB Ex. 5: writing about a day in the students' lives.**

MIXED ABILITIES
More support can be given by
- going first through the words which you anticipate they won't know.
- providing some simple comprehension questions to guide their reading, e.g.: How old is Susan? What does Susan want to do? When does she get up?
- talking through first what THEY do every day. You can build up a timetable on the blackboard, similar to the one in the article.
- asking the students to read silently and underline the words they understand. They can then compare with their neighbour.

The task can be made more demanding by
- asking the students to write (and act out) an interview/conversation with Susan Spencer in which she talks about her day and her life. (They can compare with Unit 4, Ex. 1.)
- asking the students to prepare five questions to ask other students about Susan Spencer's day.
- asking the students to write what they think about Susan's life and how it is different from theirs.

8 Decide ...

AtoZ DECIDE EXERCISES and DO IT YOURSELF!

This is the second *Decide* exercise in this Unit and the second *Decide* exercise which they have met. It is different from the first one in that it contains the choice of *Do it yourself!* If you have already done Supplementary Unit B *Making an Exercise Box,* students can use the *Ideas list* to make their own exercises. Alternatively, they can do something different. (See **AtoZ DO IT YOURSELF**.)

MIXED ABILITIES
Students are likely to find Ex. 8.1 easier than Ex. 8.2.

9 Your Language Record

AtoZ LANGUAGE RECORD

Students can now turn to the *Language Record* and write down the meanings of the words. (It is not intended that they translate the example sentences.)

Time to spare?

AtoZ TIME TO SPARE?

If some students finish before others, they can move on to the *Time to spare?* exercises.

> **Advance notice!**
> Unit 5 requires the students to collect pictures (magazine pictures, drawings, photographs, etc.) before their Unit 5 lesson. You may like to look at Unit 5, Exs. 1–3 now so that you can plan ahead for this.

4 Language focus

Verb + '-ing'; adverbs;
classroom phrases

Advance notice!
Unit 5 requires the students to decide what pictures they need and to collect those pictures before their Unit 5 lesson. You may like to plan time for this, while the students are working on Unit 4. See Unit 5, Exs. 1–3.

---

1 RESEARCHING THE CLASSROOM: GROUPWORK

Some questions to think about during the coming lessons.

- Do you think the groupwork tasks are successful? If not, what exactly goes wrong? Why is this?
- Do the students use their mother tongue a lot in the group? If so, do you think this is a problem? Can you

think of any ways to encourage them to use English?
- Which *kinds of tasks* are most successfully done in groupwork? Which *kinds of tasks* are least successfully done in groupwork?

See **AtoZ** GROUPWORK for further ideas.

---

2 TEACHING NOTES FOR UNIT 4

Important note: If you haven't already done so, sometime very soon, we recommend that you do the Supplementary Units at the back of the Student's Book and that you complete the Parcel of English Registration Card (see page 19 and page 141).

Overview of the Unit

Unit 4 focuses on the use of 'special verbs' (like, hate, start, stop, etc.) and adverbs. The mother tongue is used to draw the students' attention to the form of adverbs in their own language, since this often has a direct equivalent in English. The *Out and about with English* section (Exercise 4) presents and practises useful classroom language. The Unit includes the first *Do it yourself!* exercise (Exercise 5) in which students can plan what they will do after Unit 7.

Timing

Below are very approximate timings (in minutes) for each step. *These will vary considerably from class to class.* You can note down any revised timings here and show your anticipated lesson divisions.

1	Susan Spencer, the swimmer	12
2	I love swimming	
2.1	Some 'special' verbs	5
2.2	What do you think?	10
2.3	Write about your opinions	10
3	'Quickly', 'suddenly', and 'quietly'	
3.1	What do you say?	8
3.2	How to form adverbs	10
3.3	Practice	10
3.4	Play a game!	10
4	Out and about with English	
4.1	What can you say?	5
4.2	In class	15
4.3	If you don't know, ask!	10
5	Do it yourself!	10
6	Your Language Record	(at home) 10

(See also **AtoZ** TIMING.)

What you need

A cassette player and the Class Cassette for Exercise 1 and Exercise 4.2.

Mixed-ability classes and supplementary worksheets

Exercises 1, 2.2, and 3.4 have additional notes for mixed-ability classes.

Language worksheet 4.1 provides extra practice with special verbs (verbs + '-ing').

Language worksheet 4.2 provides extra practice with adverbs.

Say it clearly! Worksheet 1 provides practice with the pronunciation of '-ing' and '-ly/–ily'.
(See also **AtoZ** MIXED ABILITIES.)

Workbook

Unit 4 in the Workbook contains exercises to practise:

- Exercise 1: reading
- Exercise 2: writing and the verb '-ing' with the Past simple
- Exercise 3: writing and speaking in an open dialogue, talking about likes and dislikes
- Exercise 4: adverbs
- Exercise 5: classroom phrases
- Exercise 6: pronunciation of '-ly' and '-ily'

For additional notes on the use of the Workbook and Workbook answers see page 149.

Guidelines

1 Susan Spencer, the swimmer 📼

AtoZ LISTENING

You will probably need to play the cassette two or three times. The first time, you could ask students to listen with their books closed, to see how much they understand. They can then try to answer the questions from memory. You can then play the cassette again so that they can read and check. At this point, insist on the use of the verb+ '-ing' structure in their answers.

> **Answers**
> She says she loves swimming. She says she doesn't mind going to school. She says she hates doing homework. She says she stopped going out with her friends so much.

MIXED ABILITIES

More support can be given by
- playing the recording in short sections. You can stop after each section and check that the students understand.
- writing Peter Black's questions on the blackboard. You can check that the students understand the questions before you play the recording.
- reading the dialogue through with the students before you play the recording. (A student can take Peter Black's part.)

The task can be made more demanding by
- providing more detailed questions, e.g. What did she do when she was nine? What does she do for five hours a day? What doesn't she mind?
- after listening and doing the exercise, you can provide just Peter Black's part on the board. Students can then work in pairs to try to reconstruct the dialogue.
- asking the students to prepare an interview with a famous sportsperson in their country.

- **WB Ex. 1: additional reading material, using 'special verbs'.**

2 I love swimming

2.1 Some 'special' verbs

AtoZ PROCESSING TIME

Read through the comments with the students and then give them a couple of minutes to find more special verbs.

> **Answers**
> love, start, enjoy, don't mind, hate, stop.

2.2 What do you think?

AtoZ PAIRWORK and PATTERN PRACTICE

Before you put the students into pairs to do the exercise, ask two or three students what they think about some of the items listed. Insist on the correct use of verb + '-ing' in their answers.

MIXED ABILITIES

More support can be given by
- writing some of the questions in full on the blackboard with an example answer, e.g. What do you think about playing football? I hate playing football.
- going through the complete exercise before they work in pairs. They can do it across the class, with you listening and correcting.
- doing Ex. 2.3 first with the students.

2.3 Write about your opinions

A to Z WRITING

The purpose of this exercise is to consolidate the students' use of verb + '-ing' and to provide a change of pace.

- **WB Ex. 2: additional writing practice using 'special verbs'.**
- **WB Ex. 3: an open dialogue in which students talk about likes and dislikes.**
- **TB Ws 4.1: additional practice with 'special' verbs.**

3 'Quickly', 'suddenly' and 'quietly'

3.1 What do you say?

A to Z MOTHER TONGUE

You could ask the students for some more examples of adverbs in their mother tongue and/or in English.

3.2 How to form adverbs

You could give the students a few minutes to think of some more examples using the adverbs listed. (They can do this with their neighbour and note down their ideas.) Draw the students' attention to the use of 'i' in 'eas**i**ly,' etc.

> **Answers**
> dangerously   sweetly   slowly

3.3 PRACTICE

A to Z PROCESSING TIME and WRITING

The students can do this alone or with their neighbour.

You could ask them what 'language learning' notices they could put up in the classroom. (Speak clearly, Work quickly, Read carefully, etc.)

> **Answers**
> Talk quietly. Walk quickly. Drive carefully/slowly. Shout loudly. Open carefully. Read carefully.

3.4 Play a game!

A to Z GAMES

Before you play the game with the students, you can mime a few examples yourself and encourage them to guess. As they suggest ideas, say them back to them using verb + '-ing'.

You could play this game in two or three teams. Each person secretly writes down what they are going to mime. Then, within a time limit of 30 seconds or one minute they have to get their other team members to guess what they are miming. Teams can take turns to play. One point for each correct guess before the time runs out. The first team with five points wins.

> **MIXED ABILITIES**
>
> *More support can be given by*
> - reading through the list of phrases first and checking that the students understand each one. You could put translations on the board.
> - putting some more complete examples on the blackboard of what they can say. (E.g. You're driving fast. You're walking quickly.)
>
> *The task can be made more demanding by*
> - telling the students they also have to mime (and write down) WHERE they are doing the action, e.g. working hard in school/in a factory/at home/ in the countryside.
> - telling the students who are miming that they must not make any noises at all.

- **WB Ex. 4: additional practice with adverbs.**

4 Out and about with English

The *Out and about* sections in the course come at the end of every *Language focus* Unit. They provide practice in using language in various social situations.

4.1 What can you say?

The students should be able to suggest various things they can say in each situation. Collect their suggestions on the blackboard.

You write these phrases on a poster and place it on the classroom wall. You can then encourage the students to use the phrases in your lessons.

Examples: **a** What does [word] mean? What's [word] in [mother tongue]? I don't understand this word. Can you help me with this word? **b** I can't hear. Can you say it again? It's too quiet. It's not loud enough. **c** Can I have a dictionary please? Have you got a dictionary, please? Can I use the dictionary, please? **d** How do you spell [word]? How do you write [word]?

4.2 In class 📼

A to Z LISTENING

The layout of the dialogue in the Student's Book shows the teacher talking at the same time as Alison and Will.

Read through the questions with the students first and then play the cassette two or three times.

It is not necessary to spend too much time on explaining what the teacher says here, as the focus is on the language that Alison and Will are using.

Note: The symbol π (pronounced 'pie') is a mathematical symbol. It has the value 3.142. It is used to calculate the circumference of a circle. The distance across a circle is the diameter (symbol 'd'). We can calculate the circumference of a circle by multiplying the diameter by π: πd.

In the example in the recording, the diameter is 3 centimetres. This means the area is:

$3 \times \pi = 3 \times 3.142 = 9.426 \, cm$

Answers

Alison doesn't understand what π ('pi') means. Also, she doesn't know what page they have to do for homework. She asks Will: 'What did she say?', 'What does "pi" mean?', 'What page did she say?', 'What was the other page she said?'. She could say the following things to the teacher: 'Miss, I don't understand "pi". What does it mean?' Or: 'Can you explain "pi", Miss?'; 'Miss, can you explain that again please?'; 'Miss, can you say the page numbers again, please?'; 'Miss, I didn't hear. Can you say that again, please?'.

4.3 If you don't know, ask!

These phrases can be added to the poster suggested in the notes for Exercise 4.1 above.

- **WB Ex. 5: additional practice with classroom phrases.**

Answers

a How do you pronounce this word? How do you say 'pizza' in English? **b** Can you check this? I've finished. Can you look at this? **c** Can you check this? Can you look at this? **d** Can you repeat that, please? Sorry? Can you say that again, please? **e** Sorry, I didn't understand. Can you speak more slowly, please? Can you say that again, please? Can you repeat that, please?

---

5 Do it yourself!

AtoZ DO IT YOURSELF, AUTONOMY and STUDENT INVOLVEMENT

This exercise develops the idea of students planning their own work. Students are asked to plan what they would like to do after Unit 7. The amount of 'open' time you make available for the students will depend on what you feel they can handle, and what you feel you need to cover. Initially, it is probably best to allow them a limited amount of time after Unit 7, so that they can plan – for example, 20 minutes or so of classroom time.

The intention is that the students should achieve a deeper sense of involvement, control, and 'ownership' of what happens in their lessons. At this stage, it is very likely that the students' views and your own views on what it is appropriate to do in class will differ considerably. The important point in all of this, however, is that students achieve a degree of control and *accept the consequences of that*. The key to successful use of these 'DIY' sessions, therefore, is in discussion before the session, with you perhaps questioning and suggesting activities, and in EVALUATION (see **AtoZ** EVALUATION) after the session. See **AtoZ** DO IT YOURSELF! for more guidance.

For the planning/discussion stage in this Unit, put the students into small groups. Depending on the time you have available, you could either a) allow a reasonable amount of time now (10–15 minutes) and some more time later, when you are working on Units 5–6, for them to finalise their plan or b) ask the students to discuss and plan together outside of class time and tell you in a few days' time what they are thinking of doing. They can record their ideas in the space at the end of Unit 7.

6 Your Language Record

AtoZ LANGUAGE RECORD

Time to spare?

AtoZ TIME TO SPARE?

If some students finish before others, they can move on to the *Time to spare?* exercises. If some students write questions for other students to answer, these can be placed in the *Exercise Box*. (See Supplementary Unit B.)

Revision Box

AtoZ REVISION BOX

5 Activity A good life

TEACHING NOTES FOR UNIT 5

Overview of the Unit

In Unit 5, the students work together to share their ideas and make a poster about what they think makes 'a good life'. A short planning stage is needed before the actual poster-making lesson, in which the students need to decide what pictures they will collect (magazines, pictures, photographs, drawings and so on). A short evaluation stage concludes the Unit. The Unit aims to provide an opportunity to use language for communication and to stimulate the students' thinking about the world they live in.

Timing

The initial planning and collecting stages (Exercises 1–3) are intended to be done before the Unit 5 lesson. The activity itself is intended for one full lesson, although you may like to split it up over a number of lessons.

Suggested timings are:

Before the lesson		
1 What do you need for a good life?		15
2 Work in a small group		10
3 Collect some pictures	(at home)	10
In the lesson		
4 Write about your pictures		30
5 Talk about your posters		10–15
6 Evaluation		5–10

What you need

Some large sheets of paper (preferably some coloured), coloured pens, glue, scissors, and pictures (in case the students don't bring enough).

Mixed-ability classes

Exercise 4 has additional notes for mixed-ability classes.

(See also **AtoZ** MIXED ABILITIES.)

Workbook

Unit 5 in the Workbook contains the following fluency exercises:

- Exercise 1: a questionnaire about 'a good life'
- Exercise 2: a brainstorming and writing exercise

Guidelines

Before the lesson

1 What do you need for a good life?

AtoZ BRAINSTORMING, POSTERS

Before you collect ideas from the class you could give the students a few minutes to share ideas in pairs/small groups.

As students suggest ideas, you can try to push them a bit further to give examples or more detail, so that ideas come from ideas on the map. (See, for example, the way that 'good health' might break down into 'good food' and 'exercise'.)

2 Work in a small group

The purpose of the groupwork here is to help students decide who will bring which pictures.

3 Collect some pictures

This is done at home, before the Activity lesson.

In the lesson

4 Write about your pictures

AtoZ WRITING, INTERACTIVE WRITING

Before setting the students to work in groups, you could take one or two of the students' pictures and ask for ideas about what they could say about them. Write a short paragraph on the board, as an example.

Next, give them a few minutes to decide who will write what. Before they start writing, you can check that everyone has something to write about.

Encourage them to help each other in their groups.

MIXED ABILITIES

More support can be given by

- using one of the pictures that you bring to class, prepare an outline paragraph about it. The students can complete it in their own words. For example:
  This is …
  We need … because …
  I think …
  I like …
  I don't like …
- asking two students to work together to write something. They can then help each other.
- dividing the groups up so that there is a stronger student in each group. See **AtoZ** GROUPWORK.
- sitting with a group and discussing what they can write. You could perhaps write something for them and give them a few minutes to read it, before they write their own version.

The task can be made more demanding by

- asking the students to give more details and examples. Read through their work and add questions: 'Can you tell me more about …?', 'Why is … important?', and so on.
- asking the students to add 'advice' or suggestions for a good life.

5 Talk about your posters

AtoZ DISPLAYING STUDENTS' WORK

The posters can be stuck on the wall or laid out on the desks. The students can then all stand and walk around the room looking at the other posters and talking to the people who wrote them. You could make a quiz (on the board) for this stage, based on what the students have written. Students then have to find the answers as they look at the posters.

6 Evaluation

AtoZ EVALUATION

This can be done with the whole class. Emphasise the 'How can you do it better next time?' question and try to get them to suggest practical steps for the next activity they do.

6 Culture matters At school in the United States

TEACHING NOTES FOR UNIT 6

Note: Remind the students that they should be preparing something for the *Open plan* section of Unit 7.

Overview of the Unit

The main aim of the *Culture matters* Units is to give the students some understanding of how British/American society is different from their own. The Units do not intend to introduce any new structures or language areas. This first *Culture matters* Unit focuses on the school day and school life in the United States. Students get an overview of the school day, the timetable, eating arrangements and school rules. The Unit provides reading and writing tasks, with the possibility of future development.

Timing

This Unit is designed to take one class hour, except for Exercise 5, which can be developed for homework or for another lesson. Below are some suggested timings (in minutes) for each step.

1	Your school day	10
2	Lee's school	15
3	Lee's school subjects	15
4	School rules	10
5	Across cultures	10–30

(See also **AtoZ** TIMING.)

What you need

The Class Cassette and a cassette player (optionally) for Exercises 2 and 4.

Mixed-ability classes

Exercise 2 has additional notes for mixed-ability classes.

(See also **AtoZ** MIXED ABILITIES.)

Workbook

Workbook Unit 6 is the first *Help yourself!* Unit. It focuses on ways in which the students can help themselves when they are learning vocabulary. The Unit contains two ways first presented in Level 1, and one more way new to this level.

- Exercise 1: make a word bag
- Exercise 2: make a jigsaw
- Exercise 3: make a crossword

See page 149 for a special note on the *Help yourself!* Units and **AtoZ** VOCABULARY.

Background notes to schools in the United States

There is wide variety in the way schools are organised in the United States, but the following information gives a general picture. Schools are as follows:

Elementary schools	Grades 1–4	Ages 6–9
Grade schools	Grades 5–6	Ages 10–11
Junior high schools	Grades 7–9	Ages 12–14
High schools	Grades 10–12	Ages 15–17

'Schools' are not always in separate buildings or institutions. In many towns several 'schools' are combined – for example, elementary and grade schools. Many high schools include Grade 9.

In elementary schools, students generally have one main classroom where all the areas of the curriculum are covered by the same teacher (with the exceptions of Art and Gymnastics). In grade schools and above, students move to separate classrooms with different teachers for each subject. Students can take an extra-curricular subject of their choice: Vocal Music, 'Band' (marching-band instruments), Art, 'Shop' (mainly Woodwork), and, in some areas, Agricultural Education. Foreign languages are often not offered until 9th Grade.

Uniforms are not required in public schools. (Note: 'public' schools in the United States are state/government schools, but 'public' schools in Britain are private, fee-paying schools.) However, each school has its own 'dress code', such as no shorts, no T-shirts with vulgar language, no sleeveless shirts, etc. School hours are generally 8.30 or 9.00 a.m. to 2.30 or 3.00 p.m.

As in British schools, most schools have a school cafeteria where the students can buy a meal or sit down with a 'bag lunch' ★(food brought from home). There are national regulations about the food which school cafeterias can offer, and much of the food comes from subsidised agricultural produce. It is thus fairly cheap.
★ British English = 'packed lunch'.

Guidelines

1 Your school day

AtoZ DISCUSSION

If your students all regularly attend the same school where you teach, then the questions listed in the Student's Book are likely to be self-evident. Some alternative questions for discussion are:

- what is your favourite day?
- when is the best time of the day for you?
- when do you feel most awake/tired?
- what do you usually eat in the break?
- what do you usually do in the break?
- how do you think the school day could be improved?

2 Lee's school 📼

AtoZ READING and PROCESSING TIME

The students can read this text alone or with their neighbour. Ask them to make a list of the differences between Lee's day and their own.

Some points you might pick up on:

- the days and times when Lee goes to school.
- announcements from the loudspeaker.
- the 'pledge of allegiance' when everybody has to swear to support the flag.
- furniture in the classroom photograph.
- the school canteen photograph, and the availability of meals at school.

MIXED ABILITIES

More support can be given by
- going first through the vocabulary you think will cause difficulties.
- providing a bilingual wordlist.
- talking about the students' school and their school day first. Build up a short text on the paragraph, similar to the text in the book.
- asking students to read the texts and to make a list of the words/phrases they don't understand. You can then collect the 'difficult words' on the board and explain them, before you ask the students to read again.

- giving students some guiding questions, e.g. How many students are in Lee's school?; What time does Lee go to school?

The task can be made more demanding by
- asking the students to read the first two paragraphs and to write two similar paragraphs about their school.
- asking them to make a list of the precise details in the photographs which seem different from their country.
- preparing 10 questions to ask an American child about school.

3 Lee's school subjects

AtoZ PROBLEM SOLVING

Read through the introductory comment with the students. This explains that 'Shop' is where Lee does metalwork or woodwork.

Go through the timetable and check that the students understand what each subject is. Then, give them a minute or so to study the timetable and work out which is likely to be Lee's favourite day.

> **Answer**
> Lee's favourite day is likely to be Thursday since he has Science and Mathematics (Algebra) and 'Shop' on that day.

4 School rules 📼

AtoZ READING

Before you begin this exercise, you can ask the students if they know the rules of their school. Put some of them on the board. Ask them what they think about the rules. You can ask them to read through Lee's school rules and ask them whether they think those rules are good or bad. Which rules would they take away? Which rules would they add?

5 Across cultures

This exercise can form the starting-point for more extended writing if time is available. It would also form an ideal contribution to *A Parcel of English*. (See Supplementary Unit A.)

7 Revision and evaluation

TEACHING NOTES FOR UNIT 7

Note: Remind the students that they should have prepared something for the *Open plan* section of this Unit (see Unit 4, Ex. 5).

General note on the Revision and evaluation Units

CES contains six *Revision and evaluation* Units. These aim to revise the language covered in the preceding Units so that the students have a chance to check that they understand what they have covered before the course moves forward. The Units are of two main types: Units 7, 17 and 27 contain *revision exercises*, whilst Units 12, 22 and 32 involve the students in *test writing* (and thereby revising).

The final part of each *Revision and evaluation* Unit asks the students to look back on the work they have done and to give their opinions on how it could be improved. They are also asked to think about how they personally approach language learning.

The *Revision and evaluation* Units are linked to the Workbook as follows:

	Student's Book	Workbook
Unit 7	revision exercises	self-test
Unit 12	test writing	revision work
Unit 17	revision exercises	self-test
Unit 22	test writing	revision work
Unit 27	revision exercises	self-test
Unit 32	test writing	revision work

Overview of the Unit

The Unit first asks the students to assess their own abilities in some of the language covered in Units 3–6. Revision and practice exercises follow, so that students can see if their self-assessment is correct. In the final exercises, students can discuss the previous Units and answer a questionnaire on how they learn vocabulary. (This links directly with Unit 6 in the Workbook.)

Timing

The Unit is intended for one full lesson, with revision exercises done selectively. Suggested timings are as follows:

1	How well do you know it?	5
2	A life of luxury	15
3	What do you think?	10
4	What's the missing word?	5
5	What's the word?	5
6	Looking back at Units 3–6	
6.1	Group discussion	10
6.2	Your own ideas	3
7	Learning vocabulary	5

(See also **AtoZ** TIMING.)

What you need

No special materials are required.

Mixed-ability classes and supplementary worksheets

Language worksheet 4.1 provides extra practice with 'special verbs'. Language worksheet 4.2 provides extra practice with adverbs.

(See also **AtoZ** MIXED ABILITIES.)

Workbook

Unit 7 in the Workbook contains a test for the students to use by themselves. The test covers:

- Exercise 1: sport vocabulary
- Exercise 2: Present simple question forms
- Exercise 3: reading comprehension about daily routines
- Exercise 4: expressing likes and dislikes

For additional notes on the use of the Workbook and Workbook answers see page 149.

Guidelines

1 How well do you know it?

AtoZ TASKS IN BLOCKS and OVERVIEWING

The main aim here is to encourage the students to reflect on how much they have learnt.

Before asking students to complete the chart, look back with them at the relevant sections of the previous Units to remind them what they did.

Give the students a few minutes to tick the box. You could encourage them to *briefly* discuss/compare with their neighbour.

As an alternative, you could ask the students to make their own table (perhaps with their neighbour) showing what they think they have learned in this Theme, and how well they know it. They could then discuss this with the class, perhaps giving examples of each point listed.

Before the students start working on the exercises, it is a good idea to go through the exercises with them, so that they know exactly what they have to do in each one. After this there are a number of possibilities:

- let the students choose what they want to revise and practise – either to test themselves or to revise where they feel weakest.
- ask the students to do *two* exercises: one that they ticked 'very well' and one that they ticked 'a little'.
- get all the students to do all the exercises (this requires more time, of course).

Once the students have done an exercise, they can look back at the chart in Exercise 1 (or their own chart) to check their self-assessment.

(Students can also complete the Unit for homework.)

2 A life of luxury

AtoZ PAIRWORK

If you have time, some pairs of students can act out their conversation to the class. They can also record it on a cassette at home with a friend.

3 What do you think?

AtoZ WRITING

4 What's the missing word?

> **Answers**
> fast   slowly   beautifully   badly   well

5 What's the word?

> **Answers**
> 1 heart   2 energy   3 improves   4 blood   5 body   6 lifts
> 7 flexible   8 different   9 suddenly

6 Looking back at Units 3–6

AtoZ EVALUATION

6.1 Group discussion

This section has two parts. Exercise 6.1 involves small group discussion, while Exercise 6.2 asks students to note down their own reactions.

For this exercise, divide the students into groups of 3–4, and allocate a Unit or two Units to each group. Ask them to decide who in their group will report back to the class. Remind them that they are *talking about the Units in the book*.

For the reporting back stage, if more than one group is looking at each Unit, ask one group to report back and then ask the other group(s) if they have any other points to add.

6.2 Your own ideas

In this exercise, students write their own personal ideas. Tell them that they can do this anonymously but that you would like to read what they think. You could give them some more questions to stimulate their thoughts:

- How do they feel in their English lessons?
- Do they have any suggestions for future lessons?
- What did they like best in their English lessons so far?
- Where do they think they have most problems?
- Is it going too fast, just right or too slow?

Remember to collect in their papers!

See **AtoZ** EVALUATION and STUDENT INVOLVEMENT for details of the rationale behind evaluation activities and practical ideas on how to handle them.

7 Learning vocabulary

AtoZ AUTONOMY and DISCUSSION

This exercise asks the students think about a particular aspect of their learning – vocabulary. All students have ways of learning vocabulary, but they may not be as efficient as they could be. This exercise is intended to raise the students' awareness so as to make more use of the techniques in the Workbook (Workbook Unit 6).

Give the students a few minutes to read and answer the questions, and then a few more minutes to compare with their neighbour. You can then open a brief discussion on what they answered. Some more questions are:

- What mistakes do you often make with spelling?
- Which sounds do you think are most difficult for you?
- Which words do you often confuse?
- What is your favourite word? Do you remember when you learned it?
- How do you learn vocabulary? Can you think of any other ways you could learn or practise it?

At this point, you could ask them to turn back to Workbook Unit 6 and look at the different techniques there. For homework, you could ask them to choose a technique and learn the vocabulary from Units 3–6 (see the *Language Records*).

Open plan

The *Do it yourself!* sections are intended to provide a 'space' in the lessons that the students can truly call their own. Please see the teaching notes for Unit 4, Exercise 5 for more details.

These sections could be regarded as a minimum – there is no reason why the frequency of such 'open' lesson time should not be increased. The important point in this, however, is that a) the students discuss what they are going to do and agree it with you, and b) that they evaluate what they have done afterwards, particularly when they are deciding what they will do next time.

See **A to Z** DO IT YOURSELF for more guidance.

Theme B — Life on Earth

OVERVIEW OF THE THEME

Theme B, Life on Earth, focuses on aspects of the natural world and natural history, particularly the rainforests and dinosaur life. Students learn about the contribution that the rainforests make to the world and to human life (Unit 8), use their imagination to write shape poems about the rainforests (Unit 10), and learn about famous natural history sites in the United States (Unit 11). Grammatically, the Theme introduces 'was' and 'were'; the Past simple; regular verbs; and inviting and suggesting (Unit 9). Student decision-making is involved through *Decide* exercises in the *Topic* Unit, the *Revision and evaluation* Units and the *Open plan* section. Students also learn how to write their own tests (Unit 12).

The Theme offers cross-curricular links with Environmental Science, Natural History and Prehistory.

Using the cover page

AtoZ OVERVIEWING

Suggested time for the cover page: 10 minutes.

The cover page visually summarises the Theme and raises the students' interest in the Units which follow. Allow time for the students to look closely at the pictures. They can work alone or in pairs to answer the questions and write the Unit numbers in the boxes at the side.

> **Answers**
> 1 pictures: geyser – Unit 11; shape poem – Unit 10; dinosaur – Unit 9; rain jigsaw – Unit 8; rainforest – Unit 8.
> 2 The biggest rainforests are in South America, Africa, and South-East Asia (pages 44–5 in the Student's Book). Four types of dinosaur are: Compsognathus, Apatosaurus, Stegosaurus, and Protoceratops (page 50). A plant that grows in Java: rice (page 45).
> 3 In Unit 10 you can write poems about the rainforest.

See page 32 for additional ideas for using the cover page.

8 Topic In a rainforest

1· WHAT HAPPENED WITH UNITS 3–7?

Some questions to think about before you start Unit 8.

- If you look back at Units 3–7, are there particular sections that went very well, or not so well? Why do you think that was?
- Unit 4 introduced the idea of students helping themselves, which was followed up in the Workbook (Unit 6) and in the *Open plan* section at the end of

Unit 7. How did the students respond to this? Do they need more direction? Could they be given more room for personal responsibility? Can you experiment with trying different approaches?
- Unit 5 introduced an activity (poster-making). How did that go? Do you need to approach the activity in Unit 10 differently?

2 TEACHING NOTES FOR UNIT 8

Overview of the Unit

Unit 8 introduces the rainforests and encourages students to share what they already know. On the cassette, sounds from a rainforest stimulate the students' imagination of what it is like to be in a rainforest. Reading texts present information about the rainforests and show how they contribute to the Earth's climate. A listening text presents information about a fantastic discovery in a rainforest in Australia. The Unit also includes two *Decide* exercises, which provide a choice of tasks for the students and a song about the rainforests.

Timing

Below are some suggested timings (in minutes) for each activity. You can note down any revised timings here and show your anticipated lesson divisions.

1	What do you know about rainforests?	8
2	In the rainforest	8
3	Why are the rainforests important?	
3.1	The magazine questions	5
3.2	Read about the rainforests	15
4	Decide …	15
5	How do the rainforests make rain?	10
6	Sing a song!	10
7	The oldest living things on Earth …	
7.1	What do you think?	5

7.2	The Living Planet	10
7.3	Listen again	10
8	Decide …	15–20
9	Your Language Record	5–8

What you need

A cassette player and the Class Cassette for Exercises 2, 3.2, 5, 6 (song) and 7.2. *Exercise Box* for the *Time to spare?*

Mixed-ability classes and supplementary worksheets

Exercises 3.2, 4, 7.2, and 8 have additional notes for mixed-ability classes.

Say it clearly! Worksheet 1: provides practice with the pronunciation of '-ed': /t/, /d/, /ɪd/.

(See also **AtoZ** MIXED ABILITIES.)

Workbook

Unit 8 in the Workbook contains exercises to practise:

- Exercise 1: Vocabulary
- Exercise 2: Reading about dangers to the rainforests
- Exercise 3: Singing a song in English
- Exercise 4: Speaking in an open dialogue about the landscape and climate
- Exercise 5: Reading about tree rings
- Exercise 6: Pronunciation of /e/ and /ɑː/

Guidelines

1 What do you know about rainforests?

AtoZ DISCUSSION

Some background information: Rainforests are forests which produce rain (later, students will see how this process works). There are rainforests in Amazonia and Africa and in South-East Asia (see map). In a rainforest, the trees block out light, keeping the forest dark and very humid. Rainforests are important because they contribute to the world's climate and help to produce oxygen. They are also the home to thousands of types of plants and animals, most of which live in the trees, 30 metres from the ground. Some animals that live in rainforests: iguanas, macaws, leopards, snakes, butterflies, tree frogs, sloths, tigers. Apart from trees, many beautiful flowers live there. Rainforests are now under threat (a text later in the Unit and in the Workbook shows why). At the present rate of destruction, estimates show that there will be almost no rainforest left by 2035.

2 In the rainforest ▭

AtoZ LISTENING

The recording contains various sounds from the rainforest. Ask the students to note down their ideas about each sound and then to compare their ideas with each other.

> **Answers**
> birds   machines   rain   thunder   insects   lions

3 Why are the rainforests important?

3.1 The magazine questions

Ask the students to suggest what information they think they will find in the magazine article. You can put the points that they suggest on the blackboard and then compare them with the article after they have read through it.

3.2 Read about the rainforests ▭

AtoZ TASKS IN BLOCKS, PROCESSING TIME and READING

The exercise asks the students to read through the article in two stages. Explain the two stages to the students before they begin: first they read the article straight through and share ideas with their neighbours on what they understand; then they go back and make a list of the words/phrases they find difficult, so that they can see if they can guess the meanings. This two-stage process is intended to encourage a more active approach to reading.

After giving the students time to do this, you can collect questions or difficulties from them to go through.

MIXED ABILITIES

More support can be given by
- providing the students with a wordlist or by going through the words on the *Language Record*.
- sitting with a group of students and reading through the text with them.
- dividing the text into small sections, or taking the 'question' sections one at a time.
- putting the students in small groups, with a stronger student in each group. That student can help the others to understand.
- devising a 'skeleton' with questions for each section, which show the key ideas. Students can read and try to complete the missing information, e.g. Section 1: Rainforests cover 6% of the Earth. Where are the rainforests? Where aren't there any rainforests? Section 2: 75% of all the animals we know come from rainforests. What animals live in the rainforests? Where do they live? Is it hot or cold in a rainforest?, and so on.

The task can be made more demanding by
- asking the students to write five questions for other students to answer.
- asking the students to write a short paragraph about the rainforest (no more than 80 words, for example) using information in the text.
- writing some 'true/false/not in the text' statements for the students to check. For example:
  (i)   Rubber trees grow in Java. True, false or not in the text?
  (ii) People don't live in the rainforests.
  (iii) Birds don't live in rainforests.
- asking students to add one more sentence to every paragraph. They then compare texts with their partner.

- **WB Exs 1-4: further practice with vocabulary, reading, and speaking.**

4 Decide ...

AtoZ DECIDE and MONITORING AND GUIDING

Before the students decide which task they want to do, go through the tasks with them so that they know what each one involves. Then let them choose a task.

MIXED ABILITIES
Students are likely to find Exercise 4.1 easier than
Exercise 4.2 and Exercise 4.2 easier than Exercise 4.3.

After doing Exercise 4, you can show them that Exercise
8 is another *Decide* exercise which includes the option to
Do it yourself!

4.1 Words in groups

> **Answers**
> **Things that live in rainforests:** animals, birds, plants, trees,
> insects. **Things that we get from rainforests:** wood, air, rain,
> rubber, plants, fruits, medicines. **Words to describe
> rainforests and trees:** dark, hot, tall, wet.

After doing the exercise, you can ask the students to make
a similar exercise about cities. For example, 'Things that
live in cities', 'Things we find in cities', 'Words to
describe cities'.

4.2 True or false?

> **Answers**
> **a** False. The ground is always wet. **b** True. **c** False.
> Seventy-five per cent of all of the types of animals that we
> know live in rainforests. **d** True. **e** False. There was a very
> big rainforest in Java.

4.3 In the rainforest

5 How do the rainforests make rain? 📼
AtoZ PROCESSING TIME

> **Answers and tapescript**
> **1** Rain falls from the clouds. **2** The trees catch the rain in their
> leaves. **3** The rain runs down the outside of the tree to the
> ground. **4** The rain water goes into the ground. **5** The water
> goes into the roots. **6** From the roots, water goes up inside
> the tree to the leaves. **7** The leaves become wet. **8** The sun
> shines on the leaves and makes water vapour. **9** The water
> vapour becomes clouds.

6 Sing a song! Mother forest 📼
AtoZ SONGS

The song is also recorded on the Workbook cassette.

7 The oldest living things on Earth ...
AtoZ LISTENING

7.1 What do you think?

This stage is intended to make the listening work in
Exercise 7.2 more interactive. You can put on the

blackboard some of the ideas that students mention. After
listening to the recording, they can compare with the
ideas on the board.

7.2 The Living Planet 📼

At this point, the students only need to get a general idea
of what the recording is about. (Exercise 7.3 involves
more detail.) Anne Briggs is talking about the oldest
living things on Earth – trees. She mentions the oldest
trees – the Bristlecone Pines in California (see picture in
the Student's Book) and some trees they discovered in
Australia.

Note the pronunciation of 'Wollemi' /wɒləmiː/.

> 📼 TAPESCRIPT:
> *Fenton:* Hello. Welcome to 'The Living Planet'. My
>   name is Jack Fenton. Today, Anne Briggs, a
>   botanist, is going to tell us about the oldest
>   living things on Earth – trees.
>   Anne, where are the oldest trees?
> *Briggs:* Well, they grow in California, in the United
>   States of America. They are called the
>   Bristlecone Pines.
> *Fenton:* How old are they?
> *Briggs:* Well, some of them are over four thousand years
>   old.
> *Fenton:* Four thousand years old!
> *Briggs:* Yes, that's right. That means that they started
>   growing before people lived in towns.
> *Fenton:* Are the trees very big?
> *Briggs:* Oh, no. They grow very slowly. They take about
>   three thousand years to grow to about 14 metres.
> *Fenton:* That's not very tall.
> *Briggs:* No. The oldest *type* of tree is much, much older.
> *Fenton:* Oh yes?
> *Briggs:* Yes. In 1994, they discovered some trees in a
>   rainforest in Australia. They called them the
>   Wollemi Pines and they are more than 150
>   *million* years old.
> *Fenton:* 150 million years old!
> *Briggs:* Yes, this *type* of tree is more than 150 million
>   years old. It's the most fantastic discovery for a
>   long time. These trees started growing in
>   Australia before Australia was a continent.
> *Fenton:* What does that mean?
> *Briggs:* Well, at that time, 150 *million* years ago, all the
>   continents were part of one big continent.
>   Dinosaurs lived in many parts of the Earth. The
>   climate was very different from today. When the
>   climate changed, most of the plants and animals
>   died, but the Wollemi Pine continued growing
>   without any problem.

MIXED ABILITIES

More support can be given by

- providing the students with a copy of the tapescript which they can read before they listen. You could give them a copy with some phrases or words missing for them to complete, or a copy with only Jack Fenton's part.
- looking at the newspaper story outline in Exercise 8.1, the notes in Exercise 7.3 and the photograph of the Bristlecone Pines with the students. Ask them what they think they will hear on the recording.
- playing the recording in short sections and asking the students what they understood after each section.

The task can be made more demanding by

- asking them to listen for details. For example: Who is Anne Briggs? What is four thousand years old? How long does it take a Bristlecone Pine to grow to 14 metres? and so on.
- asking them to write a short newspaper-style summary of the interview. They can start: 'Yesterday, Anne Briggs, a famous botanist, told "The Living Planet" radio programme about …'
- stopping the recording after Anne Briggs says something and asking them to predict what Jack Fenton will say next.

7.3 Listen again

This stage involves listening for detail. When the students report back, insist on the correct pronunciation of the Past tense (see the *Say it clearly!* box in the Student's Book).

Answers

1994: She says that they discovered some trees in a rainforest in Australia.

The continents: The trees started growing when all the continents were part of one big continent.

Dinosaurs: Dinosaurs lived in many parts of the Earth (when the trees started growing).

The climate: The climate was very different then.

Plants and animals: When the climate changed, the plants and animals died, but the Wollemi Pines continued growing.

Note: The actual trees that they found are not 150 million years old. It is the *type* of tree that is 150 million years old. It has remained unchanged since the time of the dinosaurs.

- **WB Ex. 5: reading practice about tree rings and the age of trees.**

8 Decide …

AtoZ DECIDE and DO IT YOURSELF!

MIXED ABILITIES

Students are likely to find Ex. 8.2 easier than Ex. 8.1.

Read through the exercise with the students before you ask them to choose one.

8.1 A fantastic discovery

For Exercise 8.1 you can stimulate the students' imagination more by asking them what they think the Australian rainforest is like, and by going through the questions in the book, asking for ideas. They can also use the information given in Exercise 7.2, so you could give them a copy of the tapescript.

The photograph shows David Noble (see Unit 9, Exercise 4.5) holding part of a leaf from a Wollemi Pine and a fossil over 150 million years old. The exact location of the Wollemi Pines is being kept a secret to prevent people stealing or damaging the trees.

8.2 What's the word?

Answers

1 America 2 climate 3 medicines 4 danger 5 falls 6 vapour 7 trees 8 rice 9 shines 10 wet 11 rainforest

---

8.3 Do it yourself!

If you have already done Supplementary Unit B, *Making an Exercise Box*, students can use the *Ideas list* to make their own exercises.

They can also use the ideas in the *Time to spare?* box.

9 Your Language Record

AtoZ LANGUAGE RECORD

Time to spare?

AtoZ TIME TO SPARE?

9 Language focus

Past simple: 'be', regular verbs; inviting and suggesting

1 RESEARCHING THE CLASSROOM: WHAT MAKES A TASK DIFFICULT?

Some questions to think about during the coming lessons. Choose a task that the students found difficult.

- Why did they find it difficult?
- Was there a problem with the number of things they were being asked to do at the same time?
- Was there sufficient time for them to think?

- Did they understand the instructions?
- Were the examples clear?
- Did they have sufficient preparation?
- What other factors might make a task difficult?

See **A to Z** TASKS for further ideas.

2 TEACHING NOTES FOR UNIT 9

Overview of the Unit

Timing

Below are very approximate timings (in minutes) for each step.

1	When the Wollemi Pines …	10–12
2	More dinosaur facts	10
3	In the dinosaur forest	
3.1	'Was' or 'were'?	10
3.2	Spot the difference!	12
4	Some more Past tense verbs	
4.1	What do you say?	3
4.2	The rainforest in Java	10
4.3	Regular verbs	5
4.4	Say it clearly!	10
4.5	How they discovered the Wollemi Pines	12
4.6	Some more practice	10
5	Out and about with English	
5.1	What can you say?	5
5.2	Will meets Alison and Nick	12
5.3	Practice	15
6	Do it yourself!	10
7	Your Language Record	(at home) 10

(See also **A to Z** TIMING.)

What you need

A cassette player and the Class Cassette for Exercises 4.4, 4.5 (optional), and 5.2.

Mixed-ability classes and supplementary worksheets

Exercises 1, 2, 3 and 5 have additional notes for mixed-ability classes.

Language worksheet 9.1 provides extra practice with the Past simple of 'be' ('was' and 'were').

Language worksheet 9.2 provides extra practice with the regular Past simple.

Say it clearly! Worksheet 1: provides practice with the pronunciation of '-ed': /t/, /d/, /ɪd/.

(See also **A to Z** MIXED ABILITIES.)

Workbook

Unit 9 in the Workbook contains exercises to practise the following:

- Exercise 1: reading about dinosaurs
- Exercise 2: 'was/were'
- Exercise 3: Past simple with regular verbs
- Exercise 4: Past simple with regular verbs
- Exercise 5: pronunciation of '-ed'
- Exercise 6: speaking in an open dialogue (inviting and suggesting)

For additional notes on the use of the Workbook and Workbook answers see page 149.

52 Theme B

Guidelines

1 When the Wollemi Pines …

AtoZ PROCESSING TIME

Exercises 1 and 2 are designed to give the students more direct exposure with working with the regular Past simple and the past of 'be' before the language practice in Exercises 3 and 4.

> **Answers**
> All of the statements are true.

MIXED ABILITIES

More support can be given by
- dividing the students into groups. One group can look at sentences 1-4, another group at 5–8, and so on.
- providing a translation of each sentence. Students can then match the correct translation to each sentence before they decide if it is true or false.
- explaining the meaning of the verbs 'was', 'were', 'appeared', etc. before the students read.

- **WB Ex. 1: more reading about dinosaurs.**

2 More dinosaur facts

AtoZ READING, PROCESSING TIME

> **Answers**
> **a** Compsognathus **b** Apatosaurus **c** Stegosaurus
> **d** Protoceratops

MIXED ABILITIES

More support can be given by
- looking at the pictures of the dinosaurs with the students first. Ask them how they can describe each one. Put the key words on the board.
- putting on the board just the information needed to match with the pictures, e.g. **a** This dinosaur was very small, **b** This dinosaur had a small head. It walked on four legs, **c** This dinosaur had triangular plates on its back, **d** This dinosaur had bones at the back of its head. They looked like a fan.

The task can be made more demanding by
- giving them some more pictures of dinosaurs to describe.
- giving them copies of some of the texts with 'was'/'were' and some of the other verbs missing. The students can then complete them.
- asking them to classify the dinosaurs in different ways. For example: walked on two legs/walked on four legs; meat-eater/vegetarian; heavy/light; long legs/short legs, and so on.

3 In the dinosaur forest

3.1 'Was' or 'were'?

AtoZ INDUCTIVE GRAMMAR

Students can do this alone, in pairs or with the whole class.

> **Answers**
> I was, you were, he/she/it was, we were, you were, they were. There was only one …, there were many … .

3.2 Spot the difference!

Alone or in pairs the students can spot the difference. After you have gone through their answers, they can write eight sentences about the pictures.

> **Answers**
> In the morning … **1** There was a bird in the tree. **2** There was a snake in the grass. **3** There was a very small dinosaur near the tree. **4** There was a lot of grass. **5** There were two dinosaurs in the water. **6** There were two birds in the sky. **7** There were black clouds in the sky. **8** There were fish in the water.

MIXED ABILITIES

More support can be given with the following extra activity.
Put some times and days on the board. For example:

5.00 7.30
1.00 4.00
7.00

Monday Tuesday Wednesday Thursday Friday
Saturday Sunday

morning afternoon evening

You can then ask them questions before they work in pairs to ask each other.

– Where were you at five o'clock on Thursday morning?
– I was in bed!

- **WB Ex. 2 and Language worksheet 9.1: more practice with 'was'/'were'.**

4 Some more Past tense verbs

4.1 What do you say?

AtoZ MOTHER TONGUE

You may be able to identify examples of 'regular' Past tense verbs in the students' mother tongue.

4.2 The rainforest in Java

AtoZ INDUCTIVE GRAMMAR

> **Answers**
> Verbs from Unit 8, Ex. 3.2 section 4: be – was, were; chop – chopped, want – wanted, plant – planted, live – lived, go – went, disappear – disappeared. The point to notice is that many of the verbs end with '-ed'.

4.3 Regular verbs

> **Answers**
> Some more regular verbs from Ex. 1: appear – appeared,
> move – moved, crash – crashed, discover – discovered.

4.4 Say it clearly! 🔊

AtoZ PRONUNCIATION

You will probably need to play the recording two or three
times. Insist on the correct pronunciation as you go
through the answers.

> **Answers**
> washed /t/; wanted /ɪd/; stayed /d/; played /d/; looked /t/;
> visited /d/; liked /t/; decided /ɪd/.

4.5 How they discovered the Wollemi Pines 🔊

AtoZ PATTERN PRACTICE, MONITORING AND GUIDING

> **Answers**
> worked, visited, walked, wanted, climbed, discovered,
> looked, collected, looked, compared, started, lived.

4.6 SOME MORE PRACTICE

You can ask for ideas from the students before they begin
writing and also ask them to write a few more sentences
of their own.

Students could also write some more sentences about
themselves for other students to guess whether they are
true or false. They can use the verbs that they found in
Exercises 4.2 and 4.3.

- **WB Exs 3 and 4 and Language worksheet 9.2: more practice with
  Past simple regular verbs.**

5 Out and about with English

5.1 What can you say?

Some example phrases: Do you want to come to my
house tomorrow? Would you like to come to my house
tomorrow? What are you doing tomorrow? Why don't
you come to my house tomorrow?

5.2 Will meets Alison and Nick 🔊

AtoZ LISTENING

> **Answers**
> Nick is Alison's cousin. Nick is rather rude to Will and
> dismisses Will's opinion. They plan to meet at Will's house
> later.

5.3 PRACTICE

MIXED ABILITIES

More support can be given by
- giving the students an outline of a conversation using
  the questions in the book. For example:
  A: Hello. How are you?
  B:
  A: What are you doing?
  B:
  A: Would you like to … etc.
- giving them a complete dialogue in the wrong order.
  They put it in the correct order and then act it out.
- giving them an outline of the conversation in Ex. 5.2
  which they can recreate and act out. For example:
  Will: Hi, Alison! What …
  Alison: Hi, Will. We're going … This is …, my …
  and so on.

The task can be made more demanding by
- giving the students some information that they have
  to include in their conversation. They mustn't show
  each other the information they have. For example:
  Student A: You're going to the cinema. You want
  your friend to come. You don't like swimming.
  Student B: You're going swimming. You want your
  friend to come. You only like action films.

- **WB Ex. 6: an open dialogue to practise inviting and suggesting.**

6 Do it yourself!

**AtoZ DO IT YOURSELF, AUTONOMY and STUDENT
INVOLVEMENT**

See the Teaching Notes to Unit 4, Exercise 5.

7 Your Language Record

AtoZ LANGUAGE RECORD

Time to spare?

AtoZ TIME TO SPARE?

Revision Box

The *Revision Box* provides revision practice with the
Present continuous if you feel that students need it.

> **Answers**
> **1** Subject + 'be' + verb + '-ing' **2 – 3** Example sentences:
> Two dinosaurs are fighting. The tree is breaking. A dinosaur is
> falling. The snake is going into the water. The fish are
> jumping. The bird is laying an egg. The sun is shining. A
> dinosaur is eating grass.

Activity 10 Poems from the rainforest

| Note: Remind the students that they should be preparing something for the *Open plan* section after Unit 12.

TEACHING NOTES FOR UNIT 10

Overview of the Unit

Unit 10 shows the students how they can write simple poems about the rainforest. The students first think about the rainforest and the words they can remember from Units 8 and 9 and share ideas with their neighbour. The cassette recording includes some South American music to stimulate their thinking. They then brainstorm ideas with the class about what it is like to be in the rainforest before they develop those ideas in some simple poems.

| Note: Some students may react negatively to writing poems, so you could do the activity without actually referring to the book or without using the word 'poem' until they have finished (if at all). This kind of activity is valuable because it develops a feeling for personal expression in English, focusing on the meaning and impact of words. (See also **AtoZ** STUDENT INVOLVEMENT.)

Timing

Unit 10 is intended for one full lesson, but you may decide to split it up over a number of lessons. Suggested timings are:

1 The things you remember	10
2 Your words	5
3 In the rainforest	10
4 A poem	20
5 Show your poems	10
6 Evaluation	5

What you need

The Class Cassette and a cassette player for Exercises 1 and 4. If you intend to put the complete poems on the wall, you will need large poster paper (e.g. A3), scissors, glue, pens and coloured A4 pape (optional).

Workbook

Unit 10 in the Workbook contains some more poems to read and some more ideas to stimulate poem writing.

Guidelines

1 The things you remember 📼

AtoZ BRAINSTORMING, MUSIC

The purpose of this exercise is to draw together the language the students learned in Units 8 and 9. The cassette includes a short section of music which you could have playing as the students come into class.

There are a number of ways you can do the exercise:

- draw the idea map from the book on the board and ask the students to work individually to complete their own. Play the music while they are working. You could then collect ideas after the music has stopped.
- put the idea map on the board and ask students to come out to add to it. This could be done silently after the first person comes out (offer the chalk to different students). Play the music while they are writing on the board.

The music is flute, pipe and drum music from Peru.

2 Your words

If students have completed the ideas map individually, they can now compare.

3 In the rainforest

AtoZ DISCUSSION

You can use the questions to lead a discussion. You could first ask them to imagine they are in the rainforest now and collect their ideas on the board. Some questions you can ask them: Imagine that you are in a rainforest now.

What can you hear? What can you see? Is it nice there? How do you feel? What is above you? What is below you? Where are you, exactly? Are you alone?

Then you can ask them to imagine it is the time of the dinosaurs: *Let's imagine it's 150 million years ago, the time of the dinosaurs. What can you see? What can you hear?* and so on. Collect their ideas on the board.

4   A poem

AtoZ MONITORING AND GUIDING

If you want to avoid referring to poems, you can say 'Let's write about the rainforest. Look!', and put one of the examples on the board (or one of your own). Ask the students to write their ideas in a shape (e.g. a tree, a bird, a leaf, an insect, or an animal). They can first write, then draw an outline and then copy the words around it.

The example in the book shows how they can rework their ideas as they write.

While they are writing (alone or in groups), go around the room. (If you have students who really don't want to do it, they can do a *Time to spare?* exercise, or something from the *Exercise Box*. See **AtoZ** STUDENT INVOLVEMENT.)

5   Show your poems

AtoZ DISPLAYING STUDENTS' WORK

Discuss with the students if they would like to put their work up somewhere, put it in a book or look at each other's work in a small group. Students may wish to finish off their work at home first, however.

6   Evaluation

AtoZ EVALUATION

The question to emphasise here is 'Would you like to do it again?' (perhaps about another topic). If there are only some students who would like to do it again, you could offer them a chance within the next few lessons when other students are working on something else.

11 Culture matters Discover America!

Physical Geography and Natural History in the United States of America

Note: Remind the students that they should be preparing something for the *Open plan* section of Unit 12.

TEACHING NOTES FOR UNIT 11

Overview of the Unit

This Unit focuses on the landscape and natural features of the United States. Students get an overview of the geography of the United States, and learn about three well-known places there: Dinosaur National Monument, the Grand Canyon and Yellowstone National Park. The Unit provides reading and writing tasks, with the possibility of further development ('Across cultures', Exercise 5).

Timing

This Unit is designed to take one class hour, except for Exercise 5 'Across cultures', which can be developed for homework or for another lesson. Below are some suggested timings (in minutes) for each step.

1	Landscape in your country	5
2	Landscape in the United States	20
3	Three places to visit	20
4	Where are they?	10
5	Across cultures	10–30

(See also **AtoZ** TIMING.)

What you need

The Class Cassette and a cassette player for Exercises 2 (optional), 3 (optional) and 4.

Mixed-ability classes

Exercises 2 and 3 have additional notes for mixed-ability classes.

(See also **AtoZ** MIXED ABILITIES.)

Workbook

Unit 11 in the Workbook is the second *Help yourself!* Unit. It focuses on ways in which the students can help themselves when they are writing.

- Exercise 1: An experiment with two ways to approach writing: 'fast and then slow' - writing quickly before going back to check and correct; 'slow and careful', checking everything as they write.
- Exercise 2: Making a list of their common mistakes.

See page 149 for a special note on the *Help yourself!* Units and **AtoZ** WRITING.

Guidelines

1 Landscape in your country

AtoZ DISCUSSION

You could draw a rough outline map of your country on the board and mark the compass points, N, NE, E, SE, S, SW, W, NW, etc. and get the students to tell you where the forests, mountains, lakes, rivers and deserts are (if any).

2 Landscape in the United States 🔲

AtoZ READING and PROCESSING TIME

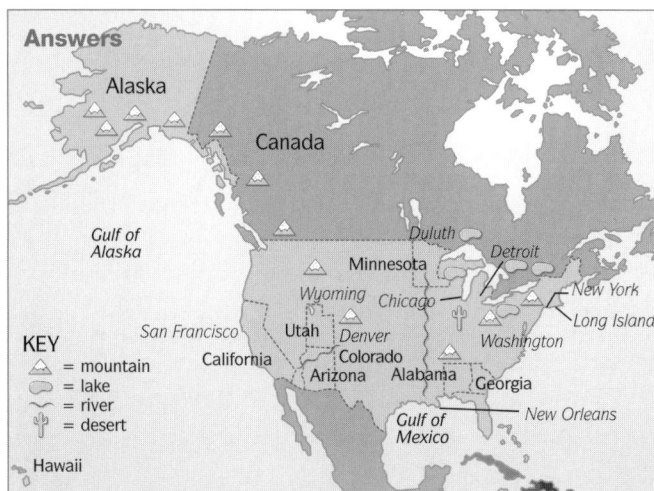

Answers

Alaska, Canada, Gulf of Alaska, Duluth, Minnesota, Detroit, New York, Wyoming, Chicago, Long Island, San Francisco, Utah, Denver, Washington, California, Colorado, Arizona, Alabama, Georgia, New Orleans, Gulf of Mexico, Hawaii

KEY
△ = mountain
🌐 = lake
〜 = river
🌵 = desert

MIXED ABILITIES

More support can be given by

- going first through the vocabulary you think will cause the students difficulties.
- providing a bilingual wordlist.
- using an outline map of their own country on the board. You can then show them how they can talk about the map using the same language that is in the article.
- asking them to read the texts and to make a list of the words/phrases they don't understand. You can then collect the 'difficult words' on the board and explain them before you ask the students to read again.
- giving them some guiding questions which focus on the items they should mark on the map, e.g. Where are the Appalachian Mountains? Where does the Mississippi river start? Where are the lakes? and so on.

The task can be made more demanding by

- asking the students to read one of the paragraphs about the United States and to write a similar paragraph about their country.
- preparing five questions to ask other students about the American landscape.
- asking them to look for specific information in various parts of the texts. For example: How long is the Mississippi? Where is the Grand Canyon? Where is Mount McKinley? How high is it?

3   Three places to visit 📼

A to Z READING

MIXED ABILITIES

More support can be given by

- going first through the vocabulary you think will cause the students difficulties.
- providing a bilingual wordlist.
- looking at the three pictures with students and asking them what they can see. You can put key words and phrases that appear in the texts on the board.
- asking the students to read just one text each or in a small group.

Answers
a The Grand Canyon **b** Dinosaur National Monument
c Yellowstone National Park

4   Where are they? 📼

A to Z LISTENING

📼 TAPESCRIPT AND ANSWERS

1 Well, here we are at the most famous geyser in the park. In about 2 minutes' time you can see the hot water shoot into the air. The water is very hot – over 100 degrees Celsius. It shoots up 46 metres into the air, every hour. Look! You can see it starting now. There it goes, up, up into the air. Now isn't that just fantastic! (Yellowstone National Park)

2 This is one of the largest skeletons in the monument. The bones that you can see here are over 150 million years old. Here you can see a complete dinosaur, the Apatosaurus. It was a really big animal! About 25 metres long, with a long, heavy body and heavy legs. You can see also that it had a very small head. It was a plant-eater and not very dangerous. A nice pet to have! (Dinosaur National Monument)

3 From here you can get one of the best views. Just look at those colours! Red, green, yellow and deep blue. Beautiful, beautiful. We can come back here later and you can see how the colours change. From here you can also see how big the canyon is. Just look over there. It's more than one-and-a-half kilometres deep and over 20 kilometres wide. Imagine, that millions and millions of years ago, the river was that big. Now, let's move on to the next point … (The Grand Canyon)

5   Across cultures

This exercise can form the starting-point for more extended writing if time is available. It would also form an ideal contribution to *A Parcel of English*. (See Supplementary Unit A.)

12 Revision and evaluation

Note: Remind the students that they should have prepared something for the *Open plan* section of this Unit (See Unit 9, Ex. 6).

TEACHING NOTES FOR UNIT 12

See Unit 7 for a 'General note on the *Revision and evaluation* Units'.

Overview of the Unit

This revision Unit has a different structure from Unit 7, which is repeated in Units 22 and 32. Instead of doing prepared revision exercises, the students build up their own test, using examples given in the Student's Book. The process of doing this has a number of important aims. It helps to make tests directly useful to learning; it helps to dispel the fear of tests which many students have; and it involves them in a deeper level of language and learning awareness.

The final part of the Unit involves an evaluation discussion of Units 8–11.

Timing

The main part of the Unit (Exercises 1–3) is intended for one full lesson, with the students' own test being used in another lesson or as homework (see below). Suggested timings are as follows. To save time, students can do the example test (Exercise 2) for homework before the lesson.

1	How well do you know it?	5–10
2	Test yourself!	15
3	Write your own test! (assembled later)	15
4	Looking back at Units 8–11	
4.1	Group discussion	15
4.2	Your own ideas	5
5	Learning to write in English	8

(See also **AtoZ** TIMING.)

What you need

No special materials needed.

Mixed-ability classes and supplementary worksheets

Language worksheet 9.1: 'was' and 'were'
Language worksheet 9.2: Past simple regular verbs

(See also **AtoZ** MIXED-ABILITY CLASSES.)

Workbook

Unit 12 in the Workbook for this Unit provides further revision exercises around the topic of volcanoes.

Exercise 1: a vocabulary puzzle
Exercise 2: speaking in an open dialogue, using the Past tense
Exercise 3: reading about volcanoes
Exercise 4: reading and gap-filling about volcanoes

Guidelines

1 How well do you know it?
AtoZ OVERVIEWING and AUTONOMY
See Unit 7, Exercise 1 for more guidance.

2 Test yourself!
AtoZ TESTS
This test is a simple model for students to write their own test. Writing their own test is useful because:

(i) In order to write the test students need to look back through what they have done and revise new vocabulary and structures.

(ii) Writing the test will encourage the students to think more deeply about the language.

(iii) Students are often terrified by tests. Showing them how they can write tests can help to break down this fear so that they can see tests as being another way to learn – rather than simply something imposed on them 'from above'.

As this is simply an example of a test, the answers are provided for students to correct. (See Student's Book page 142.)

Explain to the students that they are going to write their own test and that the test provided here is only an example. Point out where the answers are, but encourage them to try the test without looking. After doing the test, they can look back at Exercise 1.

3 Write your own test!

Divide the class into small groups (three students in each group is probably the best number) and ask the groups to choose which of the four sections they want to prepare. The students can prepare a test section, as in the example test, or they might think of other ways to make a test.

Once the students have prepared their section, collect it in. Over the next few days, you can put the sections together to make a complete test. (You will need to ensure that the test is in correct English.) The test can then be given back to the students as *their* test, which they can do in class or for homework. (Experience shows that students also learn a lot from seeing the parts which they have written in fully correct English.)

4 Looking back at Units 8–11

4.1 Group discussion

4.2 Your own ideas

AtoZ EVALUATION, AUTONOMY, STUDENT INVOLVEMENT and DISCUSSION
See Unit 7, Exercise 6.2 for further guidance.

5 Learning to write in English

AtoZ AUTONOMY and DISCUSSION
See Unit 7, Exercise 7 for further guidance.

Open plan

AtoZ DO IT YOURSELF!
See Teaching Notes to Unit 7, *Open plan* for further guidance.

Theme C

Back in time

OVERVIEW OF THE THEME

Theme C, Back in time, focuses on the topic of history and life 4,000 years ago in the Bronze Age. Students learn about how archaeologists and detectives build up a picture of what happened in the past by finding clues, making guesses and asking questions (Units 13 and 14). In Unit 15 they write a message for historians of the future, describing important events in our lifetime. The message they produce can, additionally, be used in *A Parcel of English*. Unit 16, *Culture matters*, looks at some important events in the history of the USA.

In Unit 14, the students have more opportunities to practise regular past forms and are introduced to more examples of the irregular past. The *Out and about* section presents language which students can use to react to good and bad news. Students practise listening (for general understanding and for detail), speaking (through 'brainstorming' and role play), reading and writing in short descriptive texts. The *Decide* exercises, use of the *Exercise Box* and evaluation stages continue to involve the students directly.

All the Units in the Theme offer a curricular link with History.

Using the cover page

AtoZ OVERVIEWING
Suggested time: 10 minutes

See page 32 for notes on using the cover page.

> **Answers**
> 1 Pictures: cartoon – Unit 15; Will, Alison, Helen and Nick – Unit 14; Iceman discovery – Unit 13; timeline – Unit 13; man on the moon – Unit 16.
> 2 In Units 13 and 14 students learn about life 4,000 years ago, about the Iceman, and about how historians make deductions.
> 3 In Unit 15 students produce a message for future historians, which they can bury or include in *A Parcel of English*.

Topic 13 Detectives of history

1 WHAT HAPPENED WITH UNITS 8–12?

Some questions to think about before you start Unit 13:

Pairwork

In Unit 9 Exercise 5.3 and in Unit 12 Exercise 2 the students worked in pairs.

- How did the pairwork go?
- Did the students work in the same pairs for each task?
- Do some students work better than others in pairs?
- Why do you think this is so?

There is some more pairwork in this Unit (an interview in Exercise 5.3). What different ways could you try to improve the interviews?

Evaluation

- Which part of the evaluation (Unit 12) do you think was most useful for the students?
- What did they learn from the evaluation?
- How will the results of the evaluation affect your teaching?
- How will the results of the evaluation affect the students' learning?

2 TEACHING NOTES FOR UNIT 13

Overview of the Unit

This Unit introduces history and life 4,000 years ago in the Bronze Age. Reading and listening texts present information about some major discoveries and inventions, and introduce students to a sense of chronology and the importance of discovery in history, particularly an important find in the Italian-Austrian alps. Students are exposed to some regular and irregular forms of the Past simple. The first *Decide* exercise (Exercise 5) offers a choice between vocabulary, checking understanding, and making a dialogue in pairs. The second *Decide* exercise (Exercise 9) offers a choice between deducing and writing, guided writing and *Do it yourself!*

Timing

Some suggested timings (in minutes) for each activity are as follows:

1	The history of the world	8–10
2	When did it happen?	10
3	Travel back in time!	15
4	An important discovery	
4.1	In the mountains	5
4.2	History under the ice	15
5	Decide …	15
6	Sing a song!	8–10
7	4,000 years ago they didn't have …	15
8	Clues from the past	
8.1	What can you guess?	10
8.2	Clues, guesses and questions …	10
9	Decide …	15
10	Your Language Record	(at home) 10

(See **AtoZ** TIMING.)

What you need

A cassette player and Class Cassette for Exercises 3, 4.2 (optional) and 6 (song). Also, the *Exercise Box* for the *Time to spare?*. Students need dictionaries.

Mixed-ability classes and supplementary worksheets

Exercises 4.1, 4.2, 5 and 9 have additional notes for mixed-ability classes.

Say it clearly! Worksheet 2 provides practice of /ɔː/ (saw):

(See also **AtoZ** MIXED ABILITIES.)

Workbook

The Workbook Unit contains exercises to practise the following:

- Exercise 1: vocabulary from the Unit
- Exercise 2.1: reading/listening and Past tense practice

- Exercise 3: deducing
- Exercise 4: pronunciation of /ɔː/
- Exercise 5: singing a song in English

For additional notes on the use of the Workbook and Workbook answers see page 149.

Background notes: Life 4,000 years ago and the Bronze Age

Humankind discovered metal and how to work metal about 8,000 years ago (6,000BC) in Iran and Turkey. The discovery was gradually taken by the Beaker People (who made unusual, bell-shaped cups) across Western Europe and into Scandinavia. The use of metal brought an end to the Stone Age and changed patterns of work, life and the social structure.

Archaeologists think that the process of metal-working was discovered by accident when potters started to use an oven to 'fire' (harden) their pots to make them waterproof. They also started to look for different kinds of clay to make their pots. Potters put different kinds of clay and metal into the oven (kiln) to see how they would react to the heat.

The first kinds of metals to be used were gold and copper and by 3,000BC metalsmiths learnt how to make a stronger metal by adding tin to copper. In order to find the metals, people started to mine and by 2,500BC copper and bronze were being used from Ireland to Pakistan. Bronze was the foundation of the great Minoan civilization. Craftsmen made tools, pots, jewellery and wheeled chariots from metal from about 3,250BC onwards. Recent work on the 'Iceman' (Exercise 4) showed him to have traces of copper in his hair.

Guidelines

1 The history of the world

AtoZ DISCUSSIONS and PROCESSING TIME

Give the students time to look at the pictures of the different inventions and discoveries. Check that they understand the vocabulary. Let them suggest other inventions or discoveries. Provide vocabulary where necessary and write some key words on the board.

- **WB Ex 1: more practice with vocabulary.**

2 When did it happen?

AtoZ PAIRWORK

Students work in pairs and write the event on the timeline. The students then compare their answers with the rest of the class. Exercise 3 provides a check for their answers.

- **WB Ex. 2: reading about and writing about the Egyptians.**

3 Travel back in time!

AtoZ LISTENING

The students can listen to the cassette all the way through first. Then replay the cassette in sections for students to listen to again and check their answers to Exercise 2.

> 📼 TAPESCRIPT
>
> Good morning, this is your captain speaking. Please fasten your seatbelts for your journey back in time. We will travel at 100 years per second to 4,000 years ago: 2,000BC. Please watch your television screens. This is life today – our computers and modern equipment … and now back to 1961 – the first person in space, and here in 1950 the first electronic computer. Look how big it was! Now we are in 1903. You can see the first plane flight and twenty years before – in 1880 – look! – the first electric light bulb. The year 1600 is on your screens now – this is the first telescope, and then back to 1550 you can see the first round-the-world sailing ships. One hundred years earlier, in 1450, we have the first printing press and the first books. Back now quickly one thousand years to 500AD, and you can see the wonderful Mayan city of Chichen Itza in Mexico. And now, a thousand years more … we can see some of the races of the first Olympic Games in Greece in 500BC. We can see on our televisions now the people in the Iron Age, and back another 1,000 years, I can hear the sound of the first metal. This is 2,000BC. Here we are at our time stop for today … 4,000 years ago. You can unfasten your seat belts. Let's step out of the timeship 4,000 years ago … and meet the people in their houses and at work …

A completed timeline should have the following information:

2000BC	Iron, copper and bronze tools in Europe.
500BC	The first Olympic Games.
500AD	The Mayan City of Chichen Itza in Mexico.
1450	The first printing press.
1534	Cambridge University Press began.
1550	The first round-the-world sailing ships.
1600	The first telescope.
1880	The first electric light bulb.
1903	The first plane.
1950	The first electronic computer.
1961	The first space rocket.

4 An important discovery

4.1 In the mountains

Ask the students to look at the words from the story. Give them some time – alone or in pairs – to work out what the story is about. Get them to share their ideas with the class.

MIXED ABILITIES

More support can be given by

- checking that the students are certain of the vocabulary. You could ask them to write sentences which include the word. You could also ask them if they can think of an adjective which can be used with the nouns: tourists, body, snow, police, archaeologists. They can add these to their sentences.

The task can be made more demanding by

- asking the students to write the opening paragraph of their story. Alternatively, they can write the first sentence, pass their paper to the next student who writes the next sentence, and so on. Continue in this way until the story is finished. Ask them then to check through the text for errors.

4.2 History under the ice 🔲

AtoZ READING

This is a newspaper article, so encourage the students to read the text without worrying about unknown vocabulary. Encourage them to guess words they don't know.

MIXED ABILITIES

More support can be given by

- asking students to look at the picture and the title and by encouraging them to guess what the newspaper story says. You could ask them to look through the text and to find the words which begin with capital letters (e.g. Thursday, Italy, Austria, etc.). Using those words, they can then try to guess the story.
- asking them to read the story together in pairs and to discuss together what it says. You can then collect ideas from the class, asking them 'Where does it tell you that?'
- asking them to underline all the words which they know. They can then discuss together the words/phrases which they have left blank.

The task can be made more demanding by

- asking students to follow lines of reference through the text. For example, with a pencil ask students to put a circle around the subject of the first sentence ('two people') and then read through the text until they find the next reference to the 'two people' (i.e. Helmut and Erika Simon). They can then circle those words and draw a line from the first to the second circle and so on through the text. They can do the same with the object of the sentence ('a body'). This lets them see how the text has been constructed.

5 Decide ...

AtoZ DECIDE EXERCISES and MONITORING AND GUIDING

Go through the different exercises with students so that they know what they have to do in each of them.

If they choose the vocabulary exercise, they will need a dictionary. While they are working go round and give advice where necessary.

MIXED ABILITIES

Students will probably find Ex. 5.1 easier than Ex. 5.2 and Ex. 5.2 easier than Ex. 5.3.

5.1 Check your vocabulary

AtoZ VOCABULARY

Students can decide which words they don't know at all (0% sure) and which words they are uncertain about (50% sure). Ask them to write a meaning (a synonym, a translation or picture) next to the '50% sure' words first and to compare with a neighbour, then check in the dictionary. For the '0% sure' words, ask them to make a guess from the context and then check in the dictionary. You could discuss with the students how they will try to remember the new words.

5.2 Check your understanding

> **Answers**
> 1 They found a body, an axe, a bow and twelve arrows.
> 2 On the border of Italy and Austria. 3 They called the police.
> 4 They think the body is probably over 4,000 years old.
> 5 Dust from a sandstorm melted the snow. 6 They found some bodies in Denmark which were more than 4,000 years old.

Students can write similar questions to give to their neighbour.

5.3 Interview Mr and Mrs Simon

AtoZ SPEAKING and PAIRWORK

You may need to start by reminding the students how to form questions in the Past tense with question words. The questions in Exercise 5.2 will give them some help.

One student plays the role of the police officer, the other(s) Mr and/or Mrs Simon (using the information from the article and the notepad). Go round and listen to their dialogues. When they are ready, some pairs can say the dialogues in front of the class.

Example questions
1 What did you find? What did you see first? 2 When did you find it? 3 Where did you find it/the body/the axe/the bag? 4 How did you find it? 5 Why did you tell the police in the village? Why did you pick up the axe? Why did you go for a walk in the mountains?

6 Sing a song! Pyramids and dinosaurs 🔲

AtoZ SONGS

The song is also recorded on the Workbook cassette.

7 4,000 years ago they didn't have ...

AtoZ PAIRWORK

- **WB Ex. 2: more practice with the Past simple.**

8 Clues from the past

8.1 What can you guess?

AtoZ BRAINSTORMING

Students look at the pictures. Allow them time to guess what they can learn about the Iceman and his life and times.

Answers
There are no real right or wrong answers to these questions: they are open and the students can be encouraged to deduce from clues – to be detectives!

- **WB Ex. 3: more practice in deducing.**

8.2 Clues, guesses and questions ...

Allow students time to work alone or in pairs to put the sentences together. When they have done it, you could ask them how they worked out their answers.

Answers
1 We know he had leather boots ... so he probably had cows. But what did he do with the milk? 2 We know he had arrows ... so he probably hunted wild animals. But what animals did he hunt? 3 We know now he had fire ... so he probably cooked his food. But what food did he cook? 4 We know he had a metal axe ... so he probably had iron. But how did he get it from the ground?

9 Decide ...

DECIDE and DO IT YOURSELF!

MIXED ABILITIES
Students will probably find Ex. 9.2 easier than Ex. 9.1.

9.1 Be a detective!

Possible answers
2 We know that the person ate yoghurt ... so he or she probably had cows or goats. But how did they make it? 3 We know the person had a lot of wool clothes ... so he or she probably had sheep. But how did they take the wool off? 4 We know the person made metal ... so they probably made metal tools. But which tools did they make? 5 We know the person wore a lot of gold jewellery ... so he or she was probably very rich. But why was he or she so rich?

9.2 What did they have 4,000 years ago?

Answers
1 They didn't have radio 4,000 years ago. 2 They didn't wear glasses 4,000 years ago. 3 They didn't have newspapers 4,000 years ago. 4 They didn't have blackboards 4,000 years ago. 5 They didn't have electricity 4,000 years ago. 6 They didn't have pencils and paper 4,000 years ago. 7 They didn't have running water 4,000 years ago. 8 They didn't have television 4,000 years ago.

9.3 Do it yourself!

10 Your Language Record

AtoZ LANGUAGE RECORD

Time to spare?

AtoZ TIME TO SPARE?

Advance notice!
Unit 15 requires the students to collect pictures and information before their Activity lesson. You may like to look at Unit 15 Ex. 1 now so that you can plan ahead for this.

14 Language focus

Advance notice!
Unit 15 requires the students to collect information and pictures before the Activity lesson. You may like to plan time to discuss this with the students, while they are working on Unit 14. See Unit 15, Ex. 1.

1 RESEARCHING THE CLASSROOM: HOMEWORK

Some questions to think about during the coming lessons.

- Do your students usually do all their homework? If some students frequently fail to do it, why do you think this is?
- What type of work do you usually ask them to do at home? What type of homework do you think they most enjoy?

- What do you think your students think about homework? How do you think they *experience* it? How can you find out what they think?
- How much time do you spend in the lesson correcting the homework? Do you think that this is time well spent?

See **A to Z HOMEWORK** for further ideas.

2 TEACHING NOTES FOR UNIT 14

Overview of the Unit

This Unit continues the topic of life in the past but offers further focused practice on the Past simple regular and irregular verbs, negative and questions forms. Vocabulary from Unit 13 is recycled.

Timing

Below are some suggested timings (in minutes) for each exercise.

1	Life in the past	
1.1	What do you know …?	15
1.2	Are you right?	15
2	'Had', 'went', 'saw' …	
2.1	Regular and irregular verbs	10
2.2	Some more irregular verbs	12
2.3	Questions and answers	10
2.4	A trip with your family or friends	12

3	Did they do it? No, they didn't!	
3.1	Past tense questions and negatives	12
3.2	Make a quiz!	25
3.3	Some more practice: a question bag	15
4	Out and about with English	
4.1	What can you say?	5
4.2	At the weekend	10
4.3	Practice	15
5	Do it yourself!	10–15
6	Your Language Record	(at home) 10

What you need

A cassette player and the Class Cassette for Exercises 1.2 and 4.2.

Mixed-ability classes and supplementary worksheets

Exercises 1.2 and 4.3 have additional guidelines for mixed–ability classes.

Language worksheet 14.1 practises Past simple and irregular verbs. Language worksheet 14.2 practises Past simple negative and questions.

(See also AtoZ MIXED ABILITIES.)

Workbook

Unit 14 in the Workbook contains the following exercises:

- Exercise 1.1: reading
- Exercise 1.2: Past simple irregular verbs
- Exercise 1.3: writing using the Past simple
- Exercise 2.1: Past simple questions
- Exercise 2.2: writing Past simple questions
- Exercise 3: Past simple negatives
- Exercise 4: open dialogue: giving reactions
- Exercise 5: pronunciation of /eɪ/ as in 'made', 'came' and /æ/ as in 'fat' and 'cat'

For additional notes on the use of the Workbook and Workbook answers see page 149.

Guidelines

1 Life in the past

AtoZ PROCESSING TIME, QUESTIONS and BRAINSTORMING

1.1 What do you know ...?

If you copy the diagram from the book on to the board or on a large sheet of questions, you can add beneath each question any answers that the students suggest. You can also add further questions that they can research while you are working on the Theme.

1.2 Are you right? 📼

AtoZ CHECKING ANSWERS, READING

You can decide first with the students whether they want to hear the text on the cassette before, during or after they read the text. Allow plenty of time for the students to read the text silently.

Answers to questions in Ex. 1.1
1 The village people lived in long houses. **2** They ate meat, cheese and butter. **3** They wore wool clothes and leather boots. **4** They drank milk/water. **5** They bought pots, crops and metal. **6** The children helped with the animals in the fields. **7** They travelled from village to village.

MIXED ABILITIES

More support can be given by

- asking students to work in groups of three. Each student reads one section of the text and underlines/copies out the key sentence in the section. Each student then tells the others about the sentence/paragraph in his/her mother tongue.
- asking students to look at the pictures first and write down words which describe the pictures. They then look at the texts to find their words.
(See previous Units for further ideas (e.g. Unit 8, Ex. 3.2.)

The task can be made more demanding by

- asking students to make their own 'cloze' text. Ask students to place a piece of paper over the last words at the end of each line. As they read, they write down what they think the word under the paper is. They can compare their words with each other or with the original.
- asking the students to read the title and look at the pictures and, before they read the text, to write down what information they expect to read about. This can be done as an idea map. Students can then read the text and match their prediction with the text.
(See previous units for further ideas, e.g. Unit 8, Ex. 3.2.)

- **WB Ex. 1.1:** more reading practice.

2 'Had', 'went', 'saw' ...

2.1 Regular and irregular verbs

AtoZ INDUCTIVE GRAMMAR, DEDUCTIVE GRAMMAR

- **WB Ex. 1.2:** more practice with the irregular Past simple.

2.2 Some more irregular verbs

AtoZ GRAMMAR

Students may remember the Past simple of 'have', 'go' and 'see'. Encourage them to look back at the text in Exercise 1.2 and to use the irregular verb list on page 149. Students write their own sentences for each verb. You can write some of their sentences on the board.

- **WB Ex. 1.3:** more writing practice.

2.3 Questions and answers

Answers
1e 2d 3a 4b 5c

2.4 A trip with your family or friends

AtoZ PAIRWORK, SPEAKING, MONITORING AND GUIDING

Before you put the students in pairs, ask some students around the class. You can put some example sentences on the board to support their work in pairs. You could ask some students to volunteer to speak in front of the class.

3 Did they do it? No they didn't!

3.1 Past tense questions and negatives

AtoZ INDUCTIVE GRAMMAR

Read through the dialogue with the students and then give them time to look closely at the negative sentences and the questions to try and work out for themselves how both are formed. Encourage them to compare both forms with the mother tongue.

- WB Exs. 2.1 and 2.2: more practice with Past tense questions.
- WB Ex. 3.1: more practice with Past tense negatives.
- Language worksheet 14.2: practice with both Past tense questions and negatives.

3.2 Make a quiz!

AtoZ PAIRWORK GAMES

3.3 Some more practice: a question bag

AtoZ GAMES

You could play this as a game in teams, or in groups of four or six.

4 Out and about with English

AtoZ SPEAKING, PAIRWORK and MONITORING AND GUIDING

4.1 What can you say?

4.2 At the weekend 📼

You could ask the students if they want to read the tapescript before, during or after they listen to the dialogue on the cassette.

- WB Ex. 4: more speaking practice.
- WB Ex. 5: more pronunciation practice.

4.3 PRACTICE

MIXED ABILITIES

More support can be given by
- asking the students to work in groups of four and to read out the dialogue together first. Then, after listening to the cassette, you can write the sentences on the board which say what Will, Helen, Nick and Alison did. ('I went to the beach', 'We played handball all day', 'I went to see the Mash boys with Helen'.) The students can then change the sentences so that they explain what they did.
  (See also Teaching Notes for Unit 9, Ex. 5.)

The task can be made more difficult by
- giving students some information which they must include in their conversation, e.g. a party on the beach, rain, lost money.
- telling them that they must include two good things and two bad things that happened during the weekend.

5 Do it yourself!

AtoZ DO IT YOURSELF, AUTONOMY and STUDENT INVOLVEMENT

See the Teaching Notes to Unit 4, Exercise 5.

6 Your Language Record

AtoZ LANGUAGE RECORD

Time to spare?

AtoZ TIME TO SPARE?

Revision Box

The *Revision Box* provides revision practice with 'was' and 'were' (see also Unit 9) if you feel that the students need revision in that area.

Answers

It was my birthday yesterday. There were a lot of presents in my room. My best present was a trip to the zoo with my friends. All my friends were very excited. In the zoo, there were a lot of monkeys. They were very friendly. There was a baby monkey. He was very funny. There were also two old monkeys. I think they were very hungry because they ate my lunch! It was very late when we came home. I was very tired.

Advance notice!

Don't forget to remind the students to bring their information and pictures for the Unit 15 Activity.

Activity 15 Discoveries for the future

Students make a booklet for future historians

TEACHING NOTES FOR UNIT 15

Overview of the Unit

In this Unit, students work in groups to produce a booklet to tell historians in the future about different aspects of life today. This involves writing short texts to describe pictures about our life today: they may also produce stories and poems. The finished message or booklet can be buried, put in a bottle and thrown out to sea, sent in *A Parcel of English* or displayed in the classroom. At the end of the activity, there is a short evaluation discussion.

Using the 'Message for the Future' in a Parcel of English

The work that the students do in this activity is ideal for the *Parcel of English* (see Supplementary Unit A). If you make contact with your 'twin' class, you can perhaps decide together what your 'messages' will focus on: events in their own country, or important events/issues of our time. This will then provide an interesting comparison when you exchange parcels. For this, you will need to:

- agree a timescale with your 'twin' class teacher.
- agree whether you will produce one big booklet from both classes to which all groups have contributed, or separate booklets/messages.
- agree what will happen to the messages once they have been exchanged.

As with all the *Activity* Units, you can make a video recording of the students working on their messages which you can include in the parcel.

Timing

Unit 15 is intended for one full lesson, but you may decide to split it up over a number of lessons. Suggested timings:

Before the lesson		
1	Discoveries for the future	
1.1	Our life today	10
1.2	Plan your message (also out of class)	10
In the lesson		
2	Write your message	30
3	Show your work to each other	15
4	Evaluation	5

What you need

Some large sheets of paper (e.g. A3) and some smaller sheets (e.g. A4). Some extra pictures of modern things (in case students don't bring enough). Coloured pens, glue, scissors.

Mixed-ability classes

Exercise 2 has additional guidelines for mixed-ability classes.

(See also **AtoZ** MIXED ABILITIES.)

Workbook

Unit 15 in the Workbook provides extra fluency practice about an Iron-Age village.

- Exercise 1: reading about an accidental discovery
- Exercise 2: comprehension
- Exercise 3: free writing

Guidelines

Before the lesson

---

1 Discoveries for the future

1.1 Our life today

AtoZ BRAINSTORMING

Before starting the brainstorming make sure that the students know what the activity is about and what they will be working towards. Write the idea maps (spidergrams) on the board and collect ideas from the students. Students may need some time alone or in pairs to think of some ideas first. They may prefer to work on one idea map ('areas of our life' or 'events in our time').

1.2 Plan your message
AtoZ GROUPWORK

Students discuss in their groups what their message will be about. If they can't agree, you can allocate either Area A or Area B to each group. Check with them the types of pictures they can collect, and the information they need to find out about the events and areas of our life.

In the lesson

2 Write your message
AtoZ INTERACTIVE WRITING, MONITORING AND GUIDING

With the students, read through the example in their books. Students can work on rough paper first, so that they can move the pictures around and correct and revise their work. Go round and help with vocabulary, spelling and grammar, but encourage them to help each other by commenting on each other's work.

They can then copy or paste their work into their booklets. The booklets can be different shapes and sizes, to make it more interesting.

MIXED ABILITIES

More support can be given by
- dividing the students in groups with a mixture of student abilities in each group. Each student can choose an area to write about which is similar to the examples given, which the rest of the group can revise or develop.
- suggesting that some students who prefer to speak rather than write make a cassette instead of writing a booklet.
- suggesting that students write about something which they are very familiar with – their school, their town, their football club.

The task can be made more demanding by
- asking students to write in more detail about a certain area or event: perhaps they would like to describe different kinds of computers, for example, or methods of travel.
- asking them to describe how they think the world is going to be different in the future.

---

3 Show your work to each other
AtoZ DISPLAYING STUDENTS' WORK

The messages/booklets can be hung on the wall or laid out on the desks. The students can then all stand and walk around the room, and look at the other students' work. You could make a quiz (on the board) for this stage, based on what the students have written. Students then have to find the answers as they look at the messages/booklets.

4 Evaluation
AtoZ EVALUATION

This can be done with the whole class. Emphasise the 'How can you do it better next time?' question and try to get them to suggest practical steps for the next activity they do. You could look ahead to Unit 20 with them now.

16 Culture matters The history of the USA

TEACHING NOTES FOR UNIT 16

Overview of the Unit

Students have an opportunity to share their own information about events in the history of the USA and learn about some other important events in American history.

Timing

Suggested timings for one lesson are:

1	The history of the USA	
1.1	What do you know?	10
1.2	Some important events …	25
2	What is it?	10

What you need

The Class Cassette for Exercise 1.2 (optional) and 2.

Workbook

Unit 16 in the Workbook is *Help yourself with pronunciation* and contains four techniques that students can use – three from Level 1, and one new technique:

- Exercise 1: Listen, look and repeat (backchaining)
- Exercise 2: Bang on the table! (word stress)
- Exercise 3: What are the important words? (sentence stress)

See page 149 for a special note on the *Help yourself!* Units. See also **AtoZ** PRONUNCIATION.

Guidelines

1   The history of the USA

AtoZ DISCUSSIONS, BRAINSTORMING and READING

1.1 What do you know?

You could collect the students' ideas and knowledge together as an idea map on the board. Write 'The History of the USA' in a circle on the board. As the students suggest information, you can write it on the

board on lines out from the circles. You could ask the students if they can categorise the information – famous people, famous events, famous natural events, and so on.

Background information

People from almost every country in the world have made a new home in the USA – notably the Irish, Germans, Italians, Poles, Chinese, Mexicans, Puerto Ricans, Costa Ricans, Scandinavians and Dutch. Native American Indians (in different tribes – for example the Sioux, the Cheyenne, Cherokee, Blackfeet, Seminole, and Apache) lived across the North American continent long before it became the USA. The USA is about 220 years old (Independence was gained in 1776).

1.2 Some important events … 📼

> **Answers**
> Before 1660: picture 7. 1620: picture 10. 1773: picture 6.
> 1776: picture 2. 1861–5: picture 1. 1876: picture 3.
> 1886: picture 4. 1909: picture 8. 1963: picture 11.
> 1965–75: picture 9. 1969: picture 5.

2   What is it?

AtoZ LISTENING

> **Answers**
> **1** 1963 (Martin Luther King) **2** 1965–75 (War in Vietnam)
> **3** 1886 (Coke) **4** 1909 (The Model T Ford) **5** 1620 (The Pilgrim Fathers arrive in America from England) **6** 1969 (The first man on the moon).

If there is time at the end of the lesson you could ask the students to choose some of the more important events and people in the history of their country to draw and write about. This could form part of *A Parcel of English*, or a collage on the classroom or corridor wall. They could perhaps record sound effects for each item.

17 Revision and evaluation

TEACHING NOTES FOR UNIT 17

See Unit 7 for a 'general note on the *Revision and evaluation* Units'.

Overview of the Unit

Exercise 1 asks the students how well they think they know the English from Units 13–16. Revision exercises then follow. Students can do some or all of these exercises, depending on time and how much revision they need. In the final part of the Unit, students think about how well they have understood the previous lessons and provide you with written feedback. The last exercise in the Unit asks the students to think about how they approach learning pronunciation.

Timing

The Unit is intended for one full lesson, with students doing exercises 2–5 selectively. However, you may want all students to do all the exercises, in which case the Unit may be split up over a number of lessons.

Approximate timings are:

1	How well do you know it?	5
2	What's the word?	10
3	All about you	15
4	The Aztecs	20
5	Possible or impossible?	15
6	Looking back at Units 13–16	
6.1	Group discussion	15
6.2	Your own ideas	4
7	Learning English pronunciation	10

What you need

No additional materials required.

Mixed–ability classes and supplementary worksheets

Language worksheet 14.1: irregular Past tense verbs
Language worksheet 14.2: Past tense questions and negatives

(See also **AtoZ** MIXED ABILITIES.)

Workbook

Unit 17 in the Workbook is a self-test focusing on the language covered in the Theme.

- Exercise 1: vocabulary
- Exercise 2: Past tense negatives
- Exercise 3: Past simple: regular and irregular verbs
- Exercise 4: Past tense questions
- Exercise 5: giving reactions

Guidelines

1 How well do you know it?

AtoZ TASKS IN GROUPS and OVERVIEWING
See Unit 7, Exercise 1 for further notes.

2 What's the word?

> **Answers**
>
> ```
> a h g t e y t w h w i j (S)
> (M A P) h e o i e y u w h (N)
> j d j k l (I C E) j d e j (O)
> j f j k w i n f k w j d (W)
> j d j (W H E E L) w h d h d
> j k j d l (B O O T) q k n e
> k d k o k (E N G I N E) f h
> (S T E A M) e o j e n w k w
> ```

Encourage students to look in the *Language Record* and in the *Wordlist/Index* to find words which they can use to make a puzzle: there are different ways they can make clues. They can draw pictures, write the word in their mother tongue, write a sentence with a gap, or mix the letters of the word up.

- **WB Ex. 1: more vocabulary practice.**

3 All about you

> **Answers**
> Open answers, but they should all be in the Past tense.

- **WB Ex. 3: more practice with Past tense regular and irregular verbs.**

4 The Aztecs

> **Answers**
> 1 When did the Aztecs live in Mexico? 2 How did they travel? 3 Where did they build their biggest city? 4 What language did they speak? 5 Did they have schools?/Did the children go to school? 6 What did they do?/What jobs did the Aztecs do? 7 How did they hunt wild animals? 8 How did they buy and sell things? 9 Did the Aztecs have writing? 10 When did the Spanish arrive in Mexico?/take control of Mexico?

- **WB Ex. 4: more practice with Past tense questions.**

5 Possible or impossible?

> **Answers**
> b Possible. They built beautiful cities and big buildings. c Possible. The cities had big buildings, squares and wide streets. d Impossible! The Aztecs weren't in Mexico 1,000 years ago. e Impossible! The Aztecs had their own language. f Possible. The Aztecs killed animals. g Possible. The Aztecs had schools. h Impossible! The Aztecs didn't have writing. i Impossible! The Aztecs didn't have guns.

- **WB Ex. 2: more practice with Past tense negatives.**

6 Looking back at Units 13–16

6.1 Group discussion

6.2 Your own ideas

AtoZ EVALUATION, AUTONOMY, STUDENT INVOLVEMENT and DISCUSSION
See Unit 7, Exercise 6 for further guidance.

7 Learning English pronunciation

AtoZ AUTONOMY and DISCUSSION
See Unit 7, Exercise 7 for further guidance.

Open plan

AtoZ DO IT YOURSELF!
See Teaching Notes to Unit 7, *Open plan* for further guidance.

Theme D
Below the clouds

OVERVIEW OF THE THEME

Theme D, Below the clouds, focuses on the topic of climate. In Units 18 and 19 students learn about different types of climate and how climate affects our lives – food, clothes and houses – and the disasters it causes – hurricanes, floods and drought. In Unit 20 (*Activity*) they make a cover of a book about climates and natural disasters. Unit 21 focuses on outdoor activities and introduces students to Youth Hostels in Britain and activities available near a Youth Hostel in the Lake District.

Unit 19 presents language areas: 'going to' and 'have to'. The *Out and about* section practises making plans and revises language used in a café. In Unit 22 (*Revision and evaluation*) students design part of a test for their class.

All four skills are practised throughout the Theme in addition to role play. There are also opportunities for creative writing. The *Decide* exercises, use of the *Exercise Box*, *Do it yourself!* section and the evaluation stages continue to involve the students directly.

All the Units in the Theme offer cross-curricular links with Geography and Environmental Science.

Using the cover page

AtoZ OVERVIEWING
Suggested time: 10 minutes

See page 32 for notes on using the cover page.

Answers

1 Pictures: book cover – Unit 20; leisure activities – Unit 21; volcano – Unit 19; disaster in Florida – Unit 18; test – Unit 22.

2 In January 1995, there was a very bad flood in The Netherlands (page 87, Student's Book). A barometer is an instrument which tells you when rain is coming (page 84, Student's Book). John didn't have any breakfast (page 92, Student's Book). Will and Helen are in the school canteen.

3 In Unit 20, the students can make the cover of a new book about world climates.

Topic 18 Climates of the world

Students talking about themselves; introductions; 'can'; a tour of the book; some useful phrases; numbers.

1 WHAT HAPPENED WITH UNITS 13–17?

Some questions to think about before you start Unit 18: the Past simple.

- Now that the students have spent some time on the Past simple, how many of them are confident about using it?
- What kinds of errors do they make when they use the Past simple? Do they make the same kinds of errors in writing and speaking, or in one skill area only?

- How easy do they find it to pronounce the three different sounds for the '-ed' ending? Do they need further practice with this?
- Can you integrate talking about the past into your work on Unit 18? (For example, talking about a natural disaster in your area.)

2 TEACHING NOTES FOR UNIT 18

Overview of the Unit

This Unit introduces the topic of climate around the world and how it affects the way we live, what we wear and what we eat. Reading texts and maps present information about the main climate types and the natural disasters they cause. The first *Decide* exercise (Exercise 4) offers a choice between practising new vocabulary, checking reading comprehension and writing. The second *Decide* exercise (Exercise 7) offers a choice between writing poems, or writing instructions, or *Do it yourself!* An optional 'experiment to try at home' shows students how to make a simple barometer.

Timing

Below are some suggested timings (in minutes) for each exercise.

1	The climate in your country	5–10
2	World climates	10–15
3	The climate and the way we live	
3.1	Climate, houses, food and clothes	20
3.2	Write about a climate	10
4	Decide …	15
5	Disaster from the climate	16
6	Sing a song!	5–10
7	Decide …	15
8	Your Language Record	(at home) 10

(See also **A to Z** TIMING.)

What you need

A cassette player and the Class Cassette for Exercises 5 (optional) and 6 (song). Also the *Exercise Box* for the *Time to spare?*

Mixed-ability classes and supplementary worksheets

Exercises 4 and 5 have additional notes for mixed-ability classes.

Say it clearly! Worksheet 2 provides practice of /iː/ (eat), /e/ (weather).

(See also **A to Z** MIXED ABILITIES.)

Workbook

The Workbook Unit contains exercises to practise the following:

- Exercise 1: vocabulary
- Exercise 2.1: reading (about winds)
- Exercise 2.2: reading (about hurricanes)
- Exercise 3: pronunciation of /iː/ (eat), /e/ (weather)
- Exercise 4: open dialogue: talking about the weather
- Exercise 5: singing a song in English

For additional notes on the use of the Workbook and Workbook answers see page 149.

Unit 18 Climates of the world   75

Guidelines

1 The climate in your country

AtoZ DISCUSSION and BRAINSTORMING

This exercise could also be done in pairs/groups first, before you collect ideas from the whole class.

Draw a large circle on the board, with the months written around it as in the Student's Book. You can write the students' ideas around the circle.

- **WB Ex. 3: more practice with pronunciation of /iː/ and /e/.**

2 World climates

AtoZ PAIRWORK and READING

Students can work alone or in pairs for this exercise. Students turn to the map on pages 152–3 in the Student's Book and read the descriptions of world climates.

> **Answers**
> Greenland: polar; Canada: tundra; China: cool/warm temperate and tundra; Great Britain: cool temperate; Spain: warm temperate; Egypt: desert; India: monsoon; Brazil: tropical.

> **Answers**
> a Monsoon b Tropical c Polar

- **WB Ex. 1: practice with vocabulary.**
- **WB Ex. 2: more practice with reading.**

Make a barometer

A barometer is an instrument which measures changes in air pressure. High air pressure is normally (but not always) associated with good weather, low pressure with bad weather.

The barometer that the students make is a very simple one that will only show strong changes in air pressure. If you make a barometer in the class, you can check it at the start of each lesson with the students. Note that the mouth of the jar must be raised (on the coins) to allow water to move in and out. The candle inside the jar burns the oxygen, to create a partial vacuum. You will then notice that the water level rises as the oxygen is burned. If you mark a scale on the side of the glass jar (for example, with a waterproof pen) it will be easier to see the changes each day. This will also give you opportunities to revise the use of comparatives: stronger, weaker, lower, higher.

When the air pressure falls, the level inside the jar falls because the water outside the jar can rise up. When the air pressure increases ('high'), the water outside the jar is pushed down and this pushes the level inside the jar up.

3 The climate and the way we live

AtoZ DISCUSSION and PAIRWORK

3.1 Climate, houses, food and clothes

Before you set the students working, look through the exercise with them. They have to put the pictures in four groups showing how climate, housing, food and clothes go together. Look at pictures A–D of the climates with them first, and discuss with them what they think it is like to live in each place. What type of houses do people there have? What do they eat? Why? What clothes do they wear?

> **Answers**
> Desert climate: A, G, L, O. Polar climate: B, F, I, P. Monsoon: D, E, K, M. Cool temperate: C, H, J, N.

Explanations: In a **desert climate** (A), it is very hot. People paint their houses (G) white to reflect the sun. Not many vegetables grow there so people eat a lot of meat and rice (L) (which they bring from other countries). They have to wear light, white clothes (O) and something on their heads because of the heat. In a **polar climate** (B), there are very few natural materials. Traditionally, Inuit people build igloos (F) from ice. (Note: igloos are rarely built now, except when hunting. Modern-day Inuit people import materials and live mainly in bungalows.) The only food that you can find there is fish, which they eat raw (I). They also make clothes from animal skins (P). In a **monsoon** climate (D), there are often floods so people build their houses on legs (E). They eat fish from the river and rice which grows there (K). The sun is very hot, so they usually have something on their heads (M). In a **cool temperate** climate (C), the weather changes a lot and it is often cold. People build houses from brick (H) to protect them from the wind and rain. They eat hot food (meat and vegetables), (J), and wear warm clothes (N) to protect them from the cold.

3.2 Write about a climate

AtoZ WRITING

With the students, talk through what they can write before you set them working. See Exercise 3.1 for examples of texts that the students can write.

4 Decide …

AtoZ DECIDE EXERCISES and MONITORING AND GUIDING

Go through the different exercises with them so that they know what they have to do in each of them.

> **MIXED ABILITIES**
> Students will probably find Ex. 4.1 easier than Ex. 4.2 and Ex. 4.2 easier than Ex. 4.3.

4.1 What's the word?

Answers

1 fall	**N**	S	F	E	**C O L D**	E	W	**W**	I	J	W			
2 cold	**I**	G	J	U	R Y H J W U O	**E**	L	P						
3 wet	**G**	K	**B E L O W**	E	W	U	Q	K	**T**	E				
4 below	**H**	T	**N E V E R**	F	I	L	T	W	H	A				
5 night	**T**	J	D	J	E K K D N P Q K O E									
6 never		H	G	H	R Y T R G E H	**F A L L**								

4.2 Linking sentences

This is the first exercise of this kind, so make sure that the students understand what they have to do.

Answers

1 **In mountain regions** there are a lot of trees. **There**, many people live in wooden houses.
2 **Countries around the Mediterranean** are warm temperate. **There**, the people eat rice or pasta.
3 It often rains very heavily in **the monsoon regions**. People **in those areas** build their houses on legs.
4 **The rainforests in Brazil** are tropical. **Here** it is hot nearly all year round.

There are examples of linking sentences in the descriptions of the following climates (pages 152–3): 1 Mountain 2 Cool temperate 3 Monsoon 4 Tropical.

4.3 Imagine ...

AtoZ WRITING, OPEN-ENDED TASKS

5 Disaster from the climate 🔲

AtoZ READING, DISCUSSION and LISTENING

Answers

1 Netherlands disaster: a cool temperate climate 2 Florida disaster: a warm temperate climate 3 Africa disaster: a desert climate

MIXED ABILITIES

More support can be given by
- asking students to work in groups of three; each student reads one text.
- asking students to work in pairs, to choose one text and to underline the words they know. They can then compare the words they don't know with each other and guess the meaning.
- encouraging students not to focus on each individual word, but to write down the key ideas/information in each text. They can then compare their notes with their partner or your notes on the board. See previous Units for further ideas (e.g. Unit 8 Ex. 3.2, Unit 13 Ex. 4).

The task can be made more demanding by
- asking students to look at the pictures and the titles and before they read, they write the words they think will be in the text.
- asking the students to think of another natural disaster (e.g. an avalanche or drought) and asking them to write about it.
- asking the students to practise reading very fast and to time themselves. Students read as fast as they can and then write down as much key information as they can. Then they can rewrite the text from their notes. See previous Units for further ideas (e.g. Unit 8 Ex. 3.2, Unit 13 Ex. 4).

- WB Ex. 2: more practice with reading.

6 Sing a song! Here comes the sun 🔲

AtoZ SONGS

The song is also recorded on the Workbook cassette.

7 Decide ...

AtoZ DECIDE EXERCISES

7.1 The words in your head

AtoZ VOCABULARY and WRITING

Students brainstorm word associations and images from some of the 'climate words' given. The focus is on their experience of the climate in their country. Students can then read their poems to the class or put them on the wall.

- WB Ex. 3: practice with pronunciation.
- WB Ex. 4: practice with speaking – about the weather.

7.2 Warning!

AtoZ READING and WRITING

Students can work alone or in pairs to first brainstorm ideas about what people should do when there is a flood, hurricane or snowstorm. You can stick their posters on the wall or in a more public place so that they can serve as real warnings. They could also write posters about other natural disasters.

7.3 Do it yourself!

8 Your Language Record

AtoZ LANGUAGE RECORD

Advance notice!
Unit 20 requires the students to have collected pictures and information before their Activity lesson. You may like to look at Unit 20 Ex. 1 now so that you can plan ahead for this.

19 Language focus

> **Advance notice!**
> Unit 20 requires the students to have collected pictures before the Activity lesson. You may like to plan time to discuss this with the students, while they are working on Unit 19. See Unit 20, Exs. 1–3.

1 RESEARCHING THE CLASSROOM: HOW DO THEY HELP THEMSELVES?

Some questions to think about during the next lessons.

- All students have their own way of trying to learn, particularly before tests. What do you think your students do to help themselves learn?
- Have you noticed them helping each other? How?
- Do you think the ways they use are effective? (Have you tried to learn in the same way?)

- What they do to learn at home? Where do they do their homework? What help do they ask for?
- When students are faced with a difficult task (for example a difficult text), what do they do?

See **AtoZ LEARNING STRATEGIES** for further ideas. In addition, the *Help yourself!* Units in the Workbook (Units 6, 11, 16, 21, 26 and 31) present ideas for students to use.

2 TEACHING NOTES FOR UNIT 19

Overview of the Unit

This Unit continues the theme of changing climates and focuses on plans to protect the Earth. It also offers practice with 'going to' – to talk about making plans for the future and about events which are certain to happen, and practice with 'have to'. The *Out and about* section sees Helen and Will in the school canteen ordering food. Vocabulary from Unit 18 is recycled.

Timing

Suggested timings (in minutes) for each activity are:

1	Our changing climate	
1.1	What is happening to the climate?	10
1.2	An international climate conference	15
2	Talking about the future	
2.1	What do you say?	5
2.2	Talking about the future in English	5–10
2.3	How to form 'going to' sentences	10
2.4	Guess!	15
3	What's going to happen?	12
4	I have to go to school every day	
4.1	They have to …	5

4.2	How to form 'have to' sentences	10
4.3	What do you have to do?	15
4.4	Play a game!	10
5	Out and about with English	
5.1	What do you say?	5
5.2	In the school canteen	10–15
5.3	Now you try it	15
6	Do it yourself!	10–15
7	Your Language Record	(at home) 10

What you need

A cassette player and the Class Cassette for Exs. 1.2 and 5.2.

Mixed-ability classes and supplementary worksheets

Exercise 1.2 has additional guidelines for mixed-ability classes.

Language worksheet 19.1 practises 'going to' and Language worksheet 19.2 practises 'have to'.

(See also **AtoZ MIXED ABILITIES.**)

Workbook

Unit 19 in the Workbook contains the following exercises:

- Exercise 1: writing using 'going to'
- Exercise 2: writing using 'have to'
- Exercise 3: an open dialogue in a café
- Exercise 4: pronunciation of /h/

For additional notes on the use of the Workbook and Workbook answers see page 149.

Guidelines

1 Our changing climate

`AtoZ` **PROCESSING TIME, DISCUSSION**

1.1 What is happening to the climate?

This discussion stage is intended to be a *brief* introduction before the listening work in Exercise 1.2.

The pictures are each intended to stimulate some ideas: planes cause pollution and tremendous heat which affects the environment. Deforestation in many parts of the world affects the production of oxygen and the climate. Planting new trees helps to reduce the problem. Aerosol sprays can damage the environment. Volcanoes produce tremendous heat and throw dust into the air which can cause 'dust rain', pollution and climate change. Factories and exhaust fumes from cars also cause the temperature to rise and affect air quality. Changes in the sun (sunspots) also affect our climate. Rising temperatures may cause ice at the poles to melt, which will lead to a rise in the level of the sea. This will cause flooding in many parts of the world, and changes in the climate. This will then affect how we live, plants and animal life, and so on.

There are many complex ideas here which the students may find difficult to express in English. As key vocabulary comes up, you can put this on the board, but it is not necessary to spend a lot of time trying to get them to explain fully in English. Some key vocabulary items are: *pollution, air, oxygen, heat, sea level, ozone layer.*

1.2 An international climate conference 🖾

`AtoZ` **LISTENING, DISCUSSION and PAIRWORK**
Before playing the recording, read through the text with the students and check that they understand what they have to do.

Divide them into pairs to listen for the information for either List A or List B. Ask them to copy the table into their exercise books before you play the recording.

🖾 **TAPESCRIPT**

Reporter: Hello from the International Climate Conference. There are representatives from over 100 countries here. Yesterday we heard about plans to help the environment. One big problem is the car. The Spanish group, for example, says it is going to ask car companies to make smaller cars. Smaller cars, they say, use less petrol. The group from the United States says it is going to change the type of petrol that we use. They are going to ask oil companies to make cleaner petrol. The groups from Italy and Germany also have plans to change the way we use cars. The Italians want to protect their historic cities. They say that many cities are going to stop car traffic in the city centre. The Germans want to make people use the public transport system more. They plan to have cheaper buses and trains. The other countries have different plans. Japan, for example, makes a lot of the world's refrigerators. The big problem is that gas in the refrigerators is bad for the environment. The Japanese group says that Japan is going to look for a different gas. The group from the United Kingdom is going to recycle more paper and glass. The group from Brazil …

Answers
List A: Spain: ask car companies to make smaller cars; Italy: stop car traffic in the city centre; Japan: look for a new gas for refrigerators. **List B:** USA: change the type of petrol we use/ask oil companies to make cleaner petrol; Germany: to have cheaper buses and trains; United Kingdom: recycle more paper and glass.

When you have played the recording two or three times, you can go through the answers using the language in the book. For example:

The Spanish group is going to ask companies to make smaller cars.

Put a few complete examples on the board.

MIXED ABILITIES

More support can be given by
- asking students to listen for information about just one country.
- brainstorming first with the students their own ideas about steps which would help climate changes.
- giving the students a copy of the tapescript so that they can read before or while they listen.

The task can be made more demanding by
- asking students not to look at the text as they listen.
- asking students to think of four or five more countries who are at the conference and to think of four or five other things these countries may do to help prevent climate changes . They can then prepare a television report like this one about their plans.

2 Talking about the future

2.1 What do you say?

AtoZ MOTHER TONGUE and GRAMMAR

Collect examples from the students in their own language so that they can notice the various ways in which they can express the future.

2.2 Talking about the future in English

Ensure that students notice that, here, 'going to' is used to talk about plans.

2.3 How to form 'going to' sentences

Point out to students the use of 'going to' in the pictures. Show them that questions are formed by inversion and negatives with 'be' + 'not'.

2.4 Guess!

AtoZ GROUPWORK

- WB Ex. 1 and Language worksheet 19.1: more practice with 'going to'.

3 What's going to happen?

AtoZ GRAMMAR

The first examples of 'going to' refer to plans. Here, 'going to' is used to express certainty.

> **Answers**
> **b** His teacher is going to be angry. **c** He is going to be cold/His parents are going to be angry **d** He is going to be late. He is going to walk to school. **e** He isn't going to play football. **f** He isn't going to catch the bus home.

4 I have to go to school every day

4.1 They have to ...

AtoZ MOTHER TONGUE

- WB Ex. 2 and Language worksheet 19.2: more practice with 'have to'.

4.2 How to form 'have to' sentences

4.3 What do you have to do?

If you have two large pieces of paper you can stick them up on the wall and collect ideas.

4.4 Play a game!

AtoZ GAMES and GROUPWORK

5 Out and about with English

5.1 What do you say?

Suggestions: Can I have …? Could I have …? May I have …? Is/Are there any …? An orange juice please. Have you got …? I'd like …

5.2 In the school canteen 📼

AtoZ LISTENING

> **MIXED ABILITIES**
> See Teaching Notes to Unit 9, Ex. 5 and Unit 14, Ex. 4 for further guidance.

5.3 Now you try it

AtoZ SPEAKING and GROUPWORK

- WB Ex. 3: more practice with speaking in an open dialogue.
- WB Ex. 4: more practice with pronunciation.

6 Do it yourself!

AtoZ DO IT YOURSELF, AUTONOMY and STUDENT INVOLVEMENT

See the Teaching Notes to Unit 4, Exercise 5.

7 Your Language Record

AtoZ LANGUAGE RECORD

Time to spare?

AtoZ TIME TO SPARE?

Revision Box

Remind the students that 'many' is used for things that you can count ('countables') and that 'much' is used for things that you can't count ('uncountables').

> **Answers**
> Helen: much; Will: many, much; Helen: much, many; Will: much; Helen: many; Will: much; Helen: much.

> **Advance notice!**
> Don't forget to remind the students to bring their pictures for the Unit 20 Activity.

Activity 20

A new book of world climates

TEACHING NOTES FOR UNIT 20

Overview of the Unit

In this Unit, the students work in groups to produce a cover for a new book about world climates. This involves thinking about the content of such a book and then writing a text to describe what the book is about (the 'blurb'). At the end there is a short evaluation discussion.

Including the book cover in a Parcel of English

See the Teaching Notes on Unit 15 for some ideas on including students' work in *A Parcel of English*.

In addition to producing the book cover, your class and 'twin' class can work on a booklet about an aspect of climate which affects both of the regions/countries that they live in, or only one. For example, droughts may be common in one region, but flooding may be frequent in the other. Alternatively, both classes can write about the same aspect of the climate and compare the ways it affects their lives. Clothes, food, work and leisure activities may be topics which could be included.

Timing

Unit 20 is intended for one full lesson, but you may decide to split it up over a number of lessons. Suggested timings are:

Before the lesson		
1 A new book about the world and its climates		10
2 Discuss and decide		10
3 Collect the pictures	(at home)	10
In the lesson		
4 Make the front of your book cover		15
5 Make the back of the cover		20
6 Look at other book covers		10
7 Evaluation		10

What you need

Some large sheets of paper or card (A4), some magazine pictures, coloured pens, crayons and glue. Some extra pictures of climates, disasters, different foods, clothes or houses (in case students don't bring enough).

Mixed-ability classes

Exercise 5 has additional guidelines for mixed-ability classes.

(See also **AtoZ** MIXED ABILITIES.)

Workbook

Unit 20 in the Workbook contains fluency exercises.

- Exercise 1: general knowledge about deserts
- Exercise 2: reading about deserts and comprehension
- Exercise 3: writing
- Exercise 4: creative writing

Guidelines

Before the lesson

1 A new book about the world and its climates

AtoZ BRAINSTORMING

Before starting the brainstorming make sure that the students know what the activity is about and what they will be working towards.

Allow time for the students to look back at Units 18 and 19 to collect ideas. Before drawing the ideas maps on the board you could let students work alone or in pairs to share ideas.

2 Discuss and decide

AtoZ GROUPWORK and DISCUSSION

Students work in groups to plan their cover – pictures, title and description (the 'blurb'). Check what they have planned to bring to their Activity lesson.

3 Collect the pictures

Remind students to bring their pictures to the next English lesson!

In the lesson

4 Make the front of your book cover
AtoZ GROUPWORK

Encourage students to think first of the contents of the book before they choose their pictures. Students lay out the pictures on their papers leaving space for the title, author and blurb.

5 Make the back of the cover
AtoZ GROUPWORK and WRITING

Students write a draft of the 'blurb' (the description on the back of the book). Encourage them to look at examples of blurbs for different kinds of books. Encourage the groups to help each other with ideas, grammar and spelling.

> **MIXED ABILITIES**
>
> *More support can be given by*
> - asking students to look back at Unit 18 Ex. 3 (The climate and the way we live) and write a blurb about clothes, houses and food in their country.
> - asking students to look back at Unit 18 Ex. 5 (Disasters). Ask students to write a blurb for a book about climate disasters, drawing on the vocabulary and sentences in the texts.
> - asking students to start by writing a blurb for each of their pictures. They can then work in pairs to take the best sentences/phrases from each to make one blurb.
>
> *The task can be made more demanding by*
> - asking students to write chapter titles and an introduction for their book.
> - asking students to write the opening paragraph of a chapter of their book.
> - asking students to focus on a specific area of climate (e.g. disasters) and to write a more detailed blurb.

6 Look at the other book covers
AtoZ DISPLAYING STUDENTS' WORK

7 Evaluation
AtoZ EVALUATION

This is the fourth activity the students have done in *CES* Level 2. While they are discussing the questions, you could ask them to think about how they have worked differently on each activity, what they have done to make each one better, and what strategies they have used to improve their writing.

21

Culture matters An outdoor life

> **Note**: Remind the students that they should be preparing something for the *Open plan* section of Unit 22.

TEACHING NOTES FOR UNIT 21

Overview of the Unit
Students learn about a range of different leisure activities all the year round in the UK and are introduced to the Youth Hostels Association. A listening task focuses on the leisure activities of an English family.

Timing
This Unit is designed to take one class hour, except for Exercise 4 'Across cultures', which can be developed for homework or for another lesson. Suggested timings for one lesson are:

1	Leisure activities in your country	10
2	Leisure activities in the United Kingdom	
2.1	An activity for every season	12
2.2	The Blake family	15
3	The Youth Hostels Association (YHA)	
3.1	What is the YHA?	10
3.2	A youth hostel holiday	15
4	Across cultures	10–30

(See also **AtoZ** TIMING.)

What you need
The Class Cassette for Exercise 2.2 and Exercise 3.1 (optional).

Mixed abilities
Exercise 3.1 has further guidelines for mixed-ability classes.

(See also **AtoZ** MIXED ABILITIES.)

Workbook
Unit 20 in the Workbook is *Help yourself with grammar* and contains three techniques that students can use, two from Level 1 and one new technique:

- Exercise 1: Making sentences from mixed-up words
- Exercise 2: Writing sentences following a pattern
- Exercise 3: Changing sentences

See page 149 for a special note on the *Help yourself!* Units and **AtoZ** GRAMMAR.

Guidelines

1 Leisure activities in your country
AtoZ DISCUSSION

2 Leisure activities in the United Kingdom

2.1 An activity for every season
AtoZ DISCUSSION and BRAINSTORMING

> **Answers**
> Cricket, fishing, gardening and tennis (spring and summer) and football (autumn/winter) are seasonal activities; the other activities are done all the year round.

2.2 The Blake family 📼
AtoZ LISTENING

> **Answers**
>
> | Activity | When do they do it? |
> |---|---|
> | Mrs Blake: | tennis (April–October) and gardening (March–November) |
> | Mr Blake: | cricket (April–September) and football (winter) |
> | Tim: | football (winter), rock climbing (all year round), fishing (summer) |
> | Tara: | cycling (all year round) |

3 The Youth Hostels Association (YHA)

3.1 What is the YHA? 📼

AtoZ READING and LISTENING

> **Answers**
> You can be any age. It's cheap to stay in a hostel.

MIXED ABILITIES

More support can be given by

- asking the students to choose to read either the text in Ex. 3.1 or in Ex. 3.2.
- writing on the board the five content areas of the text:
  a where hostels are
  b the price
  c what are youth hostels?
  d where are they?
  e what can you do?
  Ask students to write the key words and phrases for each sub-heading. Students can work in pairs and choose two sections each.

The task can be made more demanding by

- asking students to work in pairs to prepare an interview. One is a YHA representative and the other is a student representative who would like to know more about the YHA for a student journal. They can record the interview or write it down.

3.2 A youth hostel holiday

If they have time, students can look at the map, choose another youth hostel, imagine that they have been there for a holiday and write a letter or postcard to their friends/family.

> **Answers**
> Tara did seven different activities. They were: canoeing, making a raft, walking, using a map, building a tree house, climbing rocks, and cooking food. She wrote the letter on Wednesday.

4 Across cultures

AtoZ DISCUSSION

If there is time, students can draw a map of their area and write about the different outdoor activities they can do there.

22 Revision and evaluation

TEACHING NOTES FOR UNIT 22

See Unit 7 for a 'General note on the *Revision and evaluation* Units'.

Overview of the Unit

This Unit has the same structure as Unit 12.

Timing

The main part of the Unit (Exercises 1–3) is intended for one full lesson, with the students' own test being used in another lesson or as homework (see below). Suggested timings are as follows. To save time, students can do the example test (Exercise 2) for homework before the lesson.

1	How well do you know it?	5–10
2	Test yourself!	15
3	Write your own test! (assembled later)	15
4	Looking back at Units 18–21	
4.1	Group discussion	15
4.2	Your own ideas	5
5	Learning English grammar	8

What you need

No additional materials required.

Supplementary worksheets

Language worksheet 19.1: 'going to'
Language worksheet 19.2: 'have to'

Workbook

Unit 22 in the Workbook provides further revision exercises using the vocabulary and language of the Theme, the Tuareg people of the Sahel.

- Exercise 1: a vocabulary puzzle
- Exercise 2: writing using 'going to'
- Exercise 3: reading and writing with 'have to'

Guidelines

For detailed notes see Unit 12.

Theme E

Across borders

OVERVIEW OF THE THEME

Theme E, Across borders, focuses on the topic of international trade and transport. It looks at where different products are grown, mined and manufactured, and at how goods are transported across the world.

In Unit 23 students learn about different 'primary products' – raw materials and agricultural products – and where they come from and the kinds of products they are used for. Students will recognise some of the logos of the multinational companies introduced in the Unit. In Unit 25 (Activity) students make a tourist leaflet describing their region and learn something about the South-West region of England. The *Culture matters* Unit (Unit 26) gives students information about the Channel Tunnel, now joining England to France. Unit 27 – the *Revision and evaluation* Unit – gives students an opportunity to revise the language and structures of the Theme.

The language areas presented in Unit 24 are 'could' and 'would' for making requests and offers, and 'enough'. The *Out and about* section introduces phrases for 'asking the way', which is continued in Unit 29.

All the Units in the Theme offer curricular links with Geography and Economics.

Using the cover page

A to Z OVERVIEWING

Suggested time: 10 minutes

See page 32 for notes on using the cover page.

Answers

1 Pictures: agricultural products – Unit 23; map – Unit 27; lorry driver – Unit 24; mouth of Channel Tunnel – Unit 26; seaside town – Unit 25.

2 In Unit 23, students can learn about where products come from, where they are made and how they are transported. In Unit 24, students learn how to use 'could' and 'would' for making requests and offers, and 'enough'.

3 In Unit 25, they can make a leaflet about their region.

Topic 23 The global village

1 WHAT HAPPENED WITH UNITS 18–22?

Some questions to think about before you start Unit 23:

Unit 20 was the fourth *Activity* Unit in the book. In Unit 25, there is another *Activity* Unit, where students produce a leaflet about the area in which they live.

- Do all the students contribute in the Activity lessons?

- Are there some students who always seem to lead groupwork? If so, is it possible to change the groups?
- Do they need more time to prepare before you work on the activity in class?
- If you look ahead to Unit 25 now, can you see any aspects that you will need to plan for?

2 TEACHING NOTES FOR UNIT 23

Overview of the Unit

This Unit looks at the topic of international trade: where primary products come from, and where secondary products are made. Reading and listening texts present information about multinational companies and how goods are transported across the world. The first *Decide* exercise (Exercise 4) offers a choice between vocabulary and writing practice. The second *Decide* exercise (Exercise 7) offers a choice between vocabulary, writing practice and *Do it yourself!* work.

Timing

Suggested timings are:

1	In the shops	
1.1	The things you buy	8
1.2	What are they made from?	10
2	Primary products from all over the world	
2.1	What are primary products?	5
2.2	Who exports them?	10–12
2.3	Who imports them?	12
3	Play a game! International trade	10–15
4	Decide …	15
5	Across the world	
5.1	Companies from across the world	5
5.2	Some points of view	15
5.3	Good or bad?	10
6	Sing a song!	5–10
7	Decide …	15
8	Your Language Record	(at home) 10

What you need

A cassette player and the Cassette for Exercise 6 (song). Dictionaries and coloured pencils for Exercise 5.2 (optional). The *Exercise Box* for *Time to spare?* A map of the world (or see page 152).

Mixed-ability classes and supplementary worksheets

Exercises 4, 5.2 and 7 have mixed-ability notes.

Say it clearly! Worksheet 3 has practice with /ə/ and /ʃ/.

(See also **AtoZ** MIXED ABILITIES.)

Workbook

Workbook Unit 23 contains the following:

- Exercise 1: vocabulary from the Unit, as a puzzle
- Exercise 2: writing about things we make
- Exercise 3: pronunciation of /ə/ and /ʃ/
- Exercise 4: speaking in an open dialogue (shops and shopping)
- Exercise 5: singing a song in English

See page 149 for additional notes on the Workbook.

Guidelines

1 In the shops

1.1 The things you buy
AtoZ DISCUSSION
You could ask students about their favourite book, game, etc.

1.2 What are they made from?

AtoZ PAIRWORK

You will need to explain the term 'raw material'.

Ask the students to choose only two or three items. They can make two lists: the raw materials and where they think they come from. Encourage the students to guess, if they really don't know. You can put some examples on the board. For example:

They are made from:	The raw materials come from:
Posters: paper, ink, colours.	trees – Sweden? China?
Chocolate and sweets: chocolate, sugar, milk.	Africa? Brazil?

• **WB Ex. 1:** more practice with this vocabulary.

2 Primary products from all over the world

2.1 What are primary products?

AtoZ DISCUSSION

You can collect ideas from the class and put some of the words they mention on the board.

• **WB Ex. 2:** writing practice about primary products.

2.2 Who exports them?

Note: Primary products come from many different countries, so there are other possibilities.

Latin America (e.g. Mexico, Brazil, Chile)	**Asia** (e.g. India, Pakistan)	**North America** (e.g. USA, Canada)
copper (Chile)	wheat (India)	copper
cocoa	cocoa	wheat
sugar (Brazil, Cuba)	sugar (India)	leather
leather (Brazil, Argentina)	leather (India)	cotton
iron (Brazil)	cotton (India)	iron
rubber (Mexico, Brazil)	iron (China)	
	rubber (Malaysia, Indonesia)	

Europe (e.g. Britain, France, Italy)	**Australasia** (e.g. Australia, New Zealand)	**Africa** (e.g. Kenya, Tanzania, Guinea)
wheat	bauxite	copper (Zaire)
leather	wheat	cocoa
iron	iron	bauxite (Guinea)

2.3 Who imports them?

Answers
A5 B2 C4 D7 E6 F1 G3

• **WB Ex. 3:** more practice with /ə/.

3 Play a game! International trade

AtoZ GAMES

Students copy the chart into their books. In each square, they then write the name of a manufactured product, e.g. car, computer, T-shirt, loaf of bread.

Now read out the list of primary products. (See below.) Students must decide if this primary product is in any of their manufactured products. If it is, they cross it off. (To check they are right later, they can write the primary product next to the secondary product.) The first student with nine crosses shouts Bingo! and is the winner.

Primary products:
1 sugar 2 iron 3 cocoa 4 rubber 5 cotton 6 copper
7 wheat 8 leather 9 aluminium 10 wood

4 Decide ...

AtoZ DECIDE EXERCISES and MONITORING AND GUIDING

> **MIXED ABILITIES**
> Students will probably find Ex. 4.2 easier than Ex. 4.1 and Ex. 4.1 easier than Ex. 4.3.

4.1 Odd one out

Students decide which word is the 'odd one out' and write the word in the puzzle squares. They can then write a similar puzzle of their own for their partner or the class *Exercise Box*.

Answers
1 airport 2 money. All the others are natural substances.
3 games. All the others are made of paper. 4 copper. The others are countries. 5 clothes. All the others are types of clothes. 6 wheat. A primary product, the others are manufactured products. 7 expand. All the others mean 'make'. 8 cars. Cars are manufactured. All the other words are primary products. 9 Forest. All the others have water.
10 cocoa. The others are types of metal. 11 people. The others are primary products. 12 cotton. Cotton is a primary product. The other words are all manufactured products.

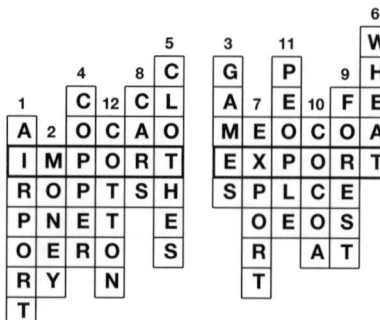

4.2 An international birthday

AtoZ WRITING

> **Example answers**
> The box is made of paper. The paper came from Sweden. The balloons are made of rubber. The rubber came from Brazil. Butter is made of milk. The milk came from … . The sugar came from India. The eggs came from … .

4.3 Buy it!

AtoZ WRITING

5 Across the world

5.1 Companies from across the world

> **Answers**
> 1 C   2 A   3 D   4 E   5 B   6 F

5.2 Some points of view

AtoZ READING, VOCABULARY

There are a lot of 'new' words here, so students will need to work out the meanings. They need three different coloured pens for this exercise, or they can mark the sentences with single underlining, double underlining, or a wavy line to show how much they understand. They can then compare with their neighbours and help each other with vocabulary and dictionary use.

MIXED ABILITIES

More support can be given by
- asking students to work in pairs: they can read six sentences each.
- asking them first to find all the sentences connected with 1 money, 2 modernisation, 3 jobs.

The task can be made more demanding by
- asking students to write about other good and bad features of multinational companies.
- asking them to look more closely at statements C, D, K and J and to think of examples.
- asking them to write and act out a conversation between two people: one person thinks multinationals are good, the other thinks they are bad.
- some students discussing what they think 'the global village' means.
- asking them to take these sentences and to make a dialogue between two people

- **WB Ex. 3: more practice with the pronunciation of /ʃ/.**

5.3 Good or bad?

> **Probable answers**
> Multinationals are 'good': B, C, D, H (?), I, J, K, L.
> Multinationals are 'bad': A, E, F, G, H (?).

6 Sing a song! Big money 🔲

AtoZ SONGS

The song is also recorded on the Workbook Cassette.

7 Decide …

MIXED ABILITIES

Students will probably find Ex. 7.2 easier than Ex. 7.1, which requires quite a wide vocabulary.

7.1 A word map

AtoZ VOCABULARY

The students can do this on a large sheet of paper and show different areas of the word map in different colours. They can then put the paper on the wall.

7.2 What's your favourite?

AtoZ WRITING

7.3 Do it yourself!

AtoZ DO IT YOURSELF!

8 Your Language Record

AtoZ LANGUAGE RECORD

Time to spare?

AtoZ TIME TO SPARE?

> **Advance notice!**
> Unit 25 requires the students to have done some reading, discussion and to have collected some pictures before their Activity lesson. You may like to look at Unit 25 Ex. 1 now, so that you can plan ahead.

24 Language focus

Advance notice!

'Unit 25 requires the students to have done some reading exercises and have collected pictures before the Activity lesson. You may like to plan time to do this with the students, while they are working on Unit 25. See Unit 25, Exs. 1–3.

1 RESEARCHING THE CLASSROOM: WHAT DO THE STUDENTS THINK?

Some questions to think about during the coming lessons:

- Think back to one particular lesson. If you asked the students what *they* thought the lesson was about, what do you think they would say? Would it be different from what *you* planned?

- If you asked your students what they thought of their English classes, what do you think they would say?
- If you took the students' opinion directly into account, do you think your lessons would alter in any way?

(See **AtoZ** STUDENT INVOLVEMENT and **AtoZ** EVALUATION for further ideas.)

2 TEACHING NOTES FOR UNIT 24

Overview of the Unit

This Unit offers grammatical and functional practice with the modals 'could' and 'would'. The Unit also introduces 'enough' and some common prepositions of place. The *Out and about* section is an introduction to asking the way which is continued in Unit 29. Vocabulary from Unit 23 is recycled.

Timing

Suggested timings (in minutes) are as follows:

1	On the road	15
2	'Could you …?'	
2.1	Making a request	5
2.2	Who says what?	12
2.3	Play a game! What do you want?	12
3	'Would you like …?'	
3.1	Making an offer	5
3.2	Make an offer	10
4	Have you got enough time?	
4.1	'Enough' in your language	10

4.2	Where do you use 'enough'?	5
4.3	What are they saying?	10
5	Out and about with English	
5.1	Around town	15
5.2	Can you tell me where it is?	15
5.3	Now you try it	10–15
6	Do it yourself!	10–15
7	Your Language Record	(at home) 10

What you need

A cassette player and the Class Cassette for Exercises 1, 2.2, and 5.2.

Mixed-ability classes and supplementary worksheets

Exercise 1 has additional guidelines for mixed-ability classes.

Language worksheet 24.1 practises 'enough' and Language worksheet 24.2 practises 'could' and 'would'.

(See also **AtoZ** MIXED ABILITIES.)

Workbook

Unit 24 in the Workbook contains the following exercises:

- Exercise 1: requests with 'could'
- Exercise 2: offers with 'would'
- Exercise 3: 'enough'
- Exercise 4: pronunciation of /ʌ/ (cut), and /ʊ/ (put)
- Exercise 5: names of places in a town and asking the way

For additional notes on the use of the Workbook and Workbook answers see page 149.

Guidelines

1 On the road 📼

AtoZ LISTENING, CHECKING ANSWERS

This is quite a long listening text. Read through the place-names on the map before playing the cassette for the first time, so that students will recognise them more easily. Check that the students know that they have to fill in the worksheet with the place-names. You could first play the cassette all the way through to familiarise the students with the voices.

MIXED ABILITIES

More support can be given by
- asking the students to work in pairs and fill out alternate sections – mornings and afternoons, or different days.
- giving the students part of the tapescript, for example, the boss's part.
- giving the students the tapescript cut up into sections. After listening once or twice, they can put the sections into the correct order before they do the tasks in the book.
- playing the recording in short sections.

The task can be made more demanding by
- asking the students to listen for exactly WHAT Ken will be taking to each place.
- giving the students some detailed questions. For example: Why can't he go to London on Tuesday? Where are the documents for Paris? Where is he going in London on Thursday?

📼 TAPESCRIPT

Ken: Good morning, boss. Where am I going this week?

Boss: Er … Portsmouth today. Now, for the rest of the week …

Ken: Yes?

Boss: Could you drive from Portsmouth to Southampton?

Ken: Today?

Boss: Yes. Have you got enough time this afternoon?

Ken: No problem.

Boss: Good. Then tomorrow morning drive to Dover. Could you pick up some washing machines there?

Ken: On Tuesday?

Boss: Yes. Tuesday morning. Take them to Paris on Tuesday afternoon.

Ken: Where are the documents?

Boss: In the Dover office, as usual. Then could you bring back a container of paper on Tuesday evening?

Ken: Er … to Paris on Tuesday afternoon and then back to London on Tuesday evening? My lorry doesn't go fast enough for that!

Boss: OK, OK. Wednesday morning. Come back to London on Wednesday morning.

Ken: Where would you like me to go then?

Boss: Yes … let me see. Right, on Wednesday afternoon could you collect some pencils in Bristol? You can get the documents at the Bristol office.

Ken: OK. That's fine. Thursday morning?

Boss: On Thursday morning could you drive back to London? Take the pencils on Thursday afternoon to the Education Office.

Ken: Fine … and then?

Boss: Well, do you think that's enough?

Ken: More than enough!

Boss: Would you like to have a rest on Friday?

Ken: Yes, I would!

Answers

Monday afternoon: Southampton; Tuesday morning: Dover; Tuesday afternoon: Paris; Wednesday morning: London; Wednesday afternoon: Bristol; Thursday morning: London; Thursday afternoon: Education Office; Friday: a rest.

2 'Could you ...?'

2.1 Making a request

AtoZ MOTHER TONGUE and TRANSLATION

Students make their own suggestions about ways of expressing this function in their own language.

2.2 Who says what? 📼

AtoZ CHECKING ANSWERS

> **Answers**
> 1E 2F 3B 4C 5D 6A

> 📟 TAPESCRIPT
> 1 Customs Officer: Could you open your suitcase please? Woman: This one? Yes, sure.
> 2 Father: Could you answer the phone, Tim? Young boy: OK, Dad.
> 3 Teacher: Could you finish this exercise for Friday please? Students: Number 4? Yes, Mrs Turner.
> 4 Teenager: Could you lend me your new cassette tonight? Teenager: Yes, no problem. Here you are.
> 5 Parent: Could you turn the music down, please? Teenager: Sorry, is it too loud?
> 6 Lorry driver: Could you tell me where Smith's Supermarket is, please? Passer-by: Turn left at the top of this road and then right.

2.3 Play a game! What do you want?

AtoZ GAMES and GROUPWORK

- WB Ex. 1 and Language worksheet 24.1: further practice with 'could'.

3 'Would you like ...?'

3.1 Making an offer

AtoZ TRANSLATION and MOTHER TONGUE

3.2 Make an offer

AtoZ PAIRWORK

> **Example answers**
> 1 Would you like to come to the park? Yes, I'd love to./ No thanks, I've got a lot of homework to do.
> 2 Would you like to come to the pop concert with me? Yes, I'd love to./No, I'm sorry, I don't like that kind of music.
> 3 Would you like a cold drink? Yes, please! I'm very thirsty. / No thanks.
> 4 Would you like an ice-cream? Yes please! I love ice-cream! / No thanks, I hate ice-cream!
> 5 Would you like to go swimming? Yes please, I love swimming! No thanks, I'm going shopping this afternoon.
> 6 Would you like a sweet?/ Yes, thanks. / No thanks.
> 7 Would you like an apple? Yes please, it looks nice. / No thanks, I don't like apples.

> 8 Would you like a piece of chocolate? Yes please! I love chocolate!/ No thanks.

- WB Ex.2 and Language worksheet 24.1: further practice with 'would'.

4 Have you got enough time?

4.1 'Enough' in your language

AtoZ INDUCTIVE GRAMMAR, MOTHER TONGUE

The main point of this discussion (picked up in Exercise 4.2) is that students notice that 'enough' comes *before* nouns and *after* adjectives.

4.2 Where do you use 'enough'?

AtoZ GRAMMAR

4.3 What are they saying?

AtoZ WRITING

> **Answers**
> 1 My trousers aren't long enough 2 I haven't got enough juice 3 It's not cold enough in the fridge 4 It's not strong enough 5 I'm not tall enough

- WB Ex. 3: further practice with 'enough'.

5 Out and about with English

5.1 Around town

AtoZ WRITING and VOCABULARY

Students work alone or in pairs. First they match the place-names with the places on the map. Then they write as many words as they can which they associate with the place or things which they can buy there.

Draw a chart on the board while the students are thinking, with all the names of the places across the top: as students suggest words, write them in the columns or ask the students to do it.

Point out the use of the possessive 's' with shop names: a baker's (= the shop of a baker); a chemist's (= the shop of a chemist), etc.

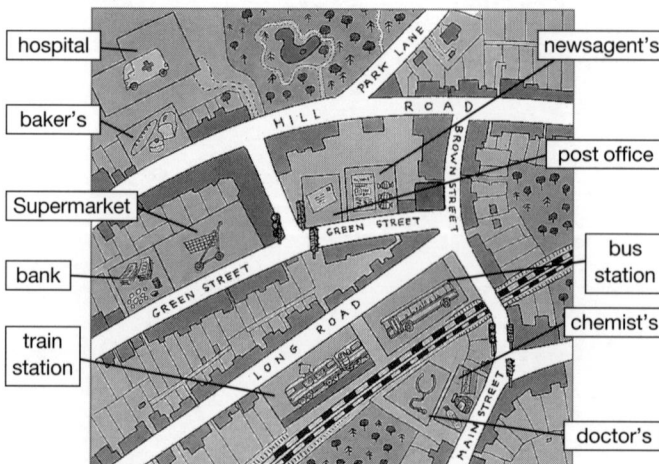

Some example answers (based on England):

hospital: get help in an emergency or after an accident, operations.
post office: buy stamps, post letters and parcels, pay bills, pay taxes.
newsagent's: buy newspapers and magazines, buy sweets.
bank: take money out and put it in, change money.
supermarket: buy food and things for cleaning.
train station: buy tickets, catch a train.
bus station: buy tickets, catch a bus.
doctor's: see a doctor if you are ill.
chemist's: buy medicines.

5.2 Can you tell me where it is? 🔊

You can ask the students to read the dialogue aloud in groups of three: Helen, Will and a man/woman.

Possible answers
Helen and Will want to go to a baker's, a supermarket, a newsagent's, a chemist's and a post office.

MIXED ABILITIES

See Teaching Notes to Unit 9, Ex. 5 and Unit 14, Ex. 4 for further guidance.

5.3 Now you try it
A to Z PAIRWORK and SPEAKING

• WB Ex. 5 and Language worksheet 24.2: further practice with asking the way.

6 Do it yourself!
A to Z DO IT YOURSELF!

7 Your Language Record
A to Z LANGUAGE RECORD

Time to spare?
A to Z TIME TO SPARE?

Advance notice!
Don't forget to remind the students to bring their pictures for the Unit 25 Activity.

Activity 25 Come to see us!

TEACHING NOTES FOR UNIT 25

Overview of the Unit

In this Unit, the students first look at a tourist leaflet about the South West of England and then work in groups to produce a tourist leaflet or poster about the area in which they live. This involves finding pictures and photographs of the region and writing short texts to describe the geography, climate, industries and the people. At the end of the activity, there is a short evaluation discussion.

Including the leaflet in a Parcel of English

See Teaching Notes for Unit 15 for some ideas on including students' work from an activity in *A Parcel of English*.

This is an ideal activity for the students to prepare to send to their 'twin' class, particularly as it will give them a sense of an audience for their leaflet. Encourage them to start thinking about what they would like to know about the region around their 'twin' class, so that they have a clearer idea of the kind of information and pictures their readers will find interesting. If possible, you could contact your link-up school in advance and find out if there is anything in particular which they would like to know about.

Timing

Unit 25 is intended for one full lesson, but you may decide to split it up over a number of lessons. Suggested timings are:

Before the lesson	
1 The South West of England	10
2 The South West – a tourist leaflet	15
3 Your own leaflet	10
In the lesson	
4 Making the leaflet	30
5 Evaluation	10

What you need

You will find it useful to have some A4 sheets of paper, some postcards, photographs, maps and information of the area (in case students don't bring enough). Coloured pens, glue, and scissors may also be useful but are not essential. A cassette player and the Class Cassette for Exercise 2 are optional.

Mixed-ability classes

Exercise 2 has additional guidelines for mixed-ability classes.

(See also **A to Z** MIXED ABILITIES.)

Workbook

Unit 25 in the Workbook contains exercises to practise:

- Exercise 1: reading about three areas in Britain
- Exercise 2: guided writing
- Exercise 3: speaking in an open dialogue

Background notes on the South West of England

The South West of England stretches from Bath and Bristol in the north, to Penzance in the South West and Southampton in the South East. It covers the counties (from south to north) of Cornwall, Devon, Dorset, Somerset, Wiltshire and Avon. In general, it is an agricultural area, famous for apples, sheep and dairy produce. The main industries are aerospace engineering in Bristol and Yeovil, leatherwork and shoes in Somerset, fishing around the coastal areas, and tourism. It is relatively underpopulated and many of its inhabitants live in small villages: many areas of Cornwall and Devon are moorland, empty of everything except sheep and ponies. Plymouth, Southampton and Bristol are major ports: Plymouth is a naval centre, Southampton takes much of the cross-channel ferry traffic to and from France, and Bristol used to be one of the main ports for importing tobacco, sugar and slaves from the West Indies. The main coastal towns, such as Penzance, Torquay ('The English Riviera', as it is sometimes called), Lyme Regis,

Weymouth and Bournemouth, are popular with tourists because of their mild climates. Tourists often visit historical sites – there is a large number of old churches and cathedrals in the small towns and villages. Others like to camp and cycle in the countryside, which is famous for its beauty and tranquillity.

Guidelines

Before the lesson

1 The South West of England

A to Z DISCUSSION

Students discuss their answers to the questions. Write key words, ideas and phrases on the board.

• **WB Ex. 3: more practice with speaking.**

2 The South West – a tourist leaflet 🔲

A to Z READING

Students can work alone or in pairs for this task.

> **MIXED ABILITIES**
>
> *More support can be given by*
> • writing on the board the key words from two texts. (e.g. *Industries*: factories, aeroplanes, shoes, cheese, butter, yoghurt; *Farming*: cows, pigs, hens, apples, fruit, cheese, cream). Students read the titles and guess which words are from which text. They then read the text, focusing on these words. Remind them that they don't have to understand every word in the text. Ask them to write five key words for the Geography and Climate texts.
> • talking about the pictures with the students, to elicit some of the key ideas in the texts.
>
> *The task can be made more demanding by*
> • asking students to choose a picture, before they read the texts, and to write down as many words as they can which they associate with that picture. They then give the words to a partner, and ask him or her to guess which picture it is.

• **WB Ex. 1: more practice with reading.**

3 Your own leaflet

A to Z BRAINSTORMING

Students suggest ideas, pictures, facts and figures about their own region which they can research and put into a leaflet. They may have different ideas from the texts on Geography, Climate, etc. They may want to discuss the audience of the leaflet, where it may be placed, how large it could be, etc. Remind students to bring pictures, postcards, and maps of the region to the next lesson!

In your lesson

4 Making the leaflet

A to Z GROUPWORK, WRITING and DISPLAYING STUDENT'S WORK

The questions in the Student's Book are intended to stimulate and guide the students' writing.

In small groups, students work on rough paper first, so that they can move the pictures around and correct and revise their work. Go round and help with vocabulary, spelling and grammar, but encourage them to help each other by commenting on each other's work.

They can then copy their work into their leaflets. They could design leaflets of different shapes and sizes.

You could put the students' work on display for a week or two so that they all have a chance to look at what they have done. You could also ask the students to think of some questions which they ask the other groups. They may want to know where they got their material and information, and what readership they were writing for.

• **WB Ex. 2: more practice with writing.**

5 Evaluation

A to Z EVALUATION

26

Culture matters Britain ~~is~~ *was* an island

Britain and the Channel Tunnel

TEACHING NOTES FOR UNIT 26

Overview of the Unit

This *Culture matters* Unit fits into the 'Across borders' Theme by giving students an opportunity to look at how the Channel Tunnel may bring Britain closer to Europe. The Unit looks at different aspects of the Channel Tunnel: its location in England and France, how it is constructed, and people's reactions to it. Exercise 5, 'Across cultures', gives students a chance to discuss their own ideas about travel to, and contact between, their own country and neighbouring countries.

Timing

Suggested timings for one lesson are:

1 Britain was an island	8
2 Through the tunnel!	12
3 One of the Wonders of the World	15
4 A good thing or a bad thing?	12
5 Across cultures	5

What you need

A cassette player and the Class Cassette for Exercise 2.

Mixed abilities

Exercise 3 has further guidelines for mixed-ability classes.

(See also **AtoZ** MIXED ABILITIES.)

Workbook

Unit 26 in the Workbook is *Help yourself with a dictionary*. It contains three ideas which the students can try when using a bilingual dictionary to help them with their English. All these techniques are new to Level 2.

- Exercise 1: What's in your dictionary? (Becoming familiar with other information available in a dictionary.)
- Exercise 2: Information about a word. (How to 'decode' the information in each entry.)

- Exercise 3: What does it mean? (Checking for different meanings of one word by using both parts of the bilingual dictionary.)

See page 149 for a special note on the *Help yourself!* Units.

Guidelines

1   Britain was an island

AtoZ DISCUSSION

Background note: About 10,000–9,000 years ago, what is now Britain was connected to France. Then, with a change in climate, the ice in the North began to melt and the sea level rose. The land between Britain and France flooded. By about 8,000 years ago, the Channel had formed and Britain had become an island.

You could allow time for students to talk about their travel and holiday experiences.

2   Through the tunnel! 📼

AtoZ LISTENING

> **Answers**
> **1** three hours **2** 300 kilometres per hour **3** 21 minutes
> **4** 130 metres under the sea

3   One of the Wonders of the World

AtoZ READING

> **Answers**
> **a** three **b** under the sea **c** six years **d** The French drill is out of the tunnel: the English drill is still in the tunnel

More support can be given by

- asking the students to skim the section on facts about the tunnel. Write the figures on the board (50 km, 130 m, 130 km, 160 km, 21, 800) and ask students to find the numbers first. Then they can write down what the numbers relate to.
- asking students to read the 'Making the tunnel' text in 90 seconds. They then have to close their books and write down (in English or their mother tongue) as much information and/or as many words or phrases as they can remember. Then write on the board some key phrases from the text (e.g. 'one of the most incredible', 'they used giant drills', 'moved slowly underground', 'took their drill out', 'their drill inside' and 'too expensive') and ask them to try to tell you what the text said about the points you put on the board.
  They can then read the text again more slowly to check if they are right.

The task can be made more demanding by

- asking the students to use the information from the texts to write a brochure persuading English people to travel through the tunnel.
- writing the facts about the tunnel in a newspaper-style article for the day the tunnel opened.
- writing some true/false questions about the article for the *Exercise Box*.

4 A good thing or a bad thing?

Answers
a bad   b good   c bad   d good   e good

You could ask students to write some more good and bad comments. They say them to the class and the class then guesses whether they are good or bad.

5 Across cultures

AtoZ DISCUSSION

You could also ask students to think of their neighbouring countries and how people currently travel across the borders. They could then suggest and design other methods of travelling to and from their country.

27 Revision and evaluation

TEACHING NOTES FOR UNIT 27

See Unit 7 for a 'General note on the *Revision and evaluation* Units'.

Overview of the Unit

This Unit has the same structure as Units 7 and 17. Exercise 1 asks the students how well they think they know the English from Units 23–26. Revision exercises then follow. Students can do some or all of these exercises, depending on time and how much revision they need. In the last exercise, students think about how well they have understood the previous lessons and provide you with written feedback.

Timing

The Unit is intended for one full lesson, with revision exercises done selectively. Suggested timings are as follows:

1	How well do you know it?	5
2	Ask someone to do something	10
3	Offering someone something	15
4	That's enough!	10
5	In the factory, on the land or in the mine?	15
6	Asking the way	12
7	Looking back at Units 23–26	
7.1	Group discussion	10
7.2	Future lessons	5
8	Learning to use the dictionary	8

What you need

No additional materials required.

Mixed-ability classes and supplementary worksheets

Language worksheet 24.1: 'could' and 'would'
Language worksheet 24.2: asking the way (1)

(See also **AtoZ** MIXED ABILITIES.)

Workbook

Unit 27 in the Workbook is a self-test focusing on the language covered in the Theme.

- Exercise 1: asking someone to do something
- Exercise 2: offering someone something
- Exercise 3: 'enough'
- Exercise 4: vocabulary
- Exercise 5: speaking in an open dialogue

Guidelines

1 How well do you know it?

AtoZ TASKS IN GROUPS and OVERVIEWING

2 Ask someone to do something

Answers
1 Could you light the fire/turn on the heating/close the window, please? 2 Could I have a drink of water, please? 3 Could I use your pencil, please? 4 Could I listen to your new cassette, please? 5 Could you say that again, please?

3 Offering someone something

Answers
1 Would you like a drink? 2 Would you like some fruit? 3 Would you like to dance? 4 Would you like a rest? 5 Yes, please. I'd love an orange juice. 6 Yes, I'd love to go. 7 No, thanks! I wouldn't. 8 Yes, I'd love to play football.

4 That's enough!

Answers
2 This jacket isn't big enough/the sleeves aren't long enough. 3 The fridge isn't cold enough. 4 There isn't enough water for the animals/us.

5 In the factory, on the land or in the mine?

Answers

Land: cocoa, cotton, rubber, sugar, wheat. Mine: bauxite, copper. Factory: aluminium, bread, car tyres, chocolate, leather, shoes, sugar, sweets, trousers, wire.

6 Asking the way

Answers

2 Excuse me, where can I find the swimming pool? 3 It's in White Road, next to the baker's. 4 Excuse me, could you tell me where the hospital is, please? 5 Excuse me, where can I find the bus station?

7 Looking back at Units 23–26

7.1 Group discussion

7.2 Future lessons

AtoZ EVALUATION, AUTONOMY, STUDENT INVOLVEMENT and DISCUSSION

See Unit 7, Exercise 6 for further guidance.

8 Learning to use the dictionary

AtoZ AUTONOMY and DISCUSSION

See Unit 7, Exercise 7 for further guidance.

Open plan

AtoZ DO IT YOURSELF

See the Teaching Notes to Unit 7, *Open plan,* for further guidance.

Theme F
Energy in our lives

OVERVIEW OF THE THEME

Theme F, Energy in our lives, focuses on the topic of energy, and the various functions it has in our lives. In Unit 28, students learn about a massive blackout in New York in 1965 and the effect that this had. They also learn about how electricity is produced and how it gets to our homes. Safety in the home with electricity is also focused on. In Unit 30, students can use their imaginations to invent unusual ways to save energy. Unit 31 concerns houses in Britain and how they use energy. In Unit 32, the final Unit of the book, students can make part of a test for the whole class and write a letter to the authors with views on the coursebook.

The language areas presented in Unit 29 are the Past continuous and the imperative. The *Out and about* section introduces further language for 'asking the way'.

The Theme offers curricular links with Physics, Social Studies, Personal and Social Education, and Environmental Science.

Using the cover page

AtoZ OVERVIEWING
Suggested time: 10 minutes

See page 32 for notes on using the cover page.

Answers
1 Pictures: New York blackout – Unit 28; invention – Unit 30; girl with hair on end – Unit 28; Will in chemist's – Unit 29; game – Unit 29.
2 The New York blackout was on 9 November 1965 (Unit 28). Atoms have electrons, neutrons, and protons (Unit 28). Frank Benson was in a lift (US English: elevator) when the blackout happened (Unit 29). Frank and Bill were going home (Unit 29).
3 In Unit 30, students can invent an unusual way to save energy.

Topic 28 Blackout!

1 WHAT HAPPENED WITH UNIT 12 AND UNIT 22?

Some questions to think about before you start Unit 28:

In Units 12 and 22, the students produced part of their own test. In Unit 32, this idea is taken further. The students are asked to look back through Theme F and first identify *what* they can test and then *how* they can test it.

• How well did the students work on test writing in Units 12 and 22?

• Do they need more time to plan for Unit 32?
• Do you perhaps need to change the way the students are grouped?

As you work through the Theme, you could perhaps make a list with the students of what things they can put in their test.

2 TEACHING NOTES FOR UNIT 28

Overview of the Unit

The Unit opens with a discussion about the uses of electricity and a reading text about the New York blackout. Students learn how electricity is produced, how it comes to their homes, and about the mysteries of static electricity. The Unit contains two *Decide* exercises (Exercises 3 and 7). Safety with electricity in the home is highlighted in Exercise 7.

Timing

Some suggested timings (in minutes) for each exercise are as follows:

1	Electricity in your town	10
2	When the lights went out …	
2.1	What happened?	12
2.2	The Great American blackout	15
2.3	What did the police say?	15
3	Decide …	20
4	Where does electricity come from?	20
5	The mysteries of electricity	
5.1	What do you know?	5
5.2	Are you right?	12
6	Sing a song!	10
7	Decide …	20
8	Your Language Record	(at home) 10

(See also **AtoZ** TIMING.)

What you need

A cassette player and the Class Cassette for Exercise 2.2 (optional), 2.3, and 6 (song). Also the *Exercise Box* for the *Time to spare?*

Mixed-ability classes and supplementary worksheets

Exercises 2.2, 3, 4, and 7 have additional notes for mixed-ability classes.
Say it clearly! Worksheet 3 provides practice with /s/.

(See also **AtoZ** MIXED ABILITIES.)

Workbook

Unit 28 in the Workbook contains exercises to practise the following:

• Exercise 1: vocabulary from the Unit, as a puzzle
• Exercise 2: writing and speaking in an open dialogue
• Exercise 3: writing a news story
• Exercise 4: pronunciation of /s/
• Exercise 5: singing a song in English

For additional notes on the use of the Workbook and Workbook answers see page 149.

Guidelines

1 Electricity in your town

AtoZ DISCUSSION and BRAINSTORMING

You could collect ideas from the students as an idea map on the board. Alternatively, you could also play this as a game in which students are put into groups. Each group gets 1 point for each idea, and 1 extra point if it's in correct English.

2 When the lights went out ...

AtoZ DISCUSSION and BRAINSTORMING

2.1 What happened?

Refer back to the list that the students produced in Exercise 1 for more ideas about what happened. Put their ideas on the board so that you can then check against their answers from Exercise 2.2.

2.2 The Great American blackout 📼

AtoZ READING

This news story is a good opportunity to introduce some of the differences between British and American English:

USA: subway   GB: underground
USA: elevator   GB: lift
USA: apartments GB: flats

> **Answers**
> The things that happened were: panic, the trains stopped working, many people were trapped in the elevators and trains, prisoners started fighting in a prison near Boston, people broke into shops and took things, the traffic lights didn't work, people had to sleep in the streets, and planes could not land at the airport.

MIXED ABILITIES

More support can be given by
* going through the vocabulary in the *Language Record* first.
* asking the students to read and underline parts of the text that they don't understand. They can then compare in small groups and help each other.
* giving the students a list of key words. They can then read through the news story and find the information for each word. Some key words: elevators, 30 million, engineers, 5.30pm, 250,000 people, a prison, police, shops, traffic signals, airport, generator.
* see previous *Topic* Units for further ideas.

The task can be made more demanding by
* asking the students to read the article once or twice. You can then give them the list of key words (see above) and ask them to write a sentence about four or five of them.
See previous *Topic* Units for further ideas.

2.3 What did the police say? 📼

Collect ideas from the students before they listen to the recording.

> 📼 TAPESCRIPT
> 'Attention please. This is the New York Police Department. Don't panic. Stay calm. If you are in a car, put your lights on. Do not get out of the car. If you are on the street, follow the police signs to a safe area. Don't run. Walk slowly and calmly. Don't push. Do not go into the subway. I repeat. This is the New York Police Department. Don't panic. Stay calm. If you are in a car, put your lights on. Do not get out of the car. If you are on the street, follow the police signs to a safe area. Don't run. Walk slowly and calmly.'

* **WB Exs. 2 and 3 : writing and speaking practice about the New York blackout.**

3 Decide ...

AtoZ DECIDE EXERCISES, OVERVIEWING and MONITORING AND GUIDING

Go through the different exercises with students so that they know what they have to do in each of them.

MIXED ABILITIES
Students will probably find Ex. 3.1 easier than Ex. 3.2 and Ex. 3.2 easier than Ex. 3.3.

3.1 Check your vocabulary
AtoZ VOCABULARY

3.2 Check how much you understand

> **Answers**
> 1 false   2 not in the story   3 false   4 false   5 false   6 true
> 7 not in the story   8 true

3.3 Make an interview

4 Where does electricity come from?

AtoZ PROCESSING TIME, READING and DISCUSSION

This is quite a complex diagram, so it would probably be best to give the students some time to read it (perhaps in pairs) before you go through it with them.

Electricity is supplied at 110 volts in some parts of the world (e.g. in North America, and much of South America) and at 220 volts in other parts (e.g. throughout Europe).

> **Answers**
> 1 c   2 b   3 d   4 a

5 The mysteries of electricity

5.1 What do you know?

The key questions to ask the students here are: Why is the paper sticking to the comb? Why is the girl's hair standing up? Why are the balloons pushing away from each other?

Background note: All of the effects shown here are the result of *static electricity*. Static electricity is electricity that is not flowing in a circuit. It is caused when two different surfaces rub together. Examples of this are the static electricity that sometimes builds up on your clothing on a clear, dry day, and lightning – the electricity that builds up inside clouds in a thunderstorm.

The diagram in Exercise 5.2 explains how the pieces of paper stick to the comb, which you should read through first.

Picture 2 in Exercise 5.1 shows a Van de Graaf generator, which the students might have learned about in their Science lessons. By turning the handle very fast, the rubber belt moves around. As it moves, static electricity builds up inside the dome at the top, up to 10 million volts. If you touch the dome, negative electrons pass into your body. This means that your body is now more negative than positive. The surplus of negative electrons in your hair repel against each other, which causes your hair to straighten out and stand on end.

Picture 3 shows two balloons pushing away from each other. If you rub a balloon against your clothing, negative electrons move from your clothing to the balloon. This produces a static electric charge. If you put two balloons with a static electric charge close together, they will repel each other.

Students can try other similar experiments: a) If you rub a plastic spoon against your clothing, you give it a negative charge. Put the spoon near to some water running from a tap, and you can cause the water to 'bend' towards the spoon; b) if you rub a balloon against your clothing, you can make it stick to the ceiling or pick up small pieces of paper.

- WB Ex. 1: vocabulary practice.

5.2 Are you right?

AtoZ READING

6 Sing a song! I didn't do it 📼

AtoZ SONGS

The song is also recorded on the Workbook Cassette.

7 Decide ...

> **MIXED ABILITIES**
> Students will probably find Ex. 7.1 easier than Ex. 7.2.

7.1 Dangers in the home

> **Answers**
> The dog is eating the wire. The baby is putting its fingers in the socket. A mouse is eating a wire. There are wires and plugs in the sink. A connection is lying in the tea or coffee. The fan is near the baby. A wire is in the toaster. The light wire is broken. The hairdryer is on the cooker.

7.2 What happened next?

AtoZ WRITING

You could ask students to first discuss ideas in pairs/groups and make notes before they try to write a short paragraph.

7.3 Do it yourself!

AtoZ DO IT YOURSELF!

8 Your Language Record

AtoZ LANGUAGE RECORD

Time to spare?

AtoZ TIME TO SPARE?

Advance notice!

Unit 30 requires the students to discuss their ideas for an invention and to draw a picture before their Activity lesson. You may like to look at Unit 30 Exs. 1–3 now so that you can plan ahead for this.

29 Language focus

Advance notice!
Unit 30 requires the students to discuss their ideas for an invention and to draw a picture (at home) before the Activity lesson. You may like to plan time for the discussion with students, while they are working on Unit 29. See Unit 30, Exs. 1–3.

1 RESEARCHING THE CLASSROOM: LEARNING THROUGH THE FOUR SKILLS

Some questions to think about during the coming lessons:

- Which of the four skills do the students use most to help themselves learn English?
- Do you think they remember new words and structures better if they talk to each other about them, or if they write them?

- What do you think the students think about writing/reading/speaking/listening? If they dislike it, why do you think that is?
- Writing is often the most neglected skill. What types of writing tasks do you ask your students to do? Do they learn a lot of English *through* writing?

See **AtoZ** FOUR SKILLS for further ideas.

2 TEACHING NOTES FOR UNIT 29

Overview of the Unit

Unit 29 begins with two listening exercises, where the students will hear and then use the Past continuous. An inductive grammar exercise and practice exercises follow, with a game in Exercise 3.5. The imperative form is also presented and practised. The *Out and about* section (Exercise 5) presents further language for asking the way.

Timing

Suggested timings (in minutes) are as follows:

1	In the blackout	15
2	Check how much you understood	10
3	A new verb form	
3.1	The verb forms you know	12
3.2	What's it for?	10
3.3	In the background	5
3.4	More practice	12
3.5	Play a game!	12

4	Do this! Don't do that!	
4.1	Don't panic!	10
4.2	Keep fit!	10
4.3	More practice	20
5	Out and about with English	
5.1	Left or right?	6
5.2	Helen, Will and the concert hall	15
5.3	Now you try it	15
6	Do it yourself!	10–15
7	Your Language Record	(at home) 10

What you need

A cassette player and the Class Cassette for Exercises 1, 2, and 5.2.

Mixed-ability classes and supplementary worksheets

Exercise 5.2 has additional guidelines for mixed-ability classes.

Language worksheet 29.1 practises the Past continuous and Language worksheet 29.2 practises language for asking the way (2).

(See also A*to*Z MIXED ABILITIES.)

Workbook

Unit 29 in the Workbook contains the following exercises:

- Exercise 1: Past continuous
- Exercise 2: Past continuous
- Exercise 3: imperatives
- Exercise 4: asking the way (2)
- Exercise 5: pronunciation of /tʃ/

For additional notes on the use of the Workbook and Workbook answers see page 149.

Guidelines

1   In the blackout 🔲

A*to*Z LISTENING

Students listen to the recording in three separate parts. Before they listen to parts B and C, they try to predict what Frank and Bill did.

The tapescript is on page 142 in the Student's Book.

2   Check how much you understood 🔲

The purpose of this exercise is to get the students to naturally produce the Past continuous in their replies.

> **Answers**
> **1** Frank was going home. **2** It stopped at about half past five. **3** He was talking to Bill. **4** They were singing a song. **5** They were helping everybody. **6** It took about an hour to come down. **7** Outside, there were thousands of people on the street. Cars weren't moving at all.

3   A new verb form

A*to*Z INDUCTIVE GRAMMAR

3.1   The verb forms you know

You can refer the students back to the relevant Units for more examples of each verb form:

Present simple: Unit 2 *Extension*, The world of people and places.
Present continuous: Unit 2 *Extension*, The world of science.
Past simple: Units 13 and 14.
'Going to': Unit 19.

> **Answers**
> Examples of the Past continuous in the tapescript are: I was going home. I was talking … People were running and shouting … We were singing … Someone was shouting … They were helping everybody … Cars weren't moving …

> **Answer**
> You can describe the Past continuous as: 'I, you, he', etc. + past of 'be' + verb '-ing'.

3.2   What's it for?

Exercise 3.3 answers the question: the Past continuous is used to describe the background action for another action.

3.3   In the background

3.4   MORE PRACTICE
A*to*Z PAIRWORK

3.5   Play a game!
A*to*Z GAMES

The completed sentences are:

A: I was walking down the street when the cars crashed.
B: He was playing a computer game when the computer exploded.
C: She was coming into the room when the water fell on her. (Child sniggering in the background.)
D: They were having dinner when she found an insect in her salad.
E: They were swimming when a monkey took their clothes.
F: They were playing football when a bird took the ball.
G: She was taking a photograph when it started to rain.
H: He was opening a box when a frog jumped out.
I: They were having dinner when a mammoth came.
J: She was playing the piano when a mouse ran out.

4   Do this! Don't do that!
A*to*Z MOTHER TONGUE

4.1   Don't panic!

4.2   Keep fit!
A*to*Z GAMES

You can play this as a game with the whole class. Give the orders quickly so that the students have to think quickly. You could allow the students one or two mistakes (write their names on the board if they make a mistake), before they have to drop out.

Some instructions that you can give are:

Touch your head! Don't touch your head! Clap your hands! Don't clap your hands! Turn round! Don't turn round! Sit down! Don't sit down! Stand up! Don't stand up! Sing a song! Don't sing! Close your eyes. Don't close your eyes! Jump! Don't jump! Smile! Don't smile! Run! Don't run! Open your books! Don't open your books! and so on.

4.3 MORE PRACTICE
AtoZ WRITING

> **Answers**
> **1** Put the headphones on your head. **2** Press the stop/eject button. **3** Put the cassette inside the cassette player. **4** Close the cassette door. **5** Press the rewind button. **6** Press the player button. **7** Listen to the music!

5 Out and about with English

5.1 Left or right?

> **Answers**
> **a** 1 **b** 5 **c** 6 **d** 4 **e** 7 **f** 2 **g** 3

5.2 Helen, Will and the concert hall 📼

> **MIXED ABILITIES**
> See Teaching Notes to Unit 9, Ex. 5 and Unit 14, Ex. 4 for further guidance.

5.3 Now you try it
AtoZ PAIRWORK and SPEAKING

- **WB Ex. 4 and Language worksheet 29.2: further practice with asking the way.**

6 Do it yourself!
AtoZ DO IT YOURSELF!

7 Your Language Record
AtoZ LANGUAGE RECORD

Time to spare?
AtoZ TIME TO SPARE?

> **Advance notice!**
> Don't forget to remind the students to bring their pictures for the Unit 30 Activity.

Revision Box

> **Answers**
> **1** Adverbs tell us how something is done.
> **2** **1** slowly **2** well **3** easily **4** fast/quickly **5** quickly

30 Activity Save your energy!

A new invention to save energy

TEACHING NOTES FOR UNIT 30

Overview of the Unit

In Unit 30, students have an opportunity to use their creative imagination to invent an unusual way of saving energy at home. An example in the Student's Book is intended to stimulate their imagination, before they brainstorm their ideas with the class. At home, they can draw a picture to illustrate their invention, before they write about it in the next class. The Unit concludes with a short evaluation discussion.

Timing

Unit 30 is best done as part of two lessons. Students can discuss their ideas, draw a picture at home, and write about it in the next lesson. Suggested timings are:

Before the lesson		
1	A strange invention	10
2	Your own inventions	10
3	At home, invent something	(at home) 10
In the lesson		
4	Explain your invention	25–30
5	Look at the other inventions	10
6	Evaluation	5

What you need

Students will need paper and coloured pencils.

Mixed-ability classes

Exercise 4 has additional guidelines for mixed-ability classes.

(See also **AtoZ** MIXED ABILITIES.)

Workbook

Unit 30 in the Workbook contains fluency practice exercises.

- Exercise 1: writing about an invention to put sugar in your drink

- Exercise 2: inventing a new way to clean your shoes, answer the telephone, or wash the dishes, and writing about it

Guidelines

Before your lesson

1 A strange invention
AtoZ DISCUSSION, PROCESSING TIME

Give the students a few minutes to try to work out what happens when the man pulls the handle, before you talk it through with them.

> **Answer**
> If you pull the handle, the electric train starts. It moves forwards and pulls the curtain open. When the train hits the bricks, the weight falls down. It pulls the bed up and the man falls into his trousers and shoes. As the bed comes up, it pulls his trousers up.

2 Your own inventions
AtoZ BRAINSTORMING

3 At home, invent something

The drawing here is explained in Exercise 4.

In the lesson

4 Explain your invention
AtoZ WRITING, GROUPWORK

5 Look at the other inventions
AtoZ DISPLAYING STUDENTS' WORK

6 Evaluation
AtoZ EVALUATION

Unit 30   Activity   **107**

31

Culture matters   Energy at home

Homes in Britain and your
country; reading,
discussing and writing

TEACHING NOTES FOR UNIT 31

Overview of the Unit

This *Culture matters* Unit focuses on how energy is
consumed in homes in Britain. It gives information
about the climate and how houses are heated. 'An energy
plan' shows how much energy electrical equipment uses.
Students can then draw an 'energy plan' of their own
house. Exercise 4 'Across cultures' asks students to
describe people's homes in their country. Written work
that they do for Exercise 4 could be included in *A Parcel
of English*.

Timing

Suggested timings for one lesson are:

1 Energy in your home		10
2 Brrrrr!		20
3 An energy plan	(at home)	10
4 Across cultures		15

What you need

A cassette player and the Class Cassette for Exercise 2.

Mixed abilities

Exercise 2 has further guidelines for mixed-ability classes.

(See also **AtoZ** MIXED ABILITIES.)

Workbook

Unit 31 in the Workbook is *Help yourself with fluency*. It
contains five ideas for students to improve their fluency in
English. The first three ideas were present in Level 1.

- Exercise 1: Phrases in a bag. A way of learning useful
  phrases
- Exercise 2: Talk to yourself. Using a cassette recorder
- Exercise 3: Have a conversation. Role play activities
  with yourself
- Exercise 4: Sing a song! Making up new words for a
  song
- Exercise 5: Practise with a friend

See page 149 for a special note on the *Help yourself!* Units.

Guidelines

1   Energy in your home
AtoZ DISCUSSION

2   Brrrrr! 🔲
AtoZ READING

MIXED ABILITIES

More support can be given by
- going through some of the 'new' vocabulary first:
  paragraph top left: generally, furniture, carpet, floor,
  curtain. Paragraph top right: heating, central heating.
  Paragraph bottom right: insulation, chimney.
  Paragraph bottom right: layer, attic, insulation.
- asking the students to read and underline parts of the
  text that they don't understand. They can then
  compare in small groups and help each other.
- giving the students a list of key words. They can then
  read through the text and find information for each
  word. Some key words: hot days, furniture, 100
  years old, chimney, central heating, rooms, glass in
  the windows.
  See previous *Topic* Units for further ideas.

The task can be made more demanding by
- asking the students to read the article once or twice.
  Give them key words (see above) and ask them to
  write a sentence about four or five of them.
- asking the students to write some questions for other
  students to answer.
- asking the students to write a brief description about
  houses in their country (see Ex. 4).
  See previous *Topic* Units for further ideas.

---

3   An energy plan

Students can draw a plan of their own home and show
where the various electrical appliances are. If, at home,
they look on the back of each electrical item (with an
adult), they can find how many 'Watts' it uses.

4   Across cultures
AtoZ WRITING

108   Theme F

32

Revision and evaluation

TEACHING NOTES FOR UNIT 32

See Unit 7 for a 'General note on the *Revision and evaluation* Units'. See Unit 12 for special notes concerning the 'design your own test' Units.

Overview of the Unit

In this, the final Unit in the book, the students have an opportunity to design a test for themselves once again. In this Unit, however, they have to decide *what* their test will be about and *how* they will test themselves.

Exercise 6 of the Unit asks the students to write to the authors, to give them their opinions of the activities and content of the book. The final exercise asks the students to think about their fluency in English.

Timing

Suggested timings are as follows.

1	What did you learn?	15
2	Who can do what?	15
3	Talk about your plan	10
4	Write your part of the test	(at home) 10
5	A test about Units 3–32 …	–
6	Write a letter to us!	15
7	Learning to be fluent	8

What you need

No additional materials are required.

Mixed-ability classes and supplementary worksheets

Language worksheet 29.1: Past continuous.
Language worksheet 29.2: asking the way (2).

(See also **AtoZ** MIXED ABILITIES.)

Workbook

Unit 32 in the Workbook is a puzzle page which practises the language from the Theme.

Guidelines

1 What did you learn?

AtoZ TASKS IN GROUPS, OVERVIEWING and TESTS

Before students start, it is a good idea to say what they will be doing, and how they will design their own test.

Collect the students' ideas on the board so that it is easier to allocate different language areas to each group.

2 Who can do what?

AtoZ GROUPWORK

Look back at Units 7, 12, 17, 22 and 27 with the students. Point out how they can test themselves.

3 Talk about your plan

AtoZ DISCUSSION

4 Write your part of the test

This is best done at home if you are short of time. You can then collect the various parts together, check them through and assemble them as the class test. See the Teaching Notes for Unit 12 for further guidance.

5 A test about Units 3–32 …

Students can exchange tests with another class or include them in a *Parcel of English*.

6 Write a letter to us!

The authors and the publishers would be *delighted* to hear from you and your students concerning your reactions to the coursebook. Feedback from teachers and students is very important in ensuring that published materials meet the needs, interests and wishes of those who use them.

7 Learning to be fluent

AtoZ AUTONOMY and DISCUSSION

See Unit 7, Exercise 7 for further guidance.

Open plan

AtoZ DO IT YOURSELF!

See the Notes to Unit 7, *Open plan* for further guidance.

Theme trail A revision game

TEACHING NOTES

This is an optical game to revise the language and the topic information in the book.

Timing

The game will take about 25–30 minutes, but it may be made shorter (reduce the number of Unit questions that need to be answered) or longer (ask students to make up some extra questions for each Unit).

What you need

Students need to play in groups of two to four. Each student will need a counter or button of a different colour from the rest of the group. Each group will also need a dice or a spinner with numbers 1–6 marked.

Guidelines

AtoZ GAMES

Preparation

The rules for playing the game are given in the Student's Book. Read through the rules with the students and check (perhaps in the mother tongue) that they understand how to play before they divide into their groups.

Playing the game

Before the students begin, make sure that they have all copied the chart into their exercise books so that they can tick [√] each Unit as they go.

Also remind them that they must cross the question number off the square on the board once the appropriate question has been asked.

The answers are given in the Student's Book on page 143, so students can check them for themselves.

An A to Z of methodology

This section contains details of some of the key areas of language teaching, particularly in relation to teaching with *CES*. You will find references to this section in the Teaching Notes for each Unit (for example: **AtoZ MOTHER TONGUE**). However, it is *not* intended that you should read all of the relevant references just to prepare one lesson or that you should read the entire section all at once! This section is for *reference*: for you to read at your leisure, as and when you wish.

Cross-references to other entries in the section are also shown in small capitals, **LIKE THIS**.

AtoZ AUTONOMY

What and why?

Autonomy has two main aspects in language teaching. The first concerns the students' *use* of the language. The ultimate goal of most language teaching is to develop the students' autonomy in their own language use. That is, to develop the ability to use the language as they need or want to. This has direct implications for the kind of tasks that students are asked to do. If students are only asked to do 'closed tasks' they are unlikely to develop the ability to use the language with ease. **OPEN-ENDED TASKS** are much more important in this respect.

The second aspect of autonomy, however, concerns how the students *learn*. If all the decisions about learning are always taken by the teacher, the students will not have the opportunity to decide things for themselves. This means that they will not develop the ability to learn by themselves or to work out what works best *for them* as individuals. In a rapidly changing world, however, these abilities are increasingly important as people are continually required to learn new skills and absorb new information. Learning how to learn should thus be a vital component in any educational course.

Practical ideas

- *CES* incorporates numerous tasks which require students to decide things for themselves, to plan and to evaluate. You can discuss these tasks with the students so that they understand the value of them in helping them to learn without your direct supervision.

- The Workbook Cassette provides a good support for the students to exercise autonomy in learning. You can spend some time discussing with the students how they use the cassette, when they listen to it, and so on.
- The *Help yourself* Units in the Workbook offer practical support in developing the students' autonomy in learning. Once the students have done one of the Units, you can return to it after a week or so and ask how many of the techniques they have used, why/why not, and so on.
- The **DO IT YOURSELF** exercises ask students to make decisions. You can increase the number of these in order to encourage the students to take more responsibility. The 'Open plan' sections after the *Revision and evaluation* Units can also be increased in frequency.
- After the students have decided something and then carried it out, it is important to **EVALUATE** what they have done. You can discuss what they did, how it went and how they could improve it next time.
- Stress to the students that there are a number of vital tools for learning. They need to have a bilingual dictionary, a grammar, notebooks, and a cassette player.
- You can discuss with the students different ways in which they can get practice (see the *Help yourself* Units).

AtoZ BRAINSTORMING

What and why?

'Brainstorming' is the name given to a number of techniques used for generating and gathering ideas. The basic principle is that the students suggest ideas which may be collected, for example, on the blackboard. During the collecting of ideas, ALL ideas suggested are noted down – only after the brainstorming is finished are the ideas discussed, grouped, or eliminated. Brainstorming can encourage students to speak out and share ideas. It also gives the teacher an immediate impression of how much the students already know about something.

Practical ideas

There are a number of different ways you can approach brainstorming.

- Write 'What do we know about (name of the topic)?' in big letters on the blackboard. Place a circle round it and some lines out from the circle. Ask the students what they know about the topic. As they say things, write them around the circle.
- Write 'What do we know about (name of the topic)?' in big letters on the blackboard. Give the students a few minutes to note down ideas by themselves. Then collect their ideas on the board.
- As above, but students work in small groups.

- As above, but play some soft **MUSIC** while they are thinking/discussing.
- Students work in groups to generate ideas and then cross-group (see **GROUPWORK**) to compare. You can use different types of **MUSIC** during these stages.
- The brainstorming can be put up on a **POSTER** and referred to and added to over a number of lessons.
- Brainstorming doesn't have to be about things they know. It can be about things they would like to know. Students can build up a question **POSTER**.
- Brainstorming can be done in English or in the **MOTHER TONGUE**.

A to Z CHECKING ANSWERS

What and why?

After students have done an exercise, it is important that they have an opportunity to check what they have done. This will give them **FEEDBACK** on their work. There are a number of ways in which you can do this.

Practical ideas

- You can go through the answers while the students look at their own work.
- Students can work together and then sit with another pair to check the answers.

- Small groups of students can go through their answers together. During this time, you can circulate around the class, helping and checking.
- You can provide an 'answer sheet' for students to check their own answers. (This can be circulated around the class while they are doing some other activity, pinned up on the board for students to check after the lesson, or written on the blackboard.)
- If students have incorrect answers, you can give hints or clues rather than simply giving the correct answers. This can help them think through the task again and learn more (see **ERROR CORRECTION**).

A to Z CURRICULUM LINKS

What and why?

One of the main features of *CES* is that it makes direct links between English language learning and the school curriculum. This happens in two ways. Firstly, there are links with broader educational aims, such as developing **PROBLEM-SOLVING** abilities, **AUTONOMY**, **QUESTIONING**, cooperative learning, and so on. Secondly, there are direct links with school subjects, such as Science, Geography, Language and so on. There are a number of reasons why this is important. Language teaching *is* a part of education, and needs to take its full educational responsibility. A cross-curricular approach also offers students an ideal opportunity to refresh and revise what they have done in other subject areas and to make links with what they have learnt so that their knowledge becomes more active. This makes both learning *and* teaching English more interesting and more memorable. Working with subject knowledge that is important and interesting in its own right makes it more likely that students will remember the language associated with it. Finally, whether language teaching has explicit links with the curriculum or not, it is clear that it can have a role in

shaping the broader attitudes and abilities of students. It thus makes sense to take this fact into account and build it into our language-teaching methodology.

Practical ideas

- Teaching English through a cross-curricular approach can mean that your role as a teacher changes. Many teachers report that cross-curricular teaching is more interesting, since it involves *their* learning as well. However, you are an *English* teacher and you cannot be expected to know all about Science, Geography and so on. Your role as a teacher, then, is to stimulate the students to find the information/answers/ explanations that they require for themselves.
- In the notes to the Units, you will find some background information on some of the topics covered in *CES*.
- You may find it useful to talk to teachers of other subject areas. As you approach a new Theme, you could find out what work the students will do or have done in that area.

- It may be possible to teach some lessons together with another subject teacher. For example, with some advance preparation, students could do Science experiments, Maths, Physical Education and so on in English. You could choose a new topic area together.

- As you begin a new Theme, you could start with a question POSTER. You can ask the students questions such as: 'What questions from History connect to this?' 'How does Geography connect to this?' 'Is Maths important for this topic?' 'How?' and so on.

AtoZ DECIDE EXERCISES

What and why?

The *Decide* exercises come in each *Topic* Unit. They give the students a choice of what they can do next. One option is usually to decide for themselves what they want to do (see DO IT YOURSELF). The students can do the *Decide* exercises alone, in pairs or in small groups. The exercises are designed as a first step in the students taking responsibility for their own learning (see STUDENT INVOLVEMENT).

Practical ideas

- Explain the choices clearly to the class before they start. Allow enough time for them to decide which task to do and how to work (alone/in pairs, etc.).
- Make sure there is enough time left in the lesson to make a start.
- While the class is working go round and offer help if needed (see MONITORING AND GUIDING).

If students finish before the others, they can use the TIME TO SPARE?, LANGUAGE RECORD and the EXERCISE BOX.

AtoZ DISCIPLINE

What and why?

One difficulty frequently encountered by teachers of secondary-age students is the problem of maintaining discipline. There are two main aspects to consider in this. The first is to ask 'What kind of discipline do I want?'. The key should be to maintain a purposeful but relaxed atmosphere in the classroom, where certain students don't disturb other students. This may mean that some so-called discipline problems are not real problems at all. As long as the overall atmosphere is conducive to learning, it may not be worth making an issue out of minor acts of 'misbehaviour'. If students were 100% compliant, we would have reason to be worried! On the other hand, discipline can, at times, become a serious problem. The important question to consider here is '*Why* are they behaving like that?'. The cause of discipline problems may lie in difficulties at home, in school, or with friends. These are likely to be beyond your control. Some causes of discipline problems, however, may lie within your classroom and you may be able to resolve them.

Practical ideas

- If the problem recurs, try to discuss it with the students. Approach the issue as *their* problem as well as yours ('We've got a problem. Our lesson/groupwork, etc. is not working, is it? What can we do about it?'). This can give them a feeling of responsibility. For this, you will need to listen to their views and be ready to make changes.
- If you have a large class, discipline problems may be caused by students who feel left out or who don't understand what is happening. Using GROUPWORK can help them feel more involved.
- Discipline problems may occur during listening activities. This may be because some students cannot hear the cassette very well. They may be 'lost' before the lesson really starts. Tell them to look at the words in the book while they listen if the room is noisy.
- If the students are restless or tired, you could start with some PHYSICAL MOVEMENT.
- The PACE and TIMING of the lessons may be too fast for some of the students and so they get lost, feel they can never catch up, and then begin to misbehave. These slower students may prefer to work individually.
- Make sure that the work of the weaker students has equal feedback.
- Try to bring about more STUDENT INVOLVEMENT, especially from those students who are causing disruption.
- To settle students down when they come into the class, you can use MUSIC or regular journal writing. A journal is a book that the students write in which you do not correct or look at unless invited to do so. The students may write anything they like about their day, their feelings, the things they have done, the things they have learnt and so on. Initially, this will be in the MOTHER TONGUE but you can encourage them to try to write in English as the course goes on.

During group or pairwork:

- Give extra help to the troublesome students.
- Get the troublesome students to work on something you know they are good at and which will give them a

feeling of achievement. You can give them some other individual responsibility for a term. For example, being in charge of the **EXERCISE BOX**, collecting in **HOMEWORK**, helping with the **DISPLAYS**, leading the

singing in **SONGS**.
- Try not to give extra English homework as a punishment; it can create the view that English is boring or difficult, or both!

AtoZ DISCUSSIONS

What and why?

Discussions can allow students the opportunity to give their own ideas and, in the later stages of the course, to practise using English to say what they want to say. They can also form a way into a topic which can stimulate the students' imagination and give the teachers an indication of how much the students already know. It is important, however – particularly when discussions are done in English – that the emphasis is always on the *ideas* which are being expressed, not on the accuracy of how it is expressed (grammar, pronunciation, etc.). A heavy focus on form can block a discussion and prevent ideas emerging.

Practical ideas

- Discussions can be approached through **BRAINSTORMING**.
- In the initial stages of the course, brief discussions can be in the **MOTHER TONGUE**. The importance of this is that it can give the students the feeling that their ideas and contributions are valued.

- As the students' abilities in English develop, you can encourage them to express their ideas in English. If the students show resistance, you might ask them 'Would you like to know how to say that in English?' and show them how they can express the same idea in English.
- Discussions in the mother tongue can be used as a way to raise the vocabulary that they will meet in English. After a brief discussion, you can put words on the board and ask if they know how to say those things in English.
- Discussions of abstract topics do not usually work well with students of this age. Discussions need a clear, concrete focus – for example, what they know about something or what they think about something with which they are very familiar.
- Discussions are probably best kept short (maximum 10 minutes). Beyond that students may lose interest or the discussion may lose its focus.
- With a clear, concrete focus, students can work briefly in small groups. Some groups can then offer feedback to the whole class.

AtoZ DISPLAYING STUDENTS' WORK

What and why?

At the end of each *Activity*, students will have produced a large piece of work (e.g. **POSTERS**, a poem, the *Parcel of English*, etc.). To give students a sense of purpose about their work it is a good idea to display it.

Practical ideas

- Pin work up on the classroom wall for a week or so and then change it. Perhaps you can display work in the corridors, in the school hall, in the school foyer, in the canteen, in the staff room or in other subject rooms (for cross-curricular links). (You can also ask students for display ideas.)
- Take a photograph of the display for reference.
- Make sure you write on the display the students' names, their class, the subject of the work and a

description of the purpose of the work (in the **MOTHER TONGUE**, if necessary).
- When you take the work down the students can either keep their work in their own 'Activity file' or put their work in a large scrapbook.
- Encourage students to help you display work.
- Display pictures as well as the writing – some students may be better at art than English!
- Some students may be sensitive about showing their work to others – it may be best to ask them if they want to.
- If a display is put up in the classroom or put out on the class tables, allow time for the students to walk around to read it. One member from each group can stand by their work to explain and talk about what they have done (see also **POSTERS**).

AtoZ DO IT YOURSELF

What and why?

'Do it yourself' is an important idea that occurs throughout *CES*. Encouraging students to do something

themselves, rather than simply using the exercises in the book, is to encourage them towards **AUTONOMY** – the ultimate goal of education. This also allows students room for their own individual interests, needs and abilities. In

Level 1, students are given the option of deciding what they want to do in each *Decide* exercise. In Level 2, this is taken one step further, where the DIY exercises in the *Language focus* Units require planning for what they will do in the 'Open plan' section at the end of the *Revision and evaluation* Units. In these exercises, the students must decide what they wish to do, in consultation with you. Initially, it is likely that the suggestions that students make for what they would like to do are not ones that you think are particularly valuable. This may not be a problem for a number of reasons. Firstly, one of the aims of allowing students to suggest something else to do is to bring about greater STUDENT INVOLVEMENT and a feeling of 'ownership' of what they are learning. Secondly, it is *only* through making decisions that students can become better at making decisions. The important point is that any suggestion they make and which they actually do is followed up by some kind of EVALUATION. This can be simply asking the students how useful they found what they did.

Practical ideas

- If students cannot think of something to do, you can *propose* something. Have a list of ideas ready. For example: choose something from the EXERCISE BOX, do some READING, look back through the previous Unit, do something from the Workbook, do a TIME TO SPARE? exercise, play one of the GAMES in the book, write some GRAMMAR rules on a POSTER, prepare something for the PARCEL OF ENGLISH, listen to a SONG.

- One or two lessons before the students come to the DECIDE EXERCISES, point out the option for them to decide for themselves. Encourage them to think of something they might like to do. Give them suggestions (see above).

- You will need to insist that what they decide to do is related to learning English!

- You could also allow some time for students to tell other students (either in small groups or to the whole class) what they have been doing.

- There are six 'Open plan' sections in Level 2. You can, however, allow the students an open space more frequently. You could, for example, allow 15 or so minutes every week or every other week. Build up a 'lesson plan' with them, on the board, a week or so before an 'Open plan' time.

AtoZ ERRORS AND ERROR CORRECTION

What and why?

Making errors is an inevitable and necessary part of language learning. It is only through making errors, and hearing the correct forms, that students can develop their own understanding of how English works. It is thus important that students have as much opportunity as possible to produce language and, with the focus on using English creatively (rather than simply repeating language), the number of errors that students make will inevitably rise. Teachers thus need to think carefully about how they will respond to these errors.

The process of absorbing a new language structure takes considerable time. Teachers cannot, therefore, expect that simply correcting an error will produce immediate results. Some errors can remain even up to very advanced levels (such as the 's' in *she lives, he goes*, etc.). A strong emphasis on error correction cannot be expected to produce students who make few errors. In fact, an over-emphasis on error correction is likely to be counter-productive as students become deterred from using – and experimenting with – new language and vocabulary. But students *do* need to have their errors pointed out to them. The key is to limit correction to a small number of points at a time and to judge when the right moment for correction is.

Practical ideas

- Correcting students when they are in the middle of saying something may produce students who are afraid to talk. You can make a note of the errors students make and go through them at the end of the discussion/lesson.

- Limit yourself to only correcting a few errors in written work or after the students speak.

- For errors in WRITING, students can be encouraged to build up a short list of their most common errors. The list can be arranged to form a mnemonic of things to check (e.g. PATTIBS = Plurals, Articles, Tenses, 'there is/are', '-ing' form, 'Be', Spelling etc.).

- In monolingual classes most students will make the same errors. You may want to have 'an error of the week' game. Choose an error which most students make, tell them what it is and write the correct version on a piece of paper on the wall. This raises the students' consciousness about this particular error. Students then have to try to not make this error all week. The student who succeeds can choose the 'error of the week' for the next week.

What and why?

There are two main ways in which evaluation is important in learning. The first way is in relation to *what* and *how much* students have learnt – such as through tests and quizzes (see TESTS). The second way, however, is in relation to *how* the students have been learning – whether groupwork, for example, is effective, whether they receive enough guidance, and so on. The first aspect of evaluation is the most common in language teaching. The second aspect is not often considered in much depth, although it is obviously extremely important. In *CES*, this second aspect of evaluation is introduced in a number of places, particularly in the *Revision and evaluation* Units, where students talk about their reactions to the preceding Units. The aim through this kind of evaluation is to involve the students more in thinking about how they are learning, to encourage them to take more control over their learning and to give you, the teacher, an insight into how the students see their English classes.

Practical ideas

- For practical ideas in the *what* and *how much* aspects of evaluation, see TESTS.
- Initially, it is likely that the students' evaluation of how they have been learning will be very superficial. Just like learning itself, evaluation requires practice. The more they do it, the better they will become at it, and the more able they will become to accept responsibility.
- Limit the time for an evaluation discussion and give the students a clear focus for any group discussion (for example, to come up with a list of their points).
- Evaluation by the students requires the teacher to be open to listen and discuss, and make changes if necessary.
- Evaluation can be done in writing directly to you. This can avoid problems with 'public' discussions.
- Avoid, initially at least, asking the students questions such as 'What things did you like?' or 'What things didn't you like?' Negative questions will produce negative answers. It is better to ask 'What do you think about …?'
- Evaluation of *how* the students have been learning/working comes mainly in the *Revision and evaluation* Units. However, you can involve the students in evaluation (oral or in writing) after any major piece of work or period of time (for example, after a *Topic* or *Language focus* Unit, or before the *Activity*).

Researching the classroom

- Before giving the students a TEST, give them a list of what they will be tested on. Then, before they do the test, ask them to write down what mark they think they will get in each part. If you do this before each test, you can see if the students' ability to assess their own strengths in English improves, and if the gap between what they *think* they will get and what they *actually* get, closes.
- After a lesson, ask the students to write down a list of what they think they learnt in that lesson. Think back over the lesson (or tape-record it) and try to identify *when* and *how* the things that they remembered came up. Do this for a few lessons to see if a pattern emerges.
- If you have one or more classes using this coursebook, you can involve one class in a lot more evaluation discussions. You can then see if more student evaluation activities produce more involved learners. You could give each class an anonymous questionnaire to discover how much time they devote to English in a week, how high their motivation is, which aspects they like best and so on. In the long term, you could also see if more student evaluation/planning activities produce better abilities in English.
- You could ask some students to keep a diary of their studies in English, of what precisely they study outside the classroom, of how long they spend on it and so on. This could also give you some idea of the LEARNING STRATEGIES they use.
- You could interview a few students to find out how they go about their studies. A word association technique is very useful in giving a 'snapshot' of the students' impressions. Read out a list of key areas in language learning, and after each one pause for a minute or so. Ask the students to note down their thoughts in relation to that area. This can be anonymous, of course. You can then collect the papers to get a picture of what is going on in the students' heads. Key areas might be: topic lessons, grammar, listening to English in class, writing in English, and so on. You could also try word association on how they feel about things to do with English, English culture and so on (which will be related to their motivation). Key areas might be: English, 'Me speaking English', English things, English-speaking people, 'my English book', 'doing English homework', and so on.

AtoZ EXERCISE BOX

What and why?

The *Exercise Box* is introduced in Unit 5 in Level 1 and in Supplementary Unit B in Level 2. It is used for the entire course. Each class can have its own *Exercise Box* (a small cardboard box or shoe box with cardboard dividers) which, ideally, should be kept in the classroom or taken to every lesson.

The purpose of the *Exercise Box* is to encourage students to write their own exercises which they keep in the *Exercise Box* for other students to use later, particularly if there is TIME TO SPARE in a lesson. Students learn a great deal from writing exercises for each other.

Practical ideas

- Refer to the IDEAS LIST for examples of kinds of exercises that students can write. Students can write a neat, correct version of their exercise on a blank postcard. They should put the answers on the back.
- The TIME TO SPARE? section gives students a chance to write an exercise and/or answer an exercise from the *Exercise Box*.
- Use the *Exercise Box* if some students finish a task before the others.
- The *Exercise Box* will gradually build up to offer a source of revision and/or remedial work.
- For easy reference, label the exercises, showing what Unit they come from. You can divide the box into sections for each Unit. You may want to colour code the exercises for difficulty.
- You can add your own exercises to the box, of course.

AtoZ FEEDBACK

What and why?

In learning, one of the most important factors is a feeling that you are getting somewhere. For some students, learning at school can seem like an endless list of exercises, in which they move from one task to the next. This can lead to a lack of a sense of direction in their learning or a feeling that there is no value in it. It is important, therefore, that students receive feedback on what they have done and that their effort is recognised and valued. Feedback may focus on the *form* of what they have done (spelling, grammar, neatness, etc.) or on its *content* (its message, the opinions and ideas expressed). As teachers, we typically respond to the form aspect, but it is only through the content aspect that we can really recognise our students as individuals with their own ideas.

Practical ideas

- Feedback can come from other students as well as from the teacher. Allowing time for students to show their work to each other (if they wish – this may be a sensitive point) can allow them an opportunity to have pride in their work, ask questions about things they are unsure of, and share ideas.
- If the students are engaged in a large activity, such as in the *Activity* Units, allow some time at the end for them to DISPLAY THEIR WORK.
- Feedback between students is best done in pairs or threes with students who are friends with each other.
- Feedback between students can be given a clear focus by asking them to produce a *single* re-written version of their work which draws on what each of them has done. For example, if they have completed a guided piece of writing, they can produce a new version which has corrected spellings, grammar, extra ideas, etc.
- In feedback to each other, students may be over-critical or focus only on the form aspect. One way to overcome this is to insist that they make positive suggestions for improvement. Comments may also be limited to two or three points.
- Feedback to you, as the teacher, can be gained through the EVALUATION activities.

AtoZ FLUENCY

What and why?

Many language learning tasks focus on accuracy. These are often 'closed' exercises in which there is only one correct answer. Fluency tasks, on the other hand, are more open. They encourage the learners to take risks and be more creative with the language because there is no 'right' or 'wrong' answer (see OPEN-ENDED TASKS). At lower language levels, language teaching has traditionally emphasised accuracy, believing that fluency comes once the grammar has been mastered. In *CES*, however, both accuracy and fluency are emphasised right from the beginning. Developing fluency is important in building up the students' confidence and maintaining a sense of achievement in being able to say something meaningful. Many students also learn more naturally through tasks which focus on *using* the language, rather than learning *about* the language. The *Topic* Units, *Activity* Units and *Culture matters* Units all aim at developing fluency. The *Language focus* Units, *Revision and evaluation* Units and exercises aim at developing accuracy.

In all four skills, confidence and fluency are linked and make the students more receptive to learning. Confidence and fluency in READING and LISTENING help students to deal with language without feeling the need to understand every word, encourage them to guess new words, and enable them to understand the main message, including the speaker/writer's attitude. Confidence and fluency in WRITING and SPEAKING allow students to get their ideas across without being restricted by an over-concern with form.

Practical ideas

- There are numerous fluency activities throughout *CES*. Compare, for example, the exercises in an

Activity Unit with the accuracy exercises in a *Language focus* Unit.
- In fluency exercises, the focus is on developing and expressing ideas. There is nothing wrong with correcting language ERRORS as they arise, but don't let this stop the main focus. Make a note of significant language errors and return to them later.
- There is only one way to become fluent and accurate at the same time: through using the language to express/understand ideas. This takes time, so you will need to expect and tolerate language errors as students develop this ability.
- In fluency-focused exercises, try to react to *what* the students say, not *how* they say it. For example, if you are marking their written work, you can add something about what they have said, your opinion on the topic, and so on.

AtoZ FOUR SKILLS

What and why?, Practical ideas

See LISTENING, SPEAKING, READING and WRITING.

Researching the classroom

- Many teachers assume that the most effective way to learn is orally (through listening and speaking). Writing and reading are seen as practice stages in learning. If you have several classes, you could involve one class in considerably more in-class writing and reading. You could then see if there appears to be a direct effect on their abilities in English. See WRITING, INTERACTIVE WRITING and READING.
- You could vary your approach to each of the skills and see if that affects what the students produce. For example, you could sometimes ask students to first write 'fluently', without stopping to check, before they go back to read and revise what they have done. At other times, you could ask them to plan what they will write and to think carefully about each sentence as they write. You could try similar experiments with the other skills. For reading, ask the students to sometimes read quickly through a text without checking words, and at other times to read carefully. For listening, you could play a text straight through

for a general impression before going back for details. At other times, you could play it in small sections. For speaking, you could sometimes ask the students to do a ROLE PLAY without preparation, and at other times you could ask them to prepare in writing first. Different students will work best in different ways. By experimenting, you can see how individual students respond to each approach.
- If the focus is on one main skill, you can see whether involving the other skills first produces a better result. For example, if you want the students to write something, you could see if their production is improved if they first read and speak about, and then listen to a text about the topic.
- Identify what you think is the students' weakest skill. You could experiment to see if it is possible to improve that skill by directly involving their stronger skills. For example, if the students seem weakest at reading, you could involve them in writing or speaking about a topic before they read about it. If writing is their weakest skill, you could ask them to read and speak about a topic first and to note down useful phrases or ideas for their own writing.

AtoZ GAMES

What and why?

At secondary school level, games are a lively way of maintaining students' interest in the language. Games in *CES* are an integral part of the course. They are fun but

also part of the learning process, and students should be encouraged to take them seriously. In general they need not be compulsory – students may prefer to do something else while another group plays a game. Most of the games in *CES* expect students to create some input before they play. This gives a sense of 'ownership' and extends the language learning element.

Practical ideas

- As with all **GROUPWORK**, the success of the game depends on clear instructions to the students. Make sure that they understand the aim of the game and the rules before they start. (Initially, these are probably best explained in the **MOTHER TONGUE**.)
- You will need to make sure that you have a supply of dice and counters permanently available.
- The best number of students for a game is probably four (six maximum) otherwise the game will move too slowly and the others will get bored while waiting for their turn.
- Students can choose a 'leader/referee' for the game before they start, to decide on disagreements.
- While they are playing you can be **MONITORING AND GUIDING**.
- Make sure they know how much time they have to play the game: 10–15 minutes is probably enough for most of the games in *CES*. Don't start a game five minutes before the end of a lesson! You can give students a 'five-minute warning' before the time is over so they can work towards the end.
- As the course progresses, you can get the students to invent their own games and design their own board.

AtoZ GRAMMAR

What and why?

An understanding of the grammar of English is crucial to the development of the students' language learning. By the time students reach secondary school age, they are able to handle and understand grammatical rules and descriptions. With the limited amount of time which the classroom provides for language learning, grammar can be a vital tool in speeding up the students' ability to produce 'correct', meaningful English. In order to see how the language 'jigsaw' fits together, it is also important that students learn to use words such as 'noun', 'verb', 'adjective', etc. This will enable the students to work things out for themselves (see **INDUCTIVE GRAMMAR**) and you, the teacher, to explain things to them.

Practical ideas

- The *Language Records* after the *Language focus* Units summarise the grammar points for the students. As the students fill them in, they provide a self-created reference for revision.
- The *Revision and evaluation* Units give students an opportunity to reflect on grammar points which they may still be uncertain about. In both Level 1 (Units 18, 23 and 33) and Level 2 (Units 12, 22 and 32), they can write their own tests as a creative practice to check their understanding.
- To make sure that students understand the metalanguage, they can write the main words – noun, verb, adjective, personal pronoun, etc. – on a poster on the wall with examples underneath, to act as a reminder.
- As they discover the main grammatical rules and structures, students can construct a **POSTER** for the wall with example sentences underneath each main rule.
- The main rules can be written on a sheet by some of the students and placed in the class **EXERCISE BOX**.
- Grammar games are often a useful way of practising language. These can be combined with **PHYSICAL MOVEMENT**. For example, to practise the comparative forms, you can ask one of the students to come towards you saying 'Peter, please come here because you are smaller/bigger/prettier/younger/older, etc. than I am.' One of the other students then invites you to walk to them and gives a reason using the comparative form. That student is then invited by another student, and so on. Similar games can be played which ask students to perform particular actions when they hear a noun, a verb or an adjective.

AtoZ GROUPWORK

What and why?

Groupwork in *CES* is based on the idea that students can learn language and information from each other. The principle of cooperative learning is basic to classroom education. It also allows teachers the opportunity to help with individual problems, for stronger and weaker students to work at their own **PACE** (see **MONITORING AND GUIDING**) and for more students to get more practice.

Practical ideas

- Before students begin groupwork, make sure they know exactly what they are expected to do. Make the focus clear with a definite outcome (for example, to write something, make a list of something).
- During the lesson note which students are working together so that you can encourage them to work with different people next time.

- After working in groups, students can be cross-grouped. This involves groups re-forming with representatives of the other groups (for example, if students are labelled A, B, C, and D in their groups, cross-groups can be formed by all the As coming together, all the Bs, all the Cs and so on). In their cross-groups, students can compare ideas.
- Three or four are probably the best numbers for groupwork.
- There are many ways to set up groups. Try to vary the basis on which you group students: i) students can choose who to work with; ii) they can turn round and work with the students behind/in front of /next to them; iii) they can be grouped according to ability; iv) they can be grouped alphabetically, according to birth months; v) they can be grouped to maintain a balance of boys and girls; vi) they can be grouped by numbering students 1, 2, 3, 4 around the class; vii) you can cut up some postcards and distribute the pieces round the class. Students have to find who has the pieces which go with theirs and thus form a group; viii) you can give out cards with names of animals (four of each). Students have to walk around the class making the noise of the animal to find out who is in their group.

Researching the classroom

- Vary the way in which you set up groups (see above). Monitor how the students work when they are grouped differently.

- If groupwork is not functioning well, ask the students to draw up their own 'Rules for Groupwork' which they will agree to follow.
- Monitor the type of TASKS which you give students in groups. Which kind of tasks produce most interaction? Do closed or OPEN-ENDED tasks produce more discussion?
- Keep a record of how the students appeared to work in their groups – well, cooperatively, noisily, unfocused, and so on. Also keep a record of the details of the groupwork: who was working with whom, what they were doing in groups, what time of day it was, when they did it in the lesson, what preceded the groupwork and so on. After a few lessons, you may be able to see a pattern in what affects the groupwork.
- Studies have shown that the way students are labelled can affect how they perform. For example, students labelled 'good students' tend to work hard, while students who are labelled 'weak' tend to find their work difficult. (This is known as 'the self-fulfilling prophecy'.) You can give each group a name which flatters them, to see if this affects the way they work. For example, 'Brilliant Students: red group', 'Brilliant Students: green group', and so on.
- If you put students into ability groups, tell the weakest students that they will find the work you give them very easy. You can see if this increases their confidence in their work.

AtoZ HOMEWORK

What and why?

In *CES*, homework gives students time to absorb, process and practise what they have learnt at school (see also *Notes on the Workbook*, page 149). It also keeps the students involved between lessons and maintains their commitment to learning English. In most courses, the amount of time available in class is simply not sufficient for language learning to take place fast enough. Extra work outside class is essential.

Practical ideas

- Before you set homework make sure that the students know which exercises they have to do and how long they are expected to spend on their homework. (No more than half an hour is recommended.)
- There are no answers in the Workbook so their homework will have to be checked in the next lesson. You will need to allow some time for this and to build it in as part of the lesson.
- There are a number of ways in which you can correct homework (see *Notes on the Workbook*).

- If you set homework, but find that students do not do it, you need to consider why this is happening. There may be a number of possible reasons. It may be too difficult or too easy. They may not have time because of other commitments. They may not see the point of it. They may not have the book! They may have other personal problems. You may be able to resolve these problems by talking to the students about it, agreeing with them when they can do their homework, discussing whether they find it too easy/difficult, and so on. Perhaps they can sometimes suggest something to do for homework. (Everybody doesn't always have to do the same thing.)

Researching the classroom

- Talk to the students about homework, what they think about it and why it is necessary. Ask them what kinds of homework they find most enjoyable. Ask for ideas of what they would like to do for homework.
- You could also find out what the students think by giving them a questionnaire, or by interviewing a few students.

- Experiment with different kinds of homework to see if it affects the students' response: homework that requires research, homework that requires them to find/make things; homework exercises; homework they can record on cassette; and so on. Many teachers have found that students respond better to homework that is *social* (i.e. that involves them in interacting with other people) rather than *solitary*.
- Experiment with how homework is organised. For example, you could give students a list of things for homework from which they can choose. You could sometimes ask them to tell you what they are going to do for homework, and get them to put it in writing.
- You could involve the students in monitoring their own homework: what they did, when they did it, where they did it, what they found difficult, and how well they performed. You can then see in what circumstances they appear to do best.

AtoZ IDEAS LIST

What and why?

The *Ideas list* is a list of types of exercises on pages 150–1 in the Student's Book. The list is intended to help the students design their own practice exercises for themselves or for the EXERCISE BOX. Designing exercises increases the amount of STUDENT INVOLVEMENT with the course and their own learning, supports a general movement towards AUTONOMY and promotes deeper levels of understanding. The EXERCISE BOX is introduced in Unit 5 of Level 1 and, with it, the *Ideas list*.

Practical ideas

- Students can also use the *Ideas list* if they have TIME TO SPARE.
- You can encourage the students to bring in their own examples of English. They can then use the *Ideas list* to make some exercises for themselves and other students.
- The *Ideas list* is fairly short. Students may be able to add more examples to the list. (These can perhaps be put on the wall.) For example, students may be able to think of ideas to use with pictures, objects, listening passages, or writing.

AtoZ INDUCTIVE GRAMMAR

What and why?

GRAMMAR may be approached in two main ways: *deductively*, in which students are given a rule which they then practise (that is, they work using other people's deductions about the language), or *inductively*, in which they work out rules for themselves. Inductive grammar teaching is useful for a number of reasons. It can involve the students more fully as thinking people with ideas of their own and increase motivation. It can involve them more fully in understanding the language as they work out different rules for forming and using English. It can also help clear up misconceptions they have and make it clear to you, the teacher, what ideas they have about how grammar works. *CES* includes a number of inductive grammar tasks in the *Language focus* Units.

Practical ideas

- Some aspects of English grammar may be similar in the students' MOTHER TONGUE. Students can be asked to think about how things are expressed in their MOTHER TONGUE and when they use certain words, etc. before they are asked to think about English.
- Students can be given simple tables and asked to complete them (for example, sentences with 'don't' and 'doesn't' missing). They can then look through the Unit in the book to discover which word belongs with which subject pronoun.
- Students can briefly work in small groups/pairs to work out a rule before you ask for their ideas. If their ideas are incorrect, you can then present the correct rule or give some more examples which make them think about the rule further.

AtoZ INTERACTIVE WRITING

What and why?

Most often, the writing that students do in school is simply for the eyes of the teacher. Interactive writing involves students writing *to* and *with* other students. There are a number of reasons why this might be useful. Firstly, writing to other students can give the students a clear sense of purpose and audience for their writing – they can get FEEDBACK from the reader on how far their message has been understood. Secondly, writing with other students can give the students a clear focus for their work. Interactive writing will involve the students in asking each other about grammar, spelling, vocabulary, phrasing, etc. and so give them the chance to learn in a non-threatening atmosphere.

Practical ideas

- While students are working in groups, you can circulate around the class, reading what they have written and helping with any problems.
- Discussion during interactive writing tasks may be in the MOTHER TONGUE. This may not be a problem since one of the purposes of interactive writing is to enable students to exchange ideas. An 'English only' rule may prevent this. The important point is to insist that the writing that they produce is in English.
- Writing can be a sensitive area and some students may not want to write with other students or have their work seen by other students. In this case, students should be entitled to work alone if they wish.

AtoZ LANGUAGE RECORD

What and why?

There are *Language Record* pages at the end of the *Topic* and *Language focus* Units. These provide a record and easy reference of the language the students have covered. They are designed to be completed by the students in their own time, either in class or at home.

Practical ideas

- As students finish the *Topic* Units and *Language focus* Units, direct them to the *Language Record* at the end of the Unit.
- Initially, allow time in class for students to complete it. They can also do it for HOMEWORK.
- Students don't have to wait until the end of the lesson to fill it in. If they have TIME TO SPARE, they can fill it in.
- While they are working on the *Language Record*, you can go round MONITORING AND GUIDING.
- Encourage students to think of their own examples for the sentences. This will support the *picture dictionary* sections in the Workbook.

AtoZ LEARNING STRATEGIES

What and why?

Learning strategies are the techniques individual students use to help themselves learn. Classroom research has identified three main types of strategies: *meta-cognitive* strategies, such as planning, evaluating and monitoring language use; *cognitive* strategies used in actually 'doing the learning', such as guessing words, repeating, learning things by heart, and working out rules; and *social* strategies, such as working with others, asking for help and so on. All students come to their English lessons with their own learning strategies. They learn many of these through their other schoolwork, through watching people, and by being told what to do. Learning strategies are very personal – what works for one person may not work for another person. Since the strategies students use are influenced by teaching and by others, students may not be using the best strategies for *them*. Teaching tends to emphasise particular approaches to learning (e.g. an emphasis on copying). Students are unlikely to be aware of what the alternatives might be and may assume that the way they learn and are taught is the only way.

Learning about learning is part of the process of education and provides an understanding which is transferable to other subjects, other areas of life and beyond school. It is also important in bringing about STUDENT INVOLVEMENT.

Practical ideas

- *CES* includes exercises which use various kinds of learning strategies. *Meta-cognitive* strategies are involved in the DECIDE and DO IT YOURSELF exercises, such as the 'Open plan' at the end of each Theme of Level 2. *Cognitive* strategies are developed all through the materials and, in particular, in the *Help yourself* Units in the Workbook. *Social* strategies are involved in the numerous GROUPWORK and individual tasks, the encouragement to ask others and share ideas, and to use resources from outside the classroom.
- As you introduce a *Help yourself* Unit from the Workbook, discuss with students the strategies that they use. Encourage them to try a new strategy and discuss the results with them a few lessons later.
- Before giving a test, discuss with the students *how* they will revise.
- When they choose a *Decide* exercise, ask them why they chose *that* one.
- You could make a *Help yourself* POSTER with ideas from the students about how they revise for tests, how they do their HOMEWORK, how they check their work, what they do to learn English in their free time, and so on.
- There are few 'right' or 'wrong' ways to learn a language. Some students may feel happier, for example, looking at a model before they write, while others prefer to 'write from the top of their heads'. The important point is that students are aware of the

possibilities. Every now and again, discuss with the students how they are going to do an exercise and allow a variety of learning approaches. In some cases, this may include looking at the answers *first,* for example.

Researching the classroom

Learning strategies generally take place inside the students' heads, so it is very difficult to find out precisely what strategies they are using. However, there are ways to get a better picture and to determine if students are using the most effective strategies.

- At the end of each lesson ask students to note down (in the mother tongue) what they thought the main point of the lesson was, what they learnt from the lesson, which exercise helped them the most/least and what they found easiest/most difficult. Collect in the papers. This will give you an idea of what *they* focus on. This may not be the same as what you think is important. (For example, one teacher who did this after a 'grammar lesson', found that the students actually thought the lesson was about 'vocabulary'. In such cases, it's not surprising that the students don't learn the key grammar points.) If this is the situation in your class, you may find it useful to discuss it with the students.

- As part of their homework, ask students to write down exactly *what* they did, how they approached it, where they did their homework, who with, what they used (dictionary, cassette, a friend, etc.) to help them complete it. Collect in their papers.
- You can prepare a brief questionnaire to find out what your students do when they are learning. For example:
  (i) What makes it easier for you to understand the cassette?; (ii) When you are reading in English and you see a new word, what do you do?; (iii) How do you revise for a test?; (iv) How do you remember English spelling?
- Alternatively, you could make an 'Always', 'Often', 'Sometimes', 'Never' questionnaire. See the *Revision and evaluation* Units in the Student's Book.
- A better idea might be to ask the students to design a questionnaire for another class, perhaps called 'How do you learn?'. This will not only give the students very useful language practice, but will also tell you a lot about what *they* think is important.
- Watch them! After you have set the students working, watch what they do. You could focus on one or two students and notice the steps that they go through, what seems to be slowing them down or helping them, and so about. Afterwards, you could start a general discussion on this.

AtoZ LISTENING

What and why?

In common with the other skills of **WRITING**, **READING** and **SPEAKING**, there are two main roles for listening in language teaching. The first is as a *goal* of teaching. It is important for students to develop the listening skill in order to understand spoken English, whether on TV, radio or in speaking to people. The second role, however, is as a *means* of learning. Listening can provide further sources of input and can help the students remember the words, phrases, grammar, etc. that they are learning. By working on listening tasks, students can become closely involved with the language and, in doing so, develop their general language proficiency. Handled well, listening can thus form a very important element in the course.

Practical ideas

- In the early stages, the emphasis is probably best placed on listening as a *means* of learning rather than as a *goal* of learning. This means that rather than treating listening as 'comprehension' exercises, students can listen to texts they have read and discussed as a way of consolidating their learning. They can also look at the text while they are listening.

- For listening to work well, students have to be able to hear! If you are in a noisy classroom, close doors, windows, turn off fans, etc. while you are playing the cassette.
- With larger classes, students can listen in smaller groups while the other students are doing something else.
- Unless you are conducting a test, you can allow the students to listen again if they wish or to pause the tape to check the meaning. Listening in this case will be useful for learning English generally.
- Control of the cassette player can be passed to a student. Other students may then feel freer to ask for things to be replayed or paused.
- Before the end of a lesson, you can play the listening passage again as a way of recapping what you have done.
- If the students are doing a listening comprehension exercise, they can work in pairs with one of the students listening for answers to some of the questions and the other student listening for answers to the other questions. They can then compare afterwards.

AtoZ MIXED ABILITIES

What and why?

All classes are 'mixed-ability' classes. All classes consist of individual students with different personalities and interests. All students also, themselves, have 'mixed abilities'. For example, some students may find writing easier than speaking, or vice versa. Some students find one particular task or approach more appealing than other tasks or approaches. It is also important to distinguish two aspects of 'ability': language ability and language-learning ability. The first aspect refers to how much language the students actually know/understand at a particular point in time. The second aspect refers to their ability to learn. A student may be weak in English, for example, but given appropriate support may be able to learn quickly. This suggests that some 'mixed-ability' classes may be the result of particular approaches to teaching (the ability to learn or the ability to be taught?). For this reason, teachers need to adopt a flexible methodology that allows for a variety of learning styles and abilities (see LEARNING STRATEGIES).

Practical ideas

- One key principle in teaching mixed-ability groups is *transparency*. Try to make sure that *all* students understand what is happening in the lesson, for example by OVERVIEWING before beginning a lesson or a new task.
- There are a number of ways in which you can approach teaching groups of mixed language and learning ability: i) stronger/average/weaker students can be given completely different tasks at different levels of difficulty; ii) students can be given tasks on the same topic at varying levels of difficulty (see below); iii) students can be involved in OPEN-ENDED TASKS which allow them to respond at their own level of ability. In principle, approaches ii) and iii) are better, since they avoid students feeling left out. Approach iii), additionally, allows students to develop more freely without being restricted by the tasks themselves.
- To provide tasks at varying levels of difficulty on the same topic, text, etc., think about how a task can be made more challenging or how more support can be given. In the Teaching Notes for all the *Topic* and *Language focus* Units there are ideas for making these kinds of adjustments to the key exercises in the Units.
- At the back of this Teacher's Book, there are additional, photocopiable *Language worksheets* for each grammar point in the *Language focus* Units.
- The TIME TO SPARE? exercises at the end of each *Topic* and *Language focus* Unit provide further tasks for varying levels of ability.
- The exercises in the DECIDE boxes encourage students to make choices about what they need to do and to work at their own pace.
- In GROUPWORK, try to mix students so that students of all abilities can work together.
- See further ideas under LISTENING, SPEAKING, READING and WRITING.

AtoZ MONITORING AND GUIDING

What and why?

In many of the activities in *CES*, students will be working in small groups or pairs. This way of working has many advantages, in that it gives students a chance to work at their own pace, to ask each other for help, to share ideas and to get more language practice. Small groupwork and PAIRWORK, however, can run the danger of students wasting their time together as they become distracted, talk about or do things other than requested, or produce work which is full of errors. For this reason, monitoring and guiding by the teacher is very important.

Practical ideas

- Before setting students to work in pairs/groups, check that they understand fully what they are going to do. You can go through one or two examples with the whole class first.
- While they are working, go round the class. You can check whether they are having any problems, check the work they have done, give extra ideas where necessary, and generally keep them on the task.
- While going round the class, you can also note down common errors that you notice. You can then spend a short time at the end of the lesson, going through a few of these.
- You also make a note of which students seem to be working well together and which seem to be having problems. Next time, you can vary the way you set up GROUPWORK accordingly.
- Before students start working, you can put some TASKS IN BLOCKS. When students have finished the work, they can move on to something from the EXERCISE BOX, look back at previous Units, or choose to DO IT YOURSELF.

AtoZ MOTHER TONGUE

What and why?

The mother tongue plays an important role in all language learning. Firstly, it is an important tool for the teacher to clarify explanations, give instructions and provide translations. At the beginning of the course, many of the instructions about classroom activities will need to be given in the mother tongue to make sure that the students know what they are expected to do.

Secondly, the mother tongue is a primary learning tool for the students. As with all other kinds of learning, a large part of language learning involves relating what you are learning to what you already know, in this case the mother tongue. Studies show that all beginning students use the mother tongue as a resource consciously and subconsciously in language-learning activities. Thus, the tasks and activities in *CES* provide opportunities for the students to TRANSLATE sentences and texts into the mother tongue so that they can compare the form and meaning of the two languages and ensure that the *correct* meanings are learnt.

Practical ideas

- Students may also use the mother tongue because they feel embarrassed about speaking English in front of the whole class. In these cases, you can give them time to prepare what they are going to say (see PROCESSING TIME).
- If you feel the students use too much of the mother tongue (for example, in GROUPWORK), you will need to consider why this situation is arising and what you can do about it. It may be that the task is too difficult for them, not interesting enough, not clear to them, or too unstructured. You could try to discuss the problem with them, give clear examples of what they have to do, or ask for suggestions from them.
- As you gradually introduce more English into your classroom management, encourage the students to reply in English to questions like 'Where is Peter today?' or 'Are you ready?'
- You will need to decide *when* you will use the mother tongue. You might, for example, limit yourself to explanations of grammar and vocabulary and to when you are MONITORING AND GUIDING.
- You will also need to decide when you will accept the mother tongue from the students. For example, you may accept use of the mother tongue in BRAINSTORMING activities in which you translate their ideas and put them on the board.

AtoZ MUSIC

What and why?

Potentially, music can have an important role in the classroom. The use of SONGS is already very familiar to most teachers. Music, however, plays a major role in many parts of our lives. We may, for example, listen to the radio while we are working, while we are driving or waiting for something. There may be background music while we are eating or reading. We may use music to relax or to mark a change of activity (such as 'coming home from work') and so on. In similar ways, music can be used to help make the classroom more welcoming.

Practical ideas

- Choose music for the atmosphere you want to create: soft calm music if you want to calm the students down, energetic music if you want to wake them up, and so on.
- You can play music as they come into the classroom. This can help 'bring them into' English again, and relax them ready for work.
- You could use music regularly at set phases in your teaching – for example, when they are working on the *Activity* Units. Students could then suggest or bring in appropriate pieces of music.
- If there are a number of steps or phases in an activity, you can use music to mark the transition. For example, some fast music for a BRAINSTORMING phase and a slow, gentle piece of music for a writing phase.

AtoZ OPEN-ENDED TASKS

What and why?

Open-ended tasks are tasks to which there is not a single absolutely correct answer or where a variety of answers are possible. They can be distinguished from 'closed tasks', where students have to answer in a particular way. An example of an open-ended task might be where the students are asked to imagine a person standing in a pair of shoes which they are shown and then to write a description of that person. A closed task using the same type of language might be one where they are given a description with certain words missing, which they have to supply. Both closed tasks and open-ended tasks are useful in language teaching. Where students are working in groups, for example, closed tasks can force the students to discuss more in order to find the correct answer. Open-ended tasks, however, are also very valuable for a number of reasons. Since there is no single correct answer, the students can often answer at the level of their ability. This means that in **MIXED-ABILITY** classes, students can be working on the same tasks at the same time. Open-ended tasks also allow for more **STUDENT INVOLVEMENT** since the students are asked to contribute more of their own personal ideas. This means that the outcome of classroom work will be richer – there will be a variety of ideas expressed which students can further compare and discuss. In this way, the students' **AUTONOMY** in their own use of English can be developed. Open-ended tasks also allow you, the teacher, to get a good idea of what the students are capable of producing.

Practical ideas

- If, at the start of a course, you are uncertain how much English the students know, you can use the open-ended tasks in Unit 1 of both Level 1 and Level 2 of *CES*.
- You can set the students some open-ended writing tasks by asking them to write their ideas about some educationally broad **QUESTIONS**, particularly ones which require **PROBLEM SOLVING**.
- The students' answers to open-ended tasks can be included in a **PARCEL OF ENGLISH**. They will give the school or class that you send the parcel to a good idea of the range of abilities and interests in your class.
- Instead of asking the students conventional 'closed' comprehension questions about a text they have listened to or read, you can ask open-ended questions. For example, you can ask 'What do you think about …?', 'What would you do …?', 'Do you think it was good that …?', 'Why do you think he/she did that?', 'What do you think they said to each other?', 'What do you think he/she was thinking?' and so on.

AtoZ OPEN PLAN

See **DO IT YOURSELF**.

AtoZ OVERVIEWING

What and why?

A common experience of some students is that they often do not have a very clear idea of where they are in a lesson – they may have very little idea of what has just happened, an unclear idea of what they are supposed to be doing now, and no idea at all of what is going to happen next. As one teacher put it, for many students being in a classroom is rather like being put in a taxi without being told where you are going or what landmarks to look out for on the way. Overviewing is a technique which helps to give students a clearer idea of where they are in the lesson. That way, if they lose concentration for a short time, they won't lose their grip on the whole lesson (100% concentration during a whole 40–50 minute lesson requires a lot of mental effort!).

Practical ideas

- The *Take a look at Theme* … tasks on the Theme cover pages are intended to give the students an overview of what they will meet in the coming Units. The tasks require the students to look through the Theme and so familiarise themselves with its content.
- Before moving into an activity which has several steps, you can give the students an overview of what they will be doing. It will then be easier to move them on from one step to the next, once the activity has begun.
- You can place an overview of the lesson on the board at the start of the lesson, showing what they will be doing.
- You can give an overview of your next lesson, leaving open some period of time. They can then be asked to suggest ideas of things they would like to do (you could use a suggestion box for this). This will help create a feeling of **STUDENT INVOLVEMENT** in the lesson. (Have something planned, just in case!)

AtoZ PACE

What and why?

The **TIMING** and pace of any lesson are linked together. **TIMING** is concerned with the management of the time available for each class, that is, *when* certain things happen. Pace is more concerned with the rate at which the students work. All students work at a different pace and they thus need to be allowed to work at a rate at which they feel comfortable. *CES* provides a number of ways of preventing some students from falling behind because the pace is too fast and of preventing others from getting bored because the pace of the lessons is too slow.

Different types of classroom activities will naturally have a different pace. For example, oral discussion with the whole class may be experienced as 'faster' than individual writing. PAIRWORK may be experienced as more relaxed than questions and answers with the teacher. These differences in pace can be used to give variety to the shape of the lesson and thus sustain interest.

Practical ideas

- In large MIXED-ABILITY classes, different students can work on different tasks at the same time at their own pace.

- For most of the exercises, except the initial BRAINSTORMING and OVERVIEWING ones, students can work at their own pace (see MONITORING AND GUIDING).
- Certain parts of the course will allow students more opportunity to have direct control over their learning and thus their pace: the TIME TO SPARE? sections, the EXERCISE BOX, the DECIDE EXERCISES, the DO IT YOURSELF exercises and the use of GROUPWORK and PAIRWORK.
- If certain students are working at a very slow pace, you will need to ask yourself why this is and if you can or should do anything about it. For example, they may be tired, they may be confused, they may not understand the task, they may be bored, they may have things on their mind. You will then need to decide if you should intervene – for example, by encouraging them to work faster or by explaining things to them again.

AtoZ PAIRWORK

What and why?

Pairwork involves students working in pairs simultaneously. The reasons for the use of pairwork are similar to those of GROUPWORK. Pairwork allows more students to get more practice. It also provides a change of pace to a lesson and helps to sustain motivation. Students working in pairs are able to share ideas and help each other. However, pairwork can fail if it is not set up well. This can lead to students getting distracted, disenchanted with English, and, eventually, misbehaving.

Practical ideas

- Ensure that students know exactly what they have to do before they begin any pairwork activity. Run

through a few examples with the whole class. Initially at least, pairwork tasks need to have a clear, concrete focus, for example on completing an exercise, doing PATTERNED PRACTICE, preparing some INTERACTIVE WRITING, preparing questions and so on.
- For variety, different students can be paired together. Students can be moved around the room or they can be put into pairs with students to their left or right, in front or behind.
- Give the students a time limit so that they know when they have to finish.
- Students can work in pairs to produce questions, exercises, etc. for other pairs to do.
- If the task does not actually *require* pairwork, the students can choose whether they want to work in pairs or alone.

AtoZ PARCEL OF ENGLISH

What and why?

A Parcel of English is a collection of pieces of work which the students can produce and send to another class (perhaps in another country) or display in their school. It is introduced in Unit 8 of Level 1 and Supplementary

Unit A of Level 2. Cambridge University Press offers a link-up scheme for classes to make contact with classes in other countries of the world. For further details see page 19 of this book and the registration card inside the book (or on the inside front cover).

AtoZ PARTICIPATION

What and why?

Particularly in large classes, some students may seem reluctant to participate orally and contribute to the lessons. There may be a number of reasons for this. There may, for example, be a number of negative factors such as being afraid to make mistakes in front of others, feeling that they will appear stupid, fearing that they will be corrected, or otherwise lacking in confidence in front of a large group.

On the other hand, many students naturally say very little. They may feel that they learn best through listening and observing – silence is their preferred LEARNING STRATEGY. Before you insist on students participating orally in the lesson, it is best therefore to think about *why* they are not participating. What may seem a problem to you may not, in fact, be a problem to them. It is important to respect the personal preferences that different students may have.

There are, however, a number of things that you can do to improve the chances of students participating.

Practical ideas

- If there are one or two students that are persistently quiet, you could talk to them after a lesson to find out what they think about it. Alternatively, you could make up a questionnaire which *all* students can answer.
- If possible, try to arrange the seating so that all the students can see you clearly and so that they can see each other. A horseshoe arrangement or circle is best, or try and push the desks together into pairs or groups.
- Accept that some students are quiet and may feel happier contributing in a less obvious way – perhaps by producing exercises and puzzles for the EXERCISE BOX, or helping to organise the PARCEL OF ENGLISH, or bringing in pictures and 'realia' for other activities.
- Some students may dominate the class by being over-noisy or always answering questions first. If this is a problem you could divide the class into four quarters and say that you will accept an answer from each group in turn.

- Some students may be reluctant to 'act out' in class. They may prefer to record a conversation on cassette at home for you to listen to later. Don't force students to speak out loud if they are not willing or ready.
- Make sure that the students understand that many of the activities in *CES* are open-ended so that a variety of answers are acceptable and 'right'. It is what *they* think that is important.
- Encourage students to understand the importance of everyone's contribution in GROUPWORK and that the work that the quiet students do often supports the work of the more dominant ones.
- Allow students to work at their own PACE (see also TASKS IN BLOCKS). This will give the more apprehensive students an opportunity to work without pressure.
- The DECIDE EXERCISES also allow students freedom to choose what they prefer to do. Give the quieter students encouragement while they work to build up confidence.
- You could make a particular point of praising weaker or quieter students and of accepting what they say (even if this contains many errors) in an effort to build up their confidence.

A to Z PATTERN PRACTICE

What and why?

A key part of language learning is having the opportunity to use the language creatively to say real things. However, there is also an element in language learning which involves practising particular structures or forms so that students can produce them effortlessly. One way in which this can be done is through pattern practice. Students produce sentences following a particular pattern and in doing so develop their ability to control the mechanical aspects of language production. Over-used, however, pattern practice can produce students who become bored and who find it difficult to use the language to actually communicate. For this reason, *CES* includes relatively few patterned exercises.

Practical ideas

- Pattern practice exercises can be done in small groups or pairs so that students get more opportunity to speak without having to wait for the rest of the class.
- The focus of pattern practice activities is on the *form* of what is said. This is the appropriate time to ensure that things are said accurately.
- Before getting students to work in pairs/groups on a patterned exercise, go through a few examples with the whole class so they know what is expected.
- While they are working, you can be MONITORING AND GUIDING.
- Oral pattern practice exercises can also be done in writing.

A to Z PHYSICAL MOVEMENT

What and why?

Students in the early secondary years need physical activity. In school, they may often spend many hours confined to a desk as they have one lesson then another. This can lead to boredom and restlessness (with its effect on DISCIPLINE). Physical movement can also be important for other reasons. If students can be physically involved with English, it can lead to deeper, more long-lasting learning as the language becomes more 'concrete' to them and involves them as whole persons.

Practical ideas

- 'Simon Says' games, in which students have to carry out actions upon the orders of the teacher/a student can be fun. Students must only do the action if the teacher/student says 'Simon says' first. (For example: 'Simon says sit down', 'Simon says clap your hands'.)
- Basic verbs can be taught in this way, with the teacher first saying the verb and the students following the action and then the students doing the action as the teacher says the verb again.

- Students can also represent something in a group. For example, they might together form the shape of their country. They can then move to where they would like to be in their country and talk about why they want to go there. They could ask each other across the map: 'Peter, where are you?', 'I'm in Barcelona in the north east'. Students can similarly form maps of their town, maps of a jungle, and maps of their school.
- Mime is also useful. Students act out a word and the others have to guess what it is.

- You could have various items of clothing available such as hats, gloves, etc. to make role plays, acting out, mime, etc. more fun.
- Physical activity doesn't have to be related to language learning. You might start a lesson or break up a long lesson by getting the students to do something. For example shake their arms, change the shape of their face, or stand up and turn round a few times. You could combine this with MUSIC.

AtoZ POSTERS

What and why?

At various places in *CES* (particularly in the *Activity Units*), students are required to produce posters of their ideas. The production of posters is a useful technique in language teaching for a number of reasons. It gives the students a concrete focus for their work and also ensures that English (rather than only the MOTHER TONGUE) is produced as a result of their GROUPWORK. Poster production can also be a lively way of working. Students can design their posters, spend time on how they look and express their ideas graphically. They can form a welcome break from a linear presentation of ideas in which groups FEEDBACK, one after the other, to the whole class. Posters allow all groups to FEEDBACK simultaneously, thus using time more effectively. They also form a permanent record of the work that has been done that can be DISPLAYED.

Practical ideas

- For poster production you – or the students – will need to have available supplies of large sheets of paper, coloured pens, scissors, glue or adhesive tape, and something to fix them to the wall.
- Coloured sheets mounted on a white background can make posters more attractive to look at.
- Students can be asked to work on parts of their posters for HOMEWORK, once they have decided in their group what they want to write.
- Encourage them to produce a draft before they put their writing on a poster.
- Once the students are ready with their posters, you can put them up on the wall or lay them out on the desks. Students can then walk around the class, looking at the posters. You could ask one member of each group to stay by their poster to explain what they have done.
- Posters can be photographed for permanent reference. A class photograph can be taken with their poster display.

AtoZ PROBLEM SOLVING

What and why?

Learning how to approach and solve problems, and accepting that there is often more than one answer to a question or more than one way of dealing with it is a key part of both education and language learning. The ability to determine the essence of a problem, and indeed to see that there *is* a problem, is a vital ingredient in learning. In *CES*, therefore, many tasks require the students to think things through not only in relation to the structure of the language but also by drawing on their existing knowledge to help them understand new situations. For example, some exercises in which the students are asked to establish their own rules for a new grammatical structure require this kind of cognitive effort. Other exercises require students to think through *why* certain things happen, or to work out an explanation for natural phenomena.

The benefits of a problem-solving approach to teaching and learning can be significant for a number of reasons. Firstly, involving the learner in thinking things through requires more involvement and produces greater depth of understanding. This kind of 'experiential knowledge' (that is, the knowledge gained through the experience of *doing* something) often lasts longer and is more significant to the learner than knowledge which is simply 'transmitted' by the teacher or the book. The students become involved in constructing their own *individual* systems of learning and understanding. Secondly, some recent research has suggested that where students are involved in using language to understand and formulate meanings, then language may be acquired more naturally, in much the same way as infants learn their first language.

Practical ideas

- When students ask you questions, you can, from time to time, insist that they find out for themselves, by using books, asking other people or figuring it out.
- Give hints or clues in answer to their questions rather than direct answers.
- You can set a 'problem of the week' for the students. Talk to other subject teachers in your school and ask for ideas about questions you could pose. 'What if …' questions and 'How can …' questions are often useful in stimulating thought. For example: 'What would happen if we had only three hours of light each day?', 'What would happen if we started teaching Chinese instead of English in school?', 'How can we make our classroom lighter and quieter?' Even: 'How can we best learn a language?' If you set such questions, you can discuss them at a specified time later.
- You can present 'language learning' as a 'problem' to be solved. Encourage students to think of their own ways of recording and learning new vocabulary. Let students discuss and compare in class the different methods they have tried. Encourage students to discuss grammar areas which they find difficult or easy to learn and use. Encourage the students to think about and investigate *how* they go about doing exercises, reading, how they revise for a test, etc.
- Students can be encouraged to bring puzzles and problems into class. They can also put these into the EXERCISE BOX and the PARCEL OF ENGLISH.

AtoZ PROCESSING TIME

What and why?

Learning – whether it is a foreign language or any other subject – often requires great mental effort. In any 40–50 minute lesson, a student may be required to absorb a lot of new information, make connections with what he or she already knows, and then be required to use it. Each of these processes takes time. Often, when students are asked a question and they fail to answer correctly, the problem is not that they don't know or haven't understood, it is simply that they haven't been given enough time to process the question and process an answer. If students are questioned with the whole class listening and waiting, there may be pressure on them to answer as quickly as possible. This can block their ability to process the question and an answer – that is, to think. The teacher may then feel under pressure to keep the lesson moving and so turns to another student. The same situation may repeat itself several times, until finally, a student who has not been put under this direct pressure and who has thus had enough time to process the question, is able to produce a satisfactory answer. This problem may be avoided by allowing all students processing time before you call for answers.

Practical ideas

- Allow students time to do an exercise by themselves/in pairs before you call for answers.
- Give students time to plan out what they are going to say, their ideas on a topic, etc. in writing before you discuss things with the whole class.
- Tell the students in advance what they will be doing. They can then prepare at home for the lesson.
- Choose 'larger' tasks which can be done in a large space of time (such as the majority of tasks in *CES*) rather than short 'item' tasks which require immediate responses (such as comprehension questions, gap-filling exercises).

AtoZ PRONUNCIATION

What and why?

A correct and clear pronunciation is obviously of considerable importance in language learning. Without it, students may not be understood and may be poorly perceived by other English speakers. However, a good pronunciation is something which takes time to build up as there are many factors involved. Students need to hear a lot of English before they can develop a 'feel' for the sounds of English. They need to have confidence in their abilities, not feel shy and be ready to make a fool of themselves as they try to get their tongues round the different sounds. Pronunciation is thus probably best dealt with a little at a time and in the context of learning new words, structures, etc. rather than in isolation.

Practical ideas

- The *Say it clearly!* reminders in the Student's Book are intended to draw attention to some sounds that the students may have difficulty with.
- It is better to spend very short periods running through pronunciation examples and exercises rather than one long session. Perhaps the same pronunciation exercise could be done in three or four different lessons for three minutes at a time.
- It is worth discovering which are the main pronunciation problems for students of your MOTHER

TONGUE. You can then spend a little time focusing on them. A little pronunciation practice at this level goes a long way!

- Students may find stress and intonation practice easier and more interesting to respond to by doing some jazz chants or clapping as the words are stressed on the cassette. This can be done in small groups if they have the cassette recorder or briefly with all the students together.
- Students can be encouraged to do pronunciation practice at home. The *Topic* and *Language focus* Units in the Workbook contain pronunciation exercises. In addition, the Workbook contains *Help yourself with pronunciation* and presents some ideas they can use.
- **READING** aloud is a technique which is often used to check pronunciation. In our experience, however, reading aloud has very little effect in improving pronunciation. In the classroom, students typically make *more* mistakes when they read aloud than they do normally. It also wastes time for the students who have to listen and places the teacher in the role of having to correct the reader all the time. Turning the written word into sounds is quite a separate process from the production of a word in normal conversation.

AtoZ QUESTIONS

What and why?

Questions are important in language learning in three main ways. Firstly, and most obviously, the 'interrogative' is a grammatical form which students need to learn to master. For users of a foreign language, the ability to ask questions is essential. It provides the key to moving around in a new environment, integrating into a community and to finding essential information. Secondly, questions form one of the main 'tools' which teachers use to check students' comprehension and to get students to produce language. Thirdly, and more profoundly, the ability to generate questions is central to **AUTONOMY** in learning and to the students' personal *educational* development. Many types of questions used in classrooms, however, are *display questions* – that is, they require the students simply to show that they know something. This places the emphasis on reproducing isolated facts. Educational questions, on the other hand, require the students to think, to discuss, to share ideas or to investigate. They can bring about more **STUDENT INVOLVEMENT** with learning English and with their educational development in general. *CES* places particular emphasis on educational questions rather than display questions.

Practical ideas

- When beginning a new topic, you can get students to **BRAINSTORM** what they already know about it and what they would like to find out. You can get the students to produce a question **POSTER** of things they can investigate/research over the next few weeks.
- Where possible, ask **OPEN-ENDED** questions, to which various answers are possible, rather than closed display questions where only one answer is correct. For example, after reading a text, instead of asking factual questions such as 'What did the man do in the shop?' (the answer to which is in the text), you could ask 'What do you think about what he did?', 'Why do you think that?'
- Before reading a text, or after reading part of a text, you can ask the students to predict what will happen next.
- If the students have a reading text with conventional comprehension questions, you can ask them to try to answer the questions *before* they read the text, using their imagination and what they already know. They can then approach the text more actively to check their answers.
- If you get students to produce questions for each other (perhaps for the **EXERCISE BOX**), you can ask them to formulate some educational questions rather than display questions.
- You can talk to teachers of other school subjects to find out what educational questions are relevant to the Theme you are working on in *CES*. Students can then be asked to find answers to these questions over the next week or so. You can discuss what they have found out at a specified time.
- Rather than *telling* the students, you can ask them a series of questions so that they work things out for themselves. You can ask: 'Can you think of any other similar examples?', 'Why do you think it is like that?', 'When does this happen?', 'Where?', 'Does it always happen?', 'When doesn't it happen?', 'How do you think you can find out?', 'What books would you need to look in?', 'Who could you ask?' and so on.

AtoZ READING

What and why?

Similar to LISTENING, SPEAKING and WRITING, there are two main roles for reading in language learning. The first is as a *goal* of learning: 'the skill of reading'. The second is as a *means* of learning: as a way of developing the students' language proficiency and educational depth. Secondary aged students need to develop the skill of reading in English. It is through reading that they will most likely come into contact with English, particularly if they go on to higher education or are employed in international work of some kind. But reading as a *means* of learning is also important. Reading can support their language learning through contextualising and extending vocabulary, creating a mental image of correct spellings, providing models for writing, and by developing a 'feel' for English – especially if they have very few classroom hours. Reading can also be a means for developing their learning beyond just English. Through reading, the students can learn more about the world and come into contact with different ideas. For these reasons, reading needs to be encouraged right from the start. There are a number of ways you can do this.

Practical ideas

- Students may not read very much in their MOTHER TONGUE so you may need to start by encouraging reading generally. You can do this by asking, perhaps at the start of every lesson, what they have read since the last lesson. This can be anything – a newspaper headline, a story, an advert, in the MOTHER TONGUE or in English. Gradually, you can suggest that they look for things to read in English which they can tell the class about. In this way, the students can begin to see reading as something of value to share.

- You can encourage extensive reading through readers or short stories. If possible, let the students choose what they want to read. Invite (rather than demand) them to tell other students (perhaps in small groups) what they have read. They don't need to report back on everything they read.

- You can allow time for silent reading in class. Some students may like to read if they finish an exercise early or if they chose to DO IT YOURSELF for the DECIDE EXERCISES in Level 2.

- Encourage students to read other students' creative work such as stories and poems.

- Encourage the students to guess the meaning of words they don't understand. Also, stress that they don't need to understand every word in order to read something.

- Show the students how to use a dictionary so that they can read alone. (At this level, a bilingual dictionary.)

- You can also teach the students other reading skills such as SKIMMING AND SCANNING.

- One common technique is to ask students to read aloud. In *CES*, this technique is not recommended. Reading aloud is, in fact, a separate skill from reading for comprehension. Students are unlikely to need this skill – unless they become newsreaders! In the classroom, students typically make *more* mistakes when they read aloud than they do normally (particularly in PRONUNCIATION). It also wastes time for the students who have to listen and places the teacher in the role of having to correct the reader all the time. Also, since the emphasis is on production, the main skills involved in reading – guessing words, working out meaning, predicting – are not utilised.

AtoZ ROLE PLAY

What and why?

In a role play students take on the role of another person – a waiter, an adult, even a Martian or a monster. Often the situation is given (e.g. *You are in a restaurant. Order a meal.*) and perhaps some ideas of what to say. Role play is a popular method in language-learning classrooms for a number of reasons. Students of this age find it fun and quiet students are often found to speak more openly in a 'role'. In a role play students are encouraged to use communication creatively and imaginatively and they get an opportunity to use language from 'outside' the classroom. In *CES*, there are role play tasks in many parts of the course, particularly in the *Out and about* sections.

Practical ideas

- The success of every role play depends on the students knowing exactly what they have to do. Make sure that the students know the role they are going to play, some language they can use and some ideas for content.

- In general, role play works better in groups of a maximum of three or four students.

- Discuss with students how long they need to prepare their roles and whether they can prepare in pairs or alone.

- Students can prepare either in 'complete' groups for the role play (that is, one student for each character) or in character groups (that is, in small groups they share ideas of what they will each say. They then join with other students when they are ready to act out the role play).

- Some students like to make notes of what they are going to say. This creates confidence in the preparation period but encourage students to speak without reading out their notes.
- As a role play is based on 'real-life situations', if you have some 'realia' (real items) from an English speaking country these will make the role play more fun, e.g. real menus, real bus/train timetables, real/plastic English/American/Australian money, etc. Younger students often like to have 'props' – handbags, shopping bags, purses, etc.
- During the preparation stage the role of the teacher is to circulate, answering questions, checking that everyone understands, and making suggestions.
- You may need to remind students of some 'checking' and 'communication' phrases: 'Sorry? Could you say that again please?', 'What do you mean?', 'What's the word for …?'.
- During the role play itself you can listen and write notes about points which can be discussed later. If a student gets stuck, indicate to the others to help in any way they can. You can prepare a comments sheet like the one below. The students who are listening to the role play can also make a note of their own comments.

Name:

Language areas	To comment on	To praise
Grammar		
Vocabulary		
Pronunciation		
Communication		
Self-correction		
General comments		

- After the role play discuss with the class how they felt it went and then put general points on the board to avoid embarrassing individual students.
- Sometimes it is a good idea to record the role play on audio or video cassette so that you and the students can see/hear it again later.

A to Z SKIMMING AND SCANNING

What and why?

'Skimming' and 'scanning' are two different READING skills. These are practised at the start of each Theme, using the cover page tasks (*Take a look at Theme …*). Skimming means looking at a text or chapter quickly in order to have a general idea of the contents. Scanning means looking at a text to find some particular information. For example, we skim through a report to have a rough idea of what it says but we scan a page of the telephone directory to find a particular name or number. As the students become more confident of their reading ability in the MOTHER TONGUE and in English they will learn how to approach texts with different reading skills, depending on the purpose of the text and the purpose they have for reading it. Students who find reading in English discouraging may be helped by knowing that they do not have to read and understand every word of a text.

Practical ideas

- Start by explaining the difference between skimming and scanning to the students (give them the example of a telephone directory and a chapter of a History/Science textbook).
- Before the students read a text, ask them whether they think they need to skim or scan it, depending on the task.
- Students often like having races. Occasionally ask students to see who can find the information in a text first.
- Make sure the students realise that understanding every word of a text is not always necessary.
- Allow time for students to read the texts quietly to themselves in class to practise their own technique. Texts do not need to be read out loud round the class.
- Encourage students to practise skimming and scanning when they read in their mother tongue.
- Ask the students who find the answers in the 'Skim' and 'Scan' section at the beginning of each *Topic* Unit to write some more questions for the rest of the class to do.

A to Z SONGS

What and why?

In general, secondary school students like singing songs, particularly if they are melodic. They are a way of recycling language in a 'fun' format, they develop a natural sense of language achievement and can also bring about STUDENT INVOLVEMENT.

Practical ideas

- The songs in *CES* are on both the Class Cassette and the Workbook Cassette. You can point this out to the students and ask them to practise a song at home.
- You can ask the students to suggest a song that you can all sing. It is best if the song is one that they all know already so that everyone can sing. If you use songs regularly, students can take it in turns to bring in a song or decide in their groups which song they would like to sing next time.
- It is probably best to sing the song either at the very beginning or the very end of a lesson.
- Make sure you allow enough time – 10 minutes at least – to give students a chance to listen and then to sing together at least twice.
- Some students may feel shy about singing – don't force them!
- Play the song through first, if you have recorded it – make sure students can hear. If the students have the words, they can read or sing while they listen.
- In some songs the students continue by making up words of their own.

Try to vary the presentation:
- Sometimes half the class or different groups can sing the verses and the other half can sing the chorus.
- Sometimes half of the class sings alternate verses.
- Perhaps an extrovert has a wonderful voice and can sing a solo!
- Some students may have guitars and would like to play the tune along with the music.
- Perhaps at the end of the term/year, the students could give a concert to the rest of the school.

The best thing to do with a song is sing it! However, there are various teaching techniques that you can use from time to time with songs:
- Give the students the lyrics with some words missed out. The students have to listen and put in the words.
- If the song has a chorus or verses that are repeated, you can put the students into groups and give each student one sentence from the song. While they are listening, they have to put the sentences in the right order.
- Give them some questions about the song before they listen. Afterwards, they can tell you their answers.
- Sing all the verses except the last one. Give a choice of three verses for the last one (you can modify/make up your own). Students have to read it and work out which one fits the tune best.

A to Z SPEAKING

What and why?

One of the main aims of *CES* is to give students confidence in expressing themselves orally. The emphasis is, therefore, on spoken fluency rather than on spoken accuracy. This should encourage students to be confident and creative in their spoken English.

Practical ideas

- Before correcting a spoken error consider whether it could lead to misunderstanding. If not, there may be little reason to correct it. Too much ERROR CORRECTION can inhibit the students' desire to speak.
- Encourage students to give their reactions to the pictures and input at the start of a Unit. There is no need to insist on whole sentences – they may only manage a phrase or even a word. Try to react to *what* they have said rather than *how* they have said it.
- Allow space and time for the students to speak! You can record some of your lessons and calculate how much time *you* spend talking and how much time *the students* spend talking. If necessary, see if you can change the situation over the term.
- Students often find it difficult to provide a rapid spoken reply to a question without time to PROCESS an answer. Sometimes it may be useful to give the students the questions you will ask them in advance so they can prepare. At the beginning, it may be better to let students volunteer a reply rather than insist that they answer in turn.
- The quieter students may prefer to be given the choice of speaking on to a cassette at home. They could then, perhaps, give you the cassette to listen to.
- Try to ensure that different people speak each time. You can suggest that different people do the reporting back after GROUPWORK.
- If you have some students who never say anything, or who PARTICIPATE very little, you need to ask yourself why this is. It may be their preferred LEARNING STRATEGY/style (to listen and absorb), or they may feel shy, they may feel that they don't know enough, or they may feel that the lessons are dominated by other students. If the situation persists, you could talk to the students concerned to find out what they think about the situation. It may not be a problem for them at all!

What and why?

Many students – and many native English speakers – find English spelling difficult. Since English has been influenced by many other languages, it does not have a completely consistent 'fit' between the way it is spoken and the way it is written. In addition, the invention of printing in the 15th century had the effect of 'fixing' the spelling of English at a time when the language was undergoing many changes.

'Good spelling' is important. It influences the way people think of you, and your ability to communicate clearly. However, it is important not to over-emphasise spelling. For many students, spelling is something that takes care of itself as they get more exposure to English. In the initial stages of learning, a stress on correct spelling may discourage students from using the language to try to express what they want to express. Some students may have problems in spelling in their own language, and drawing attention to this in English may strengthen their feeling of failure. The best approach is probably to draw the students' attention to spellings, and to do a little practice frequently.

Practical ideas

- There are two *Help yourself with spelling* Units in the Workbook.
- Ensure that the students understand that sometimes there is little or no relationship between pronunciation and spelling in English. You can make this fun by saying, for example, 'We say two /tuː/ but we write /twəʊ/.' You get them to count in 'spelling English': /əʊneɪ/, /twəʊ/, /t h reɪ/ and so on.
- If all your students share the same MOTHER TONGUE it is likely that they make the same spelling errors. Make a list of them and, if possible, put the correct version on a POSTER on the wall. Students can then refer to this when they are writing.

- You could give the students groups of words to learn, grouped around sounds. For example, /iː/ words: sweet, feet, meat, heat, etc. Point out to students how the same sound is spelt in different ways.
- Do the spelling errors fall into groups? For example, perhaps they have trouble remembering the double consonant in some comparatives and superlatives, or perhaps they confuse 'ei' with 'ie'. With the students, you could draw up a checklist of their common errors. They can then use this checklist every time they write something.
- Encourage the students to check spellings in the *Wordlist/Index* at the back of their Student's Book.
- 'Good spelling' probably comes with READING. The more the students read, the more it may help their spelling. After the students have read a text, you could ask them to go back and focus on the words. Ask them to write down (or underline/circle) any words which they think they will have trouble spelling correctly later. Discuss with the group their choices and find out why they chose those words.
- To encourage students to look closely at common letter patterns, after they have read a text, write some two-, three- or four-letter patterns on the board (for example, '-ea-', '-ough-', '-th-'). Then individually or in teams, ask them to find as many examples as possible in the text of those letter patterns.
- Students can test each other in groups.
- Play 'Spelling Snap!', in groups of three or four. Write on one side of some cards words which they know but may find difficult. Make sure there are at least three examples of each of the letter patterns. Shuffle the cards. Each student has 10 or so cards. Students take it in turns to put one of their cards in the centre of the table and say the word on the card at the same time. If the card which follows has the same letter pattern they must shout 'Snap!'. The person with the most cards at the end is the winner.

What and why?

Student involvement is probably the single most important factor in language learning, especially with students in the early secondary school years. One of the greatest causes of drop-out and student failure in learning is that they do not feel part of their course. For this reason, the encouragement of student involvement is one of the key principles in *CES* (see the *Rationale*, pages 7–12). The aim is to involve the students as fully as possible in their English course, such that they feel it is

theirs and one which is personally relevant to them. *CES* contains numerous practical ideas in relation to student involvement. The following are some of the basic principles we have adopted.

Practical ideas

- Start from the students. When introducing a new topic, find out what the students already know about it and what they would like to know about it.

- Encourage regular **EVALUATION** of how they are learning and take steps accordingly.
- Provide choices between tasks. Students do not have to be doing the same things all the time. Allow them to **DECIDE** and make room for **DO IT YOURSELF**.
- Provide creative tasks which draw on the students' imagination, experience and personal views.

- Provide 'larger' **TASKS**, such as whole activities, where students can feel freer to work in their own way.
- Draw on the **MOTHER TONGUE** as a means of involving the students' knowledge about how language works.
- Involve students in the production of **TESTS** and make tests less threatening.
- Focus on topics which are worth learning about in their own right, and which have **CURRICULUM LINKS**.

A to Z TASKS

What and why?

The word 'task' is used in a variety of meanings in language teaching. One common use is in the sense of 'whole tasks', that is, a large classroom activity in which the students may be doing a variety of different things. In this sense, the *Activity* Units in *CES* are 'whole tasks'. The focus in 'whole task' work is usually on meaning, rather than the form of the language, although both are important (see **FLUENCY**). Many writers argue that teaching through 'whole tasks' is most effective since students can learn the language through natural processes of acquisition.

In *CES*, however, the word 'task' is used in the same way as 'exercise', to refer to any structured language-learning procedure. 'Task' in this sense will include everything from a gap-filling exercise to a poetry-writing activity. Tasks may be 'small' and may only take a few minutes (such as doing a word puzzle) or 'large' (such as making a poster) which may take a whole lesson or more. In actual fact, 'large tasks' are likely to be made up of smaller tasks. Some of the key questions in language teaching are: 'What are the most effective kinds of tasks for language learning?', 'What makes a task more or less difficult for students?', 'How do different kinds of tasks affect classroom interaction?', 'How do different kinds of tasks shape **LEARNING STRATEGIES**?' and 'What roles do different kinds of tasks place on teachers and students?'

Practical ideas

- See the *A to Z* entries on **TASKS IN BLOCKS, OPEN-ENDED TASKS, AUTONOMY, EXERCISE BOX, DECIDE EXERCISES, DO IT YOURSELF, PROBLEM SOLVING, MIXED ABILITIES, FLUENCY** and other cross-references.

Researching the classroom

- Experiment with different ways of doing similar tasks to see if that affects student performance. For example, writing can be done individually or in small groups, with or without planning and **BRAINSTORMING**, or with or without dictionary support, and so on.
- Choose two or three tasks which seem to be very different in nature. For example, a poster-making activity, a grammar discovery task and a reading comprehension task. Then choose three or four students in your class. When you come to those tasks in your teaching, watch how the students respond individually to different kinds of tasks. Do some students prefer to work in a particular way? Do they seem to achieve more from particular kinds of tasks?
- Give a lot of support initially in a particular area and then gradually reduce that support to see when it becomes difficult for the students. For example, if the students are doing listening work, you can initially teach them the language they will hear, give them an overview in their own language, let them listen with their books open, and then listen several times. Gradually reduce the support (for example, they can listen with their books closed) to see at what point it becomes difficult for them. You can then discover how much support you actually need to give.
- Do the tasks that the students do in your lessons emphasise particular **LEARNING STRATEGIES** and classroom roles? When you are planning a lesson, sometimes look back over your plan and analyse the main tasks with the following questions: 1 What role will the students take? Will they be initiating language or responding? 2 What mental process will they have to go through? (E.g. repeating, analysing, planning, recalling from memory.) 3 What is the task about? Where does most of the subject matter come from? From the book, from the students, from the teacher? If you continually get the same answers to these questions, try to identify ways in which you can change the focus of your lesson to create greater variety and learning opportunities.

AtoZ TASKS IN BLOCKS

What and why?

A situation which often arises in teaching is that students, working either in groups or alone, finish before each other. This may not be a problem. There is no particular reason, for example, why students should have to be kept 100% busy 100% of the time. In some cases, however, students may waste their time as they wait for others to catch up. This may lead to boredom, disenchantment with learning English and, in some cases, DISCIPLINE problems. Putting tasks in blocks is a technique which ensures that students have something to go on to when they finish their work.

Practical ideas

- Before students start working, you can put two or three tasks together 'in a block'. Go through the tasks, explaining what they have to do in each one. As students finish one task, they can move on to the next.
- You can also put some tasks in blocks with the TIME TO SPARE? sections and the EXERCISE BOX. Students will then have something to do when they finish the tasks.
- Putting tasks in blocks will give you more time for MONITORING AND GUIDING.
- You can give a time limit for the tasks. If they finish before, students can move on to anything else they wish, providing it is related to learning English (see TIME TO SPARE? and EXERCISE BOX).

AtoZ TESTS

What and why?

Tests can form a useful and important role in language learning. They can give both the students and the teacher a clear picture of how much the students have learnt. They can also give the students a focus or something to work towards, and thus motivation for learning. However, tests can also have many negative consequences. Some students can become very anxious about tests and this can prevent them from effective learning. Students may become so focused on the test that they lose sight of the wider goal – learning English. Learning can also become 'defensive', in which case they learn something because of the fear of the test, but rapidly forget it once the test has passed. For these reasons, tests need to be handled carefully and made more 'friendly' to the students.

Practical ideas

- Before a test, give the students a clear list of what they will be tested on. They can then be asked to rate themselves on each area of the test and compare with the marks after the test.
- Try to view a test not so much as an indication of how much the students know/don't know but as an indication of how effective classroom language teaching is. If students perform badly, this may say more about what is happening/not happening in the classroom than it does about the students.
- In both Level 1 and Level 2, students can be involved in devising their own tests (see the *Revision and evaluation* Units). If you give a list of areas that you have covered over the last few lessons, pairs of students could make up parts of the test. You can then collect them in, correct them and assemble them into a complete test. Students can learn from the process of writing the test and seeing their own corrected version. The test is then also 'theirs' rather than 'yours', and so less threatening.
- Students can be given practice tests to do at home. (There are practice tests in the Workbook.) These give the students the opportunity to test themselves without anxiety.

AtoZ TIME TO SPARE?

What and why?

Students work at a different PACE and finish exercises more quickly or slowly than others. The *Time to spare?* sections (at the end of the *Topic* and *Language focus* Units) are designed to give students something to go on with if they finish ahead of the others.

Practical ideas

- The *Time to spare?* section contains extra exercises and the option of creating an exercise for the EXERCISE BOX. Students might also want to choose to DO IT YOURSELF (in Level 2).
- Students don't need to be kept 100% busy 100% of the time. If they do finish early, they can be given the option of just relaxing, as long as they don't disturb other students. Getting more work as a reward for working hard can be very demotivating!

AtoZ TIMING

What and why?

The timing and PACE of each lesson are linked together. However, timing refers mainly to *when* things are done in the lesson. The rhythm of the lesson needs to be maintained so that students use the class time productively and enjoyably. Your timing for new activities or steps in the lesson also needs to bear in mind what the students have just been doing and how much time is left in the lesson.

Practical ideas

- Look at the timing estimates in the Teaching Notes for each Unit before you start and write your own estimates.

- Make a note during the lesson of the actual time each exercise took with each class and, if appropriate, why you think it differed from your estimates.
- Before starting an exercise tell the students how long they have. Near the end of the time warn them that the time is almost over.
- Keep an eye on the clock during the lesson: don't start a new task just before the end of the lesson!
- If there are only a few minutes left at the end of the lesson the students can work on the TIME TO SPARE? exercises, fill in their LANGUAGE RECORD, do an exercise from the EXERCISE BOX, make an exercise, play a GAME, sing a SONG, or look back through the previous Units.

AtoZ TRANSLATION

What and why?

As a technique in language learning and teaching, translation used to be very popular. In recent years, however, it has fallen out of favour. There has been concern that an over-use of translation encourages the students to produce very strange-sounding English. Too much translation can also prevent students from developing fluency in the language as they develop the habit of going through their MOTHER TONGUE. Yet, used appropriately, there are a number of reasons why translation, as a teaching technique, still offers considerable benefits. Students, especially in the initial stages, *do* translate. It is, in fact, impossible to learn anything unless you find ways of integrating it into what you already know – for the beginning student this is the MOTHER TONGUE. It is thus important that the teacher is able to ensure that students have the *correct* translation in their minds. Translation can also help students be themselves – they can express what they want to say and then learn how to say those same things in English. It is also useful as a planning device (e.g. before writing) where trying to plan *in English* would prevent the flow of ideas.

Practical ideas

- You can deal with basic vocabulary problems through translation. This saves time compared with long explanations and ensures the correct meaning is understood.
- Students can play the translation game, where a 'non-English-speaking' student says something in the MOTHER TONGUE and another student has to interpret for him/her.
- BRAINSTORMING can be done in the MOTHER TONGUE, but as you put the ideas up on the board or a POSTER, you can translate them into English. Students can then learn from seeing *their* ideas in English.
- Before doing a ROLE PLAY, WRITING a passage, preparing QUESTIONS or an exercise, students can first plan things out in their MOTHER TONGUE, all the time thinking of what they are able to say in English. Planning in the MOTHER TONGUE can prevent language problems interfering with the generating of ideas.

AtoZ VIDEO

What and why?

In general, students find the use of videos motivating and stimulating. Videos are a useful vehicle for learning more about a topic, for making cross-cultural comparisons and for making the language more memorable. *CES* is accompanied by a set of videos. These can be used together with the coursebooks or on their own. The *CES* videos are not intended simply to provide 'language models'. They aim to enrich the students' knowledge and experience of language use in relation to the topics in the course by providing interesting extension material for each of the six Themes in the Levels. See the video packs themselves for further details of the *CES* videos and accompanying worksheets. The following notes apply to the use of videos in general.

Practical ideas

- Plan ahead! Book the video and cassette. Check if a technician will be available. Watch the video and read through the video script before the lesson so that you are aware of the language, characters, topic and content.
- Prepare the students before they see the video so that they have an idea of what they are going to see. Give them a general outline of what they will see. This will make it much easier for them to follow and learn.
- You can set some tasks before the students watch the video. These can be of a general nature, about what happens in the video. After the students have watched the extract from the video all the way through, you can follow this up with further detailed tasks which require the students to listen or look for detail.
- Tip: When you start the cassette put the counter on zero so that when you rewind and replay you will find the place more easily.
- Tip: Make sure that all the students can see the screen and hear.
- Keep the video session fairly short. Ten minutes of video every week is more useful than 40 minutes every month.

Some ideas for exploiting videos:

- Play the video the first time without any sound. Ask the students what they think the people are saying.
- Students can watch the section all the way through. Rewind then play a part again. Then freeze the frame and ask them if they can remember what comes next.
- Observation: the students can do this in teams. Give them a list of items before the viewing. They have to write down who had or did them, e.g. 'Who had a red car?', 'Who had glasses?', 'Who did Peter talk to?', etc.
- After viewing the video extract once, students can work in groups to write questions for each other. They can then exchange these and watch the video again to find the answers.
- Talk about cross-cultural aspects. Ask students to write down after the viewing four things they noticed which were different from their culture (objects, buildings, clothes, food, etc.) and four things which are the same. Put them on the board. Discuss why the things are the same or different.
- In advance, choose some sentences from the video script and ask what they think the video will be about, what they will learn about and so on. They can also guess who says the sentences, why, etc.
- Students can also be involved in making their own videos.

A to Z VOCABULARY

What and why?

Vocabulary is possibly the single most important area in language learning. With a large vocabulary, a person can communicate effectively even though he/she may be very weak in grammatical knowledge. In *CES*, vocabulary development is thus emphasised. This is achieved through various vocabulary-related exercises, the LANGUAGE RECORD and the suggestions for making vocabulary exercises in the IDEAS LIST in the Student's Book, and the *Help yourself* Unit and *picture dictionary* in the Workbook. It can be expected, however, that the students' *passive* knowledge of vocabulary (their understanding) will always be greater than their *active* abilities (what they are able to produce). The same is likely to be true in the MOTHER TONGUE.

Practical ideas

- Writing vocabulary puzzles for the EXERCISE BOX, for the PARCEL OF ENGLISH or for their partner (see IDEAS LIST) also gives students time to absorb new words.
- Encourage students to compare new words with translations in the MOTHER TONGUE.
- Encourage students to guess new words in texts.
- Show the students how they can use a dictionary. This will help them build up their vocabulary outside of class time.
- You could encourage the students to keep a vocabulary notebook in which they note down words/phrases new to them and their meaning in their language.
- Students can be put into small groups to test each other on vocabulary or to devise a vocabulary test for the class.
- For each Theme, the students could gradually construct a large vocabulary puzzle. Decide in advance with the students what kind you will make (e.g. find the words, or one long word acting as the basis for all the words, a traditional crossword puzzle, a circular puzzle in which the last letter of one word is the first letter of the next, etc.) and put the plan on the wall. During the two or three weeks of the Theme each student puts a clue on the puzzle. At the end of the Theme, students write the clues and the blank puzzle in their books and do the puzzle together.
- 'I spy' is a lively vocabulary game which younger students like playing. (One student says 'I spy with my little eye something beginning with "w".' The object must be in the room. Students guess. The one to get it right has the next turn.)

What and why?

In common with **LISTENING, READING** and **SPEAKING**, there are two main roles for writing in language teaching. The first is as a *goal* of teaching. It is important for students to develop the writing skill in order to express themselves in written English in letters, messages, stories, and so on. The second role, however, is as a *means* of learning. Writing can provide further sources of practice and can help the students remember the words, phrases, grammar, etc. that they are learning. By working on writing tasks, students can become closely involved with the language and, in doing so, develop their general language proficiency. Writing can thus form a very important element in the course.

Practical ideas

- Encourage the students to keep written records of what they learn. The **LANGUAGE RECORD** will be useful in this respect. Students can also keep 'Language Notebooks' in which they note down vocabulary, phrases, grammar points, etc. They can then look at these on the bus, while waiting somewhere, at home in bed, and so on.
- Before calling on the students to do any large oral activity, such as **ROLE PLAY**, students can be encouraged to plan in writing what they are going to say.
- Where students are involved in writing as a *goal* of language learning, encourage them to go through the various stages of collecting ideas, drafting, getting **FEEDBACK** from a reader, revising and final production.
- Where possible, give the students real-life tasks which have a real audience. This could be writing a letter requesting information, the **PARCEL OF ENGLISH**, pen-friends and so on. Writing to other students can also provide an audience (see **INTERACTIVE WRITING**).
- In correcting students' writing, try not to over-correct. A page full of red ink can be very demoralising! There are a number of alternative ways of approaching correction: ask the students to underline the things they are not sure of or where they would like your help – you need only then correct the things they have identified; limit yourself to no more than six to eight points for correction; rather than focusing on the form of what they have written, respond to the message. Write a brief reply to the ideas they have expressed; rather than correcting, give hints or clues and encourage the students to correct their own work. You can use a marking scheme (e.g. Sp = spelling, WW = wrong word, and so on).

Supplementary Unit A A Parcel of English

Note
If you have done *CES 1*, please see the sections 'If you have done *CES 1* …' and 'Some questions and answers …' below. See also 'Special note on the Supplementary Units', page 19.

OVERVIEW OF THE PARCEL OF ENGLISH SCHEME

The *Parcel of English* offers not only an opportunity for students and you to make contact with another school, but also provides an active context for revision. Cambridge University Press offers a registration service which links schools in different countries with each other. In order to get the maximum benefit from the *Parcel of English*, it is recommended that you use this Supplementary Unit as soon as possible after Unit 1. See the '**Special note on the Supplementary Units**', page 19, for more information.

The first 'parcel' which the students produce in this Unit focuses on two important aspects: the place where the students live and the school they go to. Students can revise the Present tense and the vocabulary of description. Subsequent 'parcels' can include a variety of texts. (See below.)

Timing

The *Parcel of English* is quite a large activity which will last more than one lesson in total. Additionally, you and the students may like to keep it going for a number of weeks so that more material may be fed into it. The suggested timings are given below.

Before the lesson	
1 Collect some pictures	(at home)
In the lesson	
2 What is a *Parcel of English*?	5
3 What's in the *Parcel of English*?	10
4 A picture and description of me	10
5 What can you write?	5
6 Making your parcel	25

What you need

Ideally, glue, scissors, small pieces of paper (10 × 10cm – enough for the whole class. To get paper this size, fold a piece of A4 paper into six equal parts), A4 paper, sticky tape, plus postcards, maps, and photos of the town and school, in case students bring very little.

Guidelines

Before the lesson

1   Collect some pictures

Remind students to bring in a photo of themselves and pictures of their town.

In your lesson

2   What is a Parcel of English?

As a group, get the students to look at the picture of the *Parcel of English* and to discuss what they can see. Ask them to suggest what it is for. Tell the students that the *Parcel of English* is a link with another school (possibly in another country) or a school/class display.

Ask them if they would like the *Parcel of English* to go to another school in another country (if your school is in agreement – you may need to ask the permission of your head of department or head of school) in order to make a school-to-school link-up. Alternatively, you or the students may prefer to make a big display of all the work in the classroom, corridor or school hall. Or they may prefer to make a big 'scrap book' to keep in the classroom.

3   What's in the Parcel of English?

Ask students to suggest what things they could put in the parcel. Make a list on the board under the three headings – 'Our class', 'Our school', 'Our town'. If possible, suggest to the students that they may want to send audio cassettes. Let them suggest what they could include (dialogues, poems, stories, jokes, music, parts of radio programmes, etc.).

Alternatively, you could put a big piece of paper on the wall and write their suggestions on it as a reminder for them to start collecting things over the next few weeks about their town and school to put in the *Parcel of English*. Decide with the students when they think you should send the parcel, where you should keep the things to put in the parcel, and how long you should spend on the parcel.

Ideas:
Our class: a plan of the class and names of the students in each place; a picture of a view from the window; pictures of games they play, comics, well-known children's cartoon characters, etc. **Our school**: a plan of the school; names of the classes and of the teachers; photographs of important things in the school, paintings, displays, etc. **Our town**: maps, plans, postcards; bus timetables; restaurant menus; local newspaper advertisements for events; recipes of local dishes.

4 A picture and description of me

Pupils work alone for this part of the activity to write a short description of themselves. Remind them it must fit onto the small piece of paper! Go round giving help where necessary. Students can exchange papers with a partner for checking. Give out to pupils a small (10 × 10cm) piece of paper to write out the final version of their description. Stick six of these onto a piece of A4 paper.

5 What can you write?

AtoZ READING, WRITING AND GROUPWORK

Point out to the students that there are four sections to the *Parcel of English* (a–d, as given in the Student's Book). Allocate a different section to each group of students. Each group can then read the example text about their topic. Go round and give help where necessary, but encourage them to guess words and help each other.

6 Making your parcel

AtoZ MONITORING AND GUIDING

Students decide what they are going to write about in their paragraph. Everyone shares ideas but *everyone must write* an individual piece, so each student's work should have slightly different information on it. Go round giving help where necessary.

Students can then put their work and pictures/maps, etc. onto pieces of paper. If there is time, they can write more about their pictures, draw more pictures or write/draw about another subject.

Remind students to bring in more things for the *Parcel of English* if they have any.

IF YOU HAVE DONE *CES 1* ...

If you used *CES 1*, you may be in one of the following situations with regard to the *Parcel of English*.

If you started a Parcel of English with a school last year and it is going well

Excellent! You may want to look at the notes below for other ideas to improve contact this year. If you are using *CES* with another class this year, you can either ask your corresponding school to link you up with a suitable class in their school; or fill in the registration form inside the book or on the inside front cover to begin another link-up; or send work from both classes in the same parcel. See the notes below for further ideas.

If you started a Parcel of English contact last year but your corresponding school did not reply

If you would like to try again, please fill in the registration form at the front of this book and Cambridge University Press will link you up with a different school. Once you have received the name and address of a school, write to the teacher saying that you will be sending a parcel and asking for confirmation. See the example letter on page 143.

If you did not make a link with another school with the Parcel of English last year and cannot do so this year

Whether your reasons are financial or practical, it is still possible to provide a wider audience for the students' work by displaying their writing and activities on the classroom or corridor walls, or by producing a class scrapbook of students' work. (See **AtoZ** DISPLAYING STUDENTS' WORK.)

SOME QUESTIONS AND ANSWERS ABOUT THE PARCEL OF ENGLISH

If you are unsure how to organise your *Parcel of English* or have experienced or can foresee difficulties, the following answers may help.

Q: *'What shall I do once I have registered?'*

Start work on your first *Parcel of English*! As soon as you receive details of your 'twin' class in a different country, write to the teacher of that class to make contact and confirm that you are linked together. Ask for a reply. Send your *Parcel of English* once you have received an acknowledgement from your 'twin' class. Here is an example of a letter of acknowledgement.

Your FULL ADDRESS
in BLOCK CAPITALS
Telephone/Fax/e-mail
date

Dear …

Cambridge 'Parcel of English' scheme

I have just received details of your class and school from Cambridge University Press. My class is now preparing a Parcel of English to send to you. We hope to have the parcel ready to send to you by about (date).

Please write back to me and confirm that you have received your 'twin' information from Cambridge and let me know when you expect to send a Parcel to us.

With many thanks and best wishes

(signed)
(Print your name in block capitals)

Q: *'It's too expensive. Our school doesn't have much money. How can we send a Parcel of English?'*

If there are financial reasons for not sending the *Parcel of English*, some of these ideas may be useful:

- Stationery: perhaps students could bring in paper, glue and other stationery from home.
- Stamps: perhaps each student could bring in a small stamp.
- Lighten the load: perhaps the parcel could be made lighter by photocopying on both sides of the paper, writing on airmail paper, or by photocopying the photographs instead of sending the originals.
- Fund-raising: many schools in the UK now have fêtes, fairs and concerts to raise money for materials and computers. The children (and parents) make cakes and sell them at fairs to raise money. Perhaps your school could have an 'English evening' where students sing English songs, read some poems in English, or tell stories. Parents and visitors could pay a small amount for a ticket.
- Sponsorship: some local companies may pay for the cost of the postage if you include some of their advertising material in the parcel.
- Ask the students for ideas!

Q: *'The postal system is unreliable. How can we send a Parcel of English?'*

If there are problems with the postal service in your area or country you could possibly:

- Send two copies of the parcel.
- Send a postcard first to say that you are about to send the parcel.
- Send a reduced version of the parcel by fax (if the school has a fax, it should be on the registration information that you receive from Cambridge).
- Send the parcel by computer on electronic mail if you have access to this. (Universities frequently have e-mail connections to other universities worldwide. A friendly person in your local university may be able to help!)
- Use registered or special delivery.
- Investigate other (private) postal systems.
- If there is a Cambridge University Press office in your country, you could ask for their suggestions. They may have ideas about how your parcel can be sent.

Q: *'My class is very weak! I am embarrassed about the quality of their work. What can I do?'*

The standard of students' work varies enormously for a wide variety of reasons: some students start studying English at eight years old, some at 11 or 12 years old; some students have two lessons a week, some have six or more lessons a week. For some students English is their third or even fourth language, for others it may be their second; some students have extra English lessons after school; some have a native speaker assistant in the school; some students are in very small classes. All these factors play a role in the 'standard' of students' work in English. However, for the *Parcel of English* the standard of the English is not the most important factor. For the students, the excitement and the benefit of the parcel is in having contact with another school and learning about the way of life in another country. The students will be more interested in sharing real communication by discovering the similarities and differences in their lives, homes, school and hobbies than in analysing the quality of the English. Do not feel embarrassed about the quality of your students' work. It is probably not as low as you think it is! Some other ideas are:

- Include in the parcel a lot of 'real' material from your town and school: maps, pictures, timetables, postcards, photographs, bus tickets, sweets or sweet wrappers, advertisements, menus from restaurants, cinema tickets, bus and train timetables, the front page of the local paper, a copy of a school magazine, etc.
- Encourage the students to include their own drawings and pictures cut out from magazines.
- Persuade students to include the piece of work that they enjoyed doing most.
- Encourage the students to draft their writing and to correct it themselves in a group (with a little help from you), before rewriting it.
- Don't put too much emphasis on 'perfection', or the weaker students will be discouraged.
- The *Parcel of English* from a class is more than the sum of its individual parts!

Q: *'How often should I send it?'*

This will obviously depend on how many lessons each week you have with your class. However, it may be a good idea to negotiate with the students about:

- What should go in the parcel. Let the student decide if they want to include a certain piece of work in the next parcel. If they do, they can leave it in a box or drawer called *'The Parcel of English'* until it seems there is enough variety of material to send.
- How often you should send it.
- Who is to arrange it. Let the students decide who is going to help you do any photocopying, tape recording, wrapping up, etc.
- You don't need to wait to receive a parcel before you send your next one (particularly where the postal services are slow).

Q: *'I've got many different classes using* CES. *How can I do the Parcel of English activity?'*

- The easiest way would be to exchange material between the classes. Decide which classes are to be linked and exchange pieces of work as a parcel.
- The other way would be to send one *Parcel of English* which contains work from different classes to another school through the Cambridge registration system.
- Enclose a letter in the parcel which explains which classes are sending work, and the parcel which is returned can belong to all your classes.

Q: *'I haven't got much class time, so what can I put in a Parcel of English?'*

Here are some ideas so that you can collect *Parcel of English* material as part of your normal teaching:

- The *Activity* Units are ideal for producing material for a *Parcel of English*.
- At the end of each *Culture matters* Unit there is an exercise called 'Across cultures'. You can include the students' work from this exercise.
- Students can send each other exercises and puzzles which they have written for the class *Exercise Box*.
- The tests which the students write in Units 12, 22 and 32 can form part of the parcel.
- You can record and include the students' conversations from 'Out and about' exercises in the *Language focus* Units.
- Part of the homework exercises each week or two weeks can be set aside for *Parcel of English* work.
- Set aside 15 minutes every two weeks to prepare *Parcel of English* work.
- Add work on the *Parcel of English* to the choices in the 'Decide …' exercises (*Topic* Units), 'Do it yourself!' (*Language focus* Units) and 'Time to spare?' sections (*Topic* and *Language focus* Units).
- Students may want to include an audio (or video) cassette of their 'talents'. Some may play a musical instrument, sing some songs, tell some jokes, read some poetry, or record part of a radio or television programme which would be interesting for children in another school or country.
- It is always interesting to see school textbooks on History, Geography, Science and Maths from other schools and countries. Students may want to include some pages of their other subject textbooks in the parcel.
- If the school or any of the children have a video camera, some of them may like to make a short video recording of a lesson, a sports match, 'a day in the life of a student', a local festival, or a famous building or site in the region. (You will need to check whether your TVs run on the same system as the link country, e.g. PAL, SECAM, NHTSC.)
- Some children may want to write recipes for their favourite meals, or explain traditional dishes.

Q: *'What shall I do with the Parcel of English when it arrives?'*

The most important thing to do first is to write back to the teacher and class that sent it and *let them know that it has arrived.*

Your students will be looking forward to the arrival of the *Parcel of English* from the other school, especially if it is in a different country about which they know very little.

- To avoid over-excitement and frustration in the lesson, open the parcel and look at the contents *before* the lesson so you can see if you need to take in a tape recorder (if there are cassettes to listen to, for example). You could reseal the parcel and open it again in class.
- In order for the whole class to look at the material in the *Parcel of English*, it may be better to divide the class into groups and ask each group to look at one part of the contents.
- While they are looking at the contents, go round and ask each group how they will respond to their part. They may have already done some work which they want to send. Some may want to write to individual students in the other class, others may want to answer questions asked in the parcel.
- The parcel may contain exercises and puzzles for your class Exercise Box. Some students may want to try these out and send the answers in your next parcel.

Q: *'I think that it will take a lot of time. How useful is it really?'*

Much of the work that you and the students are doing in class can be included in the *Parcel of English* without doing any extra work. The *Parcel of English* adds an extra dimension to your course, the value of which is immense in terms of motivation, making English 'real', developing cross-cultural awareness, fostering friendships, peace education and more. Read through the notes on the *Parcel of English* to get an idea of what benefits it can bring.

Q: *'I don't think my students are very interested in the idea of the Parcel of English. What can I do?'*

The key to a keen class is undoubtedly a keen teacher! If you can present the *Parcel of English* as an exciting thing to do, you will undoubtedly fire the students' imagination and energy. Some ideas:

- Start by making sure that the students know what the *Parcel of English* contains, and how it works.
- Ask students what they know about other countries in the world and/or other regions or towns in their country.
- Explain that the *Parcel of English* draws on the different talents of each student in the class. It is not expected that all the students will include the same things in the *Parcel of English*; they can be encouraged to choose what they would like to send.
- Some students may be reluctant to write very much, but they may be very good at finding pictures and postcards or drawings: others may prefer to send a cassette recording of a letter or story, if they prefer to speak.
- Some students may prefer to write to one of the other students in a corresponding school on an individual 'pen-pal' basis.
- Talk about what they will be able to do with their English. Many pupils do not realise how *international* English is. The fact that they will be able to communicate with pupils in another country through English will open new worlds to them.

LINKING TEACHERS TO TEACHERS

In addition to the value of your students learning from and about students in another school or country, you may also find it worthwhile to use the *Parcel of English* as a means of sharing your teacher experiences and reactions with another teacher. Some regions have Teachers' Centres where teachers can discuss new methods or teaching issues with others, but many teachers can be very isolated in their subject and their school. The *Parcel of English* can offer an opportunity to discuss professional issues with another teacher in the same position as you.

- Start by including in the parcel a letter in English from you to the other teacher. This will give you a chance to use 'adult, communicative English' as a change from the classroom English you use every day.
- Give information about yourself, your students, your school and your region.

- You could share your ideas and reactions to the 'Researching the classroom' section. You could describe how you approach grammar, pronunciation, errors and fluency with your students.
- From the 'What happened in Units …' sections, you may want to describe some successful lessons and say why they went well; and some not-so-successful lessons, and why you think they did not work.
- You can describe the differences between different groups and the different outcomes of the activities and *Open plan* sections.
- You may be able to share videos of different lessons. (You will need to check first whether your TVs run on the same system, e.g. PAL, SECAM, NHTSC.)

Supplementary Unit B Making an Exercise Box

> **Note**
> If you have done *CES 1*, please see the sections 'If you have made an *Exercise Box* before ...' and 'If you have made one before, but ...' below.

OVERVIEW OF MAKING AN EXERCISE BOX

An *Exercise Box* is a box into which students can put exercises which they themselves have designed. These can be used by other students, when they have **AtoZ TIME TO SPARE**, for **HOMEWORK**, when they are doing a **DECIDE** exercise, or at any other time, or included in a *Parcel of English*. There are a number of reasons for getting students to design their own exercises. Firstly, in working on the design of exercises for each other, students are brought into close contact with the workings of English, vocabulary items, spellings and language use. Secondly, it provides a basis for *genuine language use* in the context of a classroom – learning English is, after all, the main reason why they are there. Thirdly, it develops the students'

sense of **AtoZ AUTONOMY** by showing them how they can learn English without the direct support and supervision of the teacher. Lastly, the degree of **AtoZ STUDENT INVOLVEMENT** which the *Exercise Box* provides can be a significant source of motivation.

In order to get the full benefit of the *Exercise Box*, it is recommended that you do this Supplementary Unit as soon as possible after Unit 1. This aims to start the students off with the *Exercise Box*. It draws on some of the exercise types listed in the *Ideas list* (page 150 in the Student's Book). Once the *Exercise Box* is established, students can contribute to and take exercises from the box throughout their course.

1 IF YOU HAVE NOT MADE AN EXERCISE BOX BEFORE WITH YOUR CLASS

Below are guidelines on the use of Supplementary Unit B in the Student's Book.

Timing
Supplementary Unit B is intended as one lesson.

1	Types of exercises	5
2	Make an exercise	20
3	Take an exercise	5
4	The *Ideas list*	10

What you need
A small cardboard box and some cards for making divisions in the box, or some folders.

Guidelines

1 Types of exercises
AtoZ IDEAS LIST
Explain first to the students what they will be doing. They will be writing exercises on separate sheets of paper. They will then put the answers on the back and put them

in the box. Other students will then be able to take out an exercise and do it in other lessons for revision, or for homework.

Get the students to look at the *Ideas list* and discuss with them what they think it is for. Give them a few minutes to find the examples in the Unit and then to see if they can do them.

2 Make an exercise
AtoZ GROUPWORK and MONITORING AND GUIDING
Before the students move into groups, check that they know what they will be doing: some will be writing a mixed-up sentence exercise, some will be writing a word-halves exercise, and some may prefer to write another kind of exercise.

As the students finish writing their exercises, they can put them into the box (NOTE: You will need to ensure that they are correct before they go into the box!) Some students will finish before others. In this case, they can work to produce another exercise of a different type.

3 Take an exercise
Remind them not to write on the paper! They can check their answers on the back.

4 The Ideas list

Once the students have exchanged exercises and have done them, you can spend some time looking through the *Ideas list* with them. Discuss with them what exercises they could make for the Units which they have done. They may also be able to suggest more ideas for exercises.

You may like to set a homework task of writing another exercise or two.

See also section 2 below for further ideas.

2 IF YOU HAVE MADE AN EXERCISE BOX BEFORE AND ARE CURRENTLY USING IT WITH YOUR CLASS

If you have been using an *Exercise Box* with your class from *CES 1* you may like to think of ways in which you can develop and diversify the students' use of it. It is important to keep the idea 'fresh' by developing it in different ways, so that the students feel a sense of progression. Some ideas are:

- Have a cassette player and a set of headphones available. If possible, you could also have a junction box which allows two or more sets of headphones to be connected. Students can then listen to the Class Cassette or the Workbook Cassette.
- Students may like to bring in songs on cassettes. Ask them to write out the words and make some exercises to do with the song.
- You could also exchange your *Exercise Box* with another class, perhaps in another school.

- Exercises from your *Exercise Box* can be included in a *Parcel of English*.
- Students can bring in short texts or stories which they have read. They can write their comments about them or make some exercises.
- Students can design various questionnaires which can be left in the *Exercise Box* and which all the students can answer over the next few weeks.
- Students can start stories which other students have to add to. The stories can be read out to the class at an agreed date.
- Students can design various puzzles to put in the box. They can also draw some 'Describe and draw' cards. (Working in pairs, one student has to describe what is on the card, while the other student draws it. They then compare to see how well the person drawing has understood, and how well the person describing has explained.)

3 IF YOU HAVE MADE ONE BEFORE, BUT HAVE DISCONTINUED USING IT WITH YOUR CLASS

If you have attempted to use an *Exercise Box* before but have dropped it, you might like to consider trying again with Level 2. It is important first, however, to think about *why* you dropped it, so that it may be more successful this time. The following notes may be useful.

1 There isn't enough time to use the Exercise Box. The students work very slowly

If your course makes it difficult for you to allocate class time to the *Exercise Box*, there are a number of things that you can do. After doing Supplementary B with the students, you can ask them to make an exercise and do one from the Box as part of their homework. You do not need to supervise the student's attempt at *producing* the exercises, only the exercises which they actually submit to the box. You can therefore delegate responsibility to the students (perhaps in groups) to add so many new exercises to the box by the end of the week/month, etc. or to a deadline agreed with the students.

You can also integrate the *Exercise Box* into your course, so that it forms part of the written work that the students do, perhaps also part of the assessed work.

2 My students' work is not of a high enough standard. Everything they do is full of errors

This is likely to be the case when the students are just starting with the *Exercise Box*. There are two main factors to consider here. Firstly, the value of the *Exercise Box* lies not so much in the language which students produce (although this is indeed important) but more in the involvement, responsibility and sense of autonomy which it gives them. This is likely to give more long-term, enduring benefits than an insistence on getting things 100% right all the time. Secondly, new ideas take time to be absorbed. For most students (and perhaps many teachers) the idea of writing an exercise will be completely new. Once they have seen what can be done and have had feedback from you, the teacher, you can expect a gradual improvement in the quality of their work.

That said, if the student's work is consistently full of errors such that it makes it difficult to work with, you could consider limiting the students to particular exercise types. The exercises in the *Ideas list* are arranged in approximate order of complexity. You could limit the students to the first few exercises at first such as matching, gapped texts, scrambled words and sentences. You should also insist that the students produce tidy, legible work which respects the proposed readers.

3   It's too difficult to organise in the classroom

If it is difficult to organise during class time, you can set writing as an exercise for homework. You can collect in the exercises in the next lesson, check them and distribute them on a sheet as homework next time. In this way, the students' homework will truly be *their* homework.

If it is difficult to use a box, exercises can be kept in envelopes or folders. Particular students could be given responsibility for taking them back and forth to class, checking the contents, etc.

4   I can't see the value of the Exercise Box. What's the point?

As explained previously, the potential of the *Exercise Box* is enormous. Similar to the *Parcel of English*, the *Exercise Box* offers an extra dimension to your course, the value of which is immense in terms of motivation, making English 'real', developing the ability to learn autonomously and the depth of student involvement. The benefits can be felt in the short term by strengthening the students' confidence and ability in English and in the long term by fostering the development of wider educational abilities. See **A to Z** **EXERCISE BOX**, **AUTONOMY** and **STUDENT INVOLVEMENT**.

5   My students don't see its value. They think it's boring

Once again, the key to a keen class is undoubtedly a keen teacher! If you can present the *Exercise Box* as an exciting thing to do, you will undoubtedly fire the students' imagination and energy. Don't, however, force the *Exercise Box* on them. Explain what it's for and try to find out what they think about it. It may be that they have not fully understood what they are expected to do. If possible, see if you can get some exercises that another class has designed – your class may like to make some exercises in return.

6   It's too much hard work! I have to correct everything

See the notes above. It is undoubtedly true that, initially, the *Exercise Box* requires teachers to monitor things carefully and check that the exercises that are made available to other students are relatively correct in their design. Much of this work, however, can be done during normal classroom time. Thus, instead of the students writing out a gap-filling exercise or answering comprehension questions, they can be designing their exercises, with the teacher circulating around the class, checking work as usual. If you a) ensure that students choose exercise types from the *Ideas list* which are appropriate to their level of ability, and b) insist that they check their work and produce neat, legible exercises, the teething troubles of the *Exercise Box* should resolve themselves over time.

Notes on the Workbook and Workbook answers

1 USING THE WORKBOOK

The Student's Workbook and cassette provide supplementary exercises for the work covered in the Student's Book. The unit numbers correspond to the units in the Student's Book. The contents of the Workbook units are summarised at the beginning of each set of unit notes in this Teacher's Book, and cross-references are given with each exercise. (The symbol • **WB Ex.** shows the relevant Workbook exercise number.)

As it is often difficult to do listening tasks thoroughly and clearly in class, there is a cassette with the Workbook. The cassette contains listening tasks for comprehension, interactive dialogues in which the students respond to questions, additional pronunciation work, and all the songs. The cassette is strongly recommended, although all the exercises can be done without the cassette – except the *Say it clearly!* exercises (*Topic* and *Language focus* Units) and Unit 16.

The Workbook may be used in class or set for homework. For this, we anticipate that students will spend about half an hour on their homework after an English lesson. If the Workbook is set for homework it is important that it receives some attention during class time. If you vary the way this is done, you can help to sustain the students' commitment to homework. (See also AtoZ HOMEWORK.)

There are a number of possible ways you can do this:

- before you set Workbook exercises for homework, explain clearly what the students have to do in each one. Write on the blackboard which exercises they are to do;
- after they have done the exercises, go through the answers with the whole class;
- collect in the Workbooks periodically to check;
- allow small groups of students to go through their answers together. During this time you can circulate around the class, helping out and checking;
- provide an 'answer sheet' for students to check their own answers (this can be circulated around the class while they are doing some other activity, pinned up on the board for students to check after the lesson, or written on the blackboard);
- get students to exchange books while you read out answers;
- encourage students to do the Workbook exercises together with another student;
- get them to record their answers to some exercises (interactive dialogues from the Workbook, for example, could be re-recorded by two pupils together).

2 SPECIAL NOTE ON THE 'HELP YOURSELF!' UNITS

There are six *Help yourself!* Units in the Workbook which cover the areas of Vocabulary (Unit 6), Writing (Unit 11), Pronunciation (Unit 16), Grammar (Unit 21), Dictionary work (Unit 26), and Fluency (Unit 31).

These are intended to give students practical ideas for learning English. The four units on Grammar, Vocabulary, Pronunciation and Fluency present the ideas given in the Workbook in *CES* Level 1, and include some further techniques. The two units on Writing and Dictionary work present new techniques to help the students.

The units have no 'right or wrong' answers which you can check, since they are designed to be of direct use to the students in *how* they approach their learning and to

support the general movement towards autonomy. The ideas presented are *suggestions* – whether or not students continue to use them will depend to a large extent on personal preference. However, students cannot make real decisions about how they learn unless they have experience to base it on; the units are designed to give students that experience.

Although the units are intended for the students to use alone, it is important, nevertheless, that they receive some attention in class. The units are rather unusual in a number of ways, so before the students do one of these units it is best if you go through (perhaps in the mother tongue) what the unit is for and what they have to do. Additionally, you could:

- discuss before they do a unit how they usually go about learning vocabulary, grammar, etc. (for example, in preparation for a test). Secondary-aged students *do* have ways that they use to learn, although they may not be as efficient as they could be.
- ask, if they have used Level 1, if they can remember any of the techniques for learning vocabulary/pronunciation/grammar/fluency presented in the Level 1 Workbook.
- discuss, after they have done a unit, what they thought about each of the ideas. If they haven't done them, discuss why.
- set a test on a language area. They can then prepare for the test using the techniques. (For example, you could give a list of words to learn, a grammar area to revise, or some social situations to prepare for.) In this way, the students may see directly how the ideas in the *Help yourself!* Units may help them.

Unit 6: *Help yourself with vocabulary*
This unit presents two techniques from Level 1 and one new idea for practising vocabulary. Exercise 1 shows students how they can make a 'word bag' of English words and their meanings, and then test themselves. Exercise 2 shows how they can make their own gap-filling exercises. Exercise 3 gives them a new idea to help learn new words by 'playing' with them to make a crossword. There are many different ideas similar to crosswords (for example, a word box, jumbled words – see the *Ideas list* in the Student's Book). Playing with words in this way helps to root them in the memory through stress-free involvement. (See also AtoZ **VOCABULARY**.)

Unit 11: *Help yourself with writing*
The two exercises in this unit are new to Level 2. Many students lack confidence in writing both in their mother tongue and English, and time spent on writing in the classroom can often be too short to experiment with different ways of increasing confidence. The writing techniques in this unit are designed to help the students develop their own approach to writing. Exercise 1 shows students two basic approaches to writing with which they can experiment: fluent writing and planned writing. Exercise 2 asks students to make a checklist of their mistakes so that they may check their work in future. (See also AtoZ **WRITING**.)

Unit 16: *Help yourself with pronunciation*
Practising pronunciation, intonation and stress in class often presents difficulties. There may be insufficient time to hear everyone, students get bored waiting for their turn, others may feel shy or embarrassed, and so on. Workbook Unit 16 presents four ways for students to practise their pronunciation at home. Exercise 1 is a 'backchaining' exercise in which the students listen and repeat, looking in a mirror as they speak. Exercises 2 and

3 introduce students to the idea of 'stress' in a sentence. Exercise 2 asks them to bang (lightly!) on the table when they hear the stressed syllable in the sentence. Exercise 3 asks them to find important words in a dialogue which need to be stressed. Exercise 4 is similar to an exercise in Unit 31 where students are asked to role play with themselves. (See also AtoZ **PRONUNCIATION**.)

Unit 21: *Help yourself with grammar*
This unit gives students three ways in which they can get extra practice with grammar. Exercise 1 is a 'cut and mix' exercise that requires students to make their own scrambled sentences to practise new structures. Exercise 2 requires the students to break a sentence down into its parts and make their own pattern to practise with it. This gives students practice not only with different sentence structures, but also in metalanguage – the language which we use to describe language. Exercise 3 gives students a chance to 'play' with a basic sentence by making changes to its form and meaning. They can make a sentence negative, interrogative, past or future, or singular or plural. (See also AtoZ **DEDUCTIVE** and **INDUCTIVE GRAMMAR**.)

Unit 26: *Help yourself with a dictionary*
The three exercises in this unit are all new to Level 2. Students are shown the hidden advantages of a bilingual dictionary. Exercise 1 familiarises students with the overall contents of their dictionaries. Exercise 2 focuses closely on the information given by each dictionary entry and asks them to use their dictionaries to check the entries for different words. Exercise 3 encourages students to use both halves of the bilingual dictionary to double check words which may have more than one meaning in either language.

Unit 31: *Help yourself with fluency*
In many classes, it is often difficult to ensure that there is enough time for all students to speak at length. Some studies have shown that in classes of 30 students with three hours of English a week, the total speaking time of an individual student may be as little as 50 minutes in a complete year. It is very difficult to build up confidence and fluency in such a small amount of time. The techniques presented here therefore show ways students can get more practice in speaking fluently outside the class. Exercise 1 is similar to the word bag idea in Unit 6, but uses complete phrases. In Exercise 2 students talk to themselves on the cassette by recording some questions. Exercise 3 asks students to role play with themselves. They can be encouraged to use props like hats or coats to help characterisation and give the exercise more fun. Most students like songs and music and Exercise 4 suggests that they make up some new English words for a song they know. Exercise 5 ask students to work with a friend to think of a situation and make up a dialogue together. (See also AtoZ **FLUENCY**.)

3 WORKBOOK ANSWERS

Unit 1 Welcome back!

1 a Maria b Vincent c Rick d Sujita

2 The world of people and places: This is Sydney. They speak *English* there. Many people think Sydney is the capital of *Australia*, but it isn't. The capital is *Canberra*. Sydney is a very beautiful city. Sydney is in the South-*East* of the country. It has a population of about *three and a half* million.

The world of science: This is our solar system. It has *nine* planets. The hottest planet is *Mercury*. The coldest planet is *Pluto*. The *Sun* is at the centre of our solar system. Our sun is a star. As far as we know, our sun is the only star that has *planets*.

The world of history: Today, there are *seven* continents in the world. They are called: *Europe, Asia, Africa, Australia*, North *America*, South *America* and *Antarctica*. Millions of years ago there was only *one* continent. We call it *Pangaea*.

The world of nature: There are five important types of animals. They are called *Mammals, Reptiles, Birds, Fishes*, and *Insects*. Mammals have *warm* blood and they give *milk* to their babies. Reptiles have *cold* blood and they lay eggs. *Insects* have got six legs. Many of them can *fly*. *Birds* also lay eggs but they have *feathers*. The last type of animal is *fish*. Their blood is *cold* and they live in *water*.

4

```
G H T G J I K I O P W E Q S F H G F G F
R H E Y G A H Y E H G A (A S I A) L F J A
A E T F A M K L B C Q W E S F A R O U N
V T F X (M E X I C O) M H N U T F E Q R I
I J (W A S H I N G T O N) T Q I D P R P M
T T H E R U D T R S T Y A J H S B I E A
Y K I O L P L K M N H B G V F C S S F L
(E X P A N D S) F T G Y H U J I K O E P S
H J U H Y A (M A M M A L) L E R T U I O U
F G T R F D E W S E D R F T (C H I N A) C
```

Unit 2 Extension The world encyclopaedia

1 Example: Words that describe the picture:
cold, snowy, empty, horrible, (windy), (beautiful), icy.
Words that don't describe the picture: (interesting), wet, exciting, (boring), tall, friendly, happy, hot, (nice), (dry), rainy, sunny, (ugly).

3 Examples: b Possible. Amundsen-Scott has got libraries, cinemas and shops. c Impossible! Amundsen-Scott doesn't have any schools or teachers. d Possible! Amundsen-Scott has got sports rooms. e Possible! Amundsen-Scott has got telephones. f Impossible! Amundsen-Scott hasn't got any trees or flowers.
g Impossible! There aren't any cars or buses.
h Impossible! Amundsen-Scott is one of the driest places in the world.

4 She is thinking of a whale.

5 1 eight 2 mammals 3 an animal 4 fish, seals, and penguins 5 150 kph 6 three weeks

6.2 1 Where does the Venus flytrap grow?
2 What do the leaves look like?/ How do the leaves look?
3 What is inside the leaves?
4 What do Venus flytraps eat?
5 Why do they eat meat?

7 Language is very important for *us*. With language, *we* can talk about different things. *We* can talk about the past, the present and the future. *We* are the only animals that have a language. Other animals can communicate but *they* can only say the same things. For example, a young bird can tell *its* mother when *it* is hungry. Monkeys make noises when *they* are in danger. *We* can't understand *them* but other monkeys know what the noises mean.

8 Examples: 2 It's a space ship! It's coming down! It's coming down on the top of Maxi Stores! 3 There's a door. There's a small door on the side of the spaceship. It's opening! It's opening! 4 I can see a head. It's looking out. 5 What! Its head and arms are coming out! 6 Oh, no! It's pulling me up to the spaceship! Oh, no! Oh, no! 7 The spaceship is leaving! 8 We're disappearing into space.

9 Starlight is faster/longer/heavier/newer/stronger/more expensive than Skywalker.

10 b Wrong. It is the hottest planet because it is very close to the sun. c Wrong. A year on Mercury is shorter than a year on Earth. d Wrong. Pluto is the smallest planet. e Wrong. The Sun is much bigger than the moon. f Wrong. We don't know if there is life on Mars. g Wrong. The first person on the moon was a man (Neil Armstrong). h True. (Valentina Tereshkova in 1963.)

Theme A

Unit 3 Sports for everybody

1 1 Monday 2 Friday 3 Saturday 4 Wednesday 5 Sunday

2

4 a 1 b 3 c 6 d 5

Unit 4 Language focus

1 1–d 2–a 3–b 4–c

4 Examples: He walks very slowly.   He drives dangerously. She runs fast.   He walks very quietly.   She works very hard.   She is shouting loudly.   He works very happily.

```
L           Q
O U         U H S       F
U H         I A L       A
D A N G E R O U S L Y
L P         T D W       T
Y P         L   L       L
  I         Y   Y       Y
  L
  Y
```

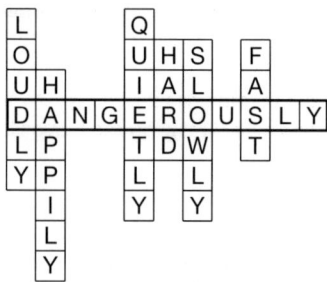

5 Examples: **a** Can I have a pen, please? Can I use your pen, please? **b** Sorry, I can't find the page. **c** Sorry, I can't hear. Can you say that again, please? **d** Can I have some more time, please? **e** Can you check this/Can you look at this, please?

Unit 7   Test yourself

1 Examples: Basketball is a very good sport for your health. It makes your body strong (√√√) and flexible (√√). Anybody can play basketball, but you need a net and a ball. You also need a lot of energy to do it (energy level: 3).

2 Examples: **1** What subjects do you study/do? **2** What time do you start school? What time do you finish school/get home from school? **3** Do you have your lunch at school? **4** Do you wear a uniform? What colour is your uniform? **5** What activities do you do after school? **6** How many students are there in your class?

3 7.30a.m. Bill gets up. 8.00a.m. He leaves the house. 8.30a.m. He arrives at work. 8.30–1p.m. He works in a factory. 1p.m. He goes home for lunch. 1.30p.m. He arrives home. 4.30p.m. He goes back to work. 4.30p.m.–8.30p.m. He trains lions in the zoo. 8.45p.m. He works in a bed factory. 11p.m. He finishes work.

4 Examples: **a** He likes cycling. **b** They love ski-ing. **c** They hate going to school. **d** He hates/doesn't like washing up. **e** She hates/doesn't like going to bed. **f** They like playing with the computer.

A picture dictionary (1)

Body: head, heart, lungs, hand, arm, blood, muscle, leg, foot/feet. Verbs: breathe, win, improve. Adjectives: strong, excellent, light. Adverbs: slowly, dangerously, happily, quietly, suddenly.

Theme B

Unit 8   Topic   In a rainforest

1 Reptile, fruit, rice, world, rubber, medicine, rain, plant, insect, forest.

2 DANGER IN THE RAINFOREST!
The rainforests are very *important* for us but they are in danger. Many animals and plants are also in danger. Look:
1 Some people *chop down* the trees. They sell the wood or *plant* things like rice.
2 Other *people* chop down the trees to start farms. They can get *a lot* of money from meat.

3 When it rains, there is a big *problem*. The rain falls but there aren't *any* trees to catch it. The water takes the soil into the *rivers*.
4 Because there aren't any trees, the rainwater does not make *clouds* again. The rivers become bigger and bigger. Many plants and animals *die*.

5 **1** Between 1500 and 1800 the climate was dry or very cold. The rings are thin. **2** The weather was wet and good for trees. **3** Trees will have more thick rings.

Unit 9   Language focus

1 Mistakes: **1** Humans were not alive at the time of the dinosaurs. **2** Dinosaurs did not fly. **3** Dinosaurs were reptiles. They did not give milk to their young. **4** Dinosaurs did not live in lakes. **5** Dinosaurs did not sleep in the winter. There weren't any winters. **6** An Apatosaurus did not eat meat. **7** Horses didn't live at the same time as dinosaurs.

2 Millions of years ago, there *were* many types of dinosaurs on Earth. Some dinosaurs *were* meat-eaters and other dinosaurs *were* plant-eaters. The biggest meat-eating dinosaur *was* probably the Tyrannosaurus Rex. It *was* about as long as four cars and as tall as the tallest giraffe today. Its head *was* about 1.2 metres long. Its teeth *were* very sharp. Its legs *were* very big but it *was* too heavy to run for a long time. It killed other dinosaurs for food. The smallest dinosaur *was* also a meat-eater. It *was* the Compsognathus. It *was* only 50cm long. It walked on two legs and it had many sharp teeth.

3 **a** They died about 65 million years ago. **b** The first people appeared about 150,000 years ago. **c** They lived on the land. **d** They lived together. **e** They walked on two legs and four legs. **f** They discovered the first dinosaur bones in England. **g** Yes, Tyrannosaurus Rex killed smaller dinosaurs. **h** No, the Tyrannosaurus Rex looked very dangerous.

4 Scientists are not sure why the dinosaurs *disappeared*. Some scientists think that the climate *changed* suddenly. Fossils of trees tell us that the temperature *dropped* a lot and that the level of the sea *dropped* also. This means that it *was* suddenly much colder. Perhaps the dinosaurs *were* too slow to change with the climate.

A new idea is that a meteor *crashed* into the Earth. Scientists *discovered* a place in Mexico where they think the meteor *crashed*. They think that there *was* a lot of dust from the meteor. The dust *landed* on the plants. Many animals – including some dinosaurs – *were* plant-eaters and perhaps the dust *killed* them. This means that there *was* nothing for meat-eating dinosaurs to eat, and so they *died*. But, as many animals from that time didn't die, we are not 100% sure what really *happened*.

Unit 12   Revision   Under a volcano

1 **a** bird **b** medicine **c** roots **d** reptiles **e** insect **f** wet **g** clouds **h** dinosaurs **i** disappeared **j** meat **k** chop down **l** rice

3 **1** F **2** F **3** F **4** F

4.1 1 was 2 was 3 opened 4 started 5 hurried 6 were 7 was 8 was 9 lived 10 decided 11 moved 12 were 13 covered 14 stopped 15 was

4.2 1 market town 2 in their beds 3 and the dust 4 the town of Pompeii 5 walk down the roads 6 for the next time

A picture dictionary (2)

Picture: tree, leaf, plant, cloud, bird, insect, ground, roots, fruit, snake, flower, wood, rubber. Adjectives: dark, hot, wet, large. Verbs: died, played, crashed, stopped, discovered, walked, liked, climbed.

Theme C

Unit 13 Topic   Detectives of history

1.1
```
n  s  l  t  W H E E L  e  t  l  w
R A D I O  e  c  h  o  d  p  m  y
q  h  x  T E L E P H O N E  t
C O M P A S S  d  g  f  d  x  w
e  i  T O O L S  s  k  f  b  a  y
n  B O A T  g  h  a  z  j  o  l  s
g  z  k  d  G L A S S  s  r  e  C
i  k  b  P L A N E  n  g  y  s  A
n  h  y  o  u  r  y  k  n  l  a  m  R
e  h  y  s  m  n  b  l  k  a  u  t  w
v  c  s  k  j  C O M P U T E R
```

2.1 1 b 2 e 3 c 4 a 5 d

2.2 1 Yes, they went to other countries. 2 They ate corn. 3 They built pyramids. 4 They found jewellery and papyrus. 5 They were farmers and soldiers. 6 They discovered it in the pyramids.

3
1 The Egyptians bought stones for jewellery from different countries … so they probably travelled. But which countries did they visit?
2 The Egyptians put food in the pyramids … so they probably believed in a new life after death. But what other things did they believe in?
3 The Egyptians had writing … so they probably had documents. But what did they write with?
4 We know the land by the river Nile was very good … so they were probably farmers. But what food did they grow?

Unit 14 Language focus

1.1 1 b 2 d 3 f 4 a 5 e 6 c

1.2 1 went 2 went 3 went, fell 4 saw 5 took 6 found 7 came

2.1 Examples:
1 When did you find the scrolls?
2 Why did you go in the cave?
3 Where did find the scrolls?
4 How did you find them?
5 What did you see on the scrolls?

Unit 15 Fluency practice   An Iron-Age village

1 1 b 2 f 3 d 4 a 5 c 6 e

2 1 Three people. 2 Because he was sure that the pots were over 3,000 years old. 3 Because they lived on the water.

Unit 17 Test yourself

1 Things that we get from animals: cheese, leather, meat, milk, wool.
Types of animals: cats, dogs, cows, sheep.
Things from nature: ice, oil, snow.

1 snow 2 leather 3 wool 4 meat

2 Questions about the Iceman
1 I don't know. He didn't wear trousers!
2 I don't know. He didn't watch television!
3 I don't know. He didn't live in a house.
4 I don't know. He didn't speak English.
5 I don't know. He didn't eat sandwiches.

3 1 played 2 tried 3 touched 4 used 5 put 6 stopped 7 tried 8 watched 9 ate

4 2 Where did the Aztecs live? 3 Who was their sun god? 4 What did they do every day? 5 Why did they kill many people? 6 What did the Aztecs do? 7 What did the rich people wear?

A picture dictionary (3)

Timelines: 1825 The first train. 1840 The first bicycle. 1880 The first electric light bulb. 1893 The first car. 1900 The first plane. 1901 The first radio. 1926 The first television. 1950 The first electronic computer. 1961 The first person in space.

Verbs: discover, print, travel, invent, disappear. Nouns: wheel, crops, snow, boots, engine, map, steam, axe, farm. Past forms: saw, wore, made, went, drank, ate.

Theme D

Unit 18 Topic   Climates of the world

1 1 warm temperate 2 tropical 3 desert 4 monsoon 5 tundra 6 tropical 7 polar

2.1 Force 1: 5, Force 2: 4, Force 3: 2, Force 4: 7, Force 5: 11, Force 6: 3, Force 7: 8, Force 8: 6, Force 9: 9, Force 10: 1, Force 11: 12, Force 12: 10.

Unit 19 Language focus

1.1 a They're going to crash. b The cat is going to eat the dinner. c The plane is going to land. d The band is going to play. e They are going to have a picnic. f The bench is going to break. g She's going to buy a bicycle.

1.2 Plans: b, c, d, e, g. Certain to happen: a, f.

2 Examples: He has to … **1** wash the dishes and pans, **2** clean the floor, **3** wash the floor, **4** turn off the radio, **5** clean the oven, **6** clean the windows, **7** take the cat outside, **8** put everything away, **9** pay for the food, **10** wash his clothes.

Unit 20 Fluency practice   In the desert

1 Answers are at the end of the Unit.

2 **1** The climate changed. The rain did not come every year.
. **2** Goats ate the plants. **3** People cut down the trees.

Unit 22 Revision   The Tuareg people

1

1 2   3   4 5 6 7 8 9   10   11   12   13
firelephantomorrowetreesahelevelightemperatenoughurricanenvironmentropical

Answer: the letters spell TEMPERATURE

2 **1** She is going to take an examination.
2 They are going to wash the car.
3 They are going to swim.
4 He is going to fall over.

A picture dictionary (4)

Label the pictures: desert, cloud, sun, flood, fire, wind, snow, ice. Verbs: burn, protect, destroy, paint, cut down, rise. Nouns: vegetables, building, canal, river, heat. Adjectives: warm, heavy, dry, strong, light, wet.

Theme E

Unit 23 Topic   The global village

1.1 **2** Tree. All the other things are made from paper.
3 Wheat. All the other things are manufactured products.
4 Bag. All the other things are clothes.
5 Cheese. All the other things are agricultural products.
6 Guitar. All the other things are electronic/play music. They don't make it.
7 Sandwich. All the other things are drinks or liquids.
8 Bicycle. All the other things have engines.
9 Sugar. All the other things are metals.
10 Swimming. All the other sports use a ball.
11 Park. All the other places are where people work.

1.2

```
    R a d i o         s w i M m i n g
  b A g               s u g A r
    W h e a t         g u i T a r
                        c h E e s e
                          t R e e
              s a n d w I c h
                        p A r k
              b i c y c L e
```

The puzzle spells 'RAW MATERIAL'

Unit 24 Language focus

1 **1** Could you open the window, please?
2 Could you take me to town, please?
3 Could you carry some books, please?
4 Could you help me (with my homework), please?

2.1 1 c 2 e 3 b 4 a 5 d 6 f

2.2 Examples: **1** Would you like a cold drink? **2** Would you like some fruit/a banana? **3** Would you like a piece of cake?

1 Would you like to play football? **2** Would you like to go to the cinema? **3** Would you like to go for a bicycle ride?

3.1 **a** They aren't old enough. **b** I'm not clever enough. **c** Have you got enough money? **d** Is that enough food? **e** I haven't got enough petrol! **f** The ladder isn't long enough.

5.1 **a**: a newsagent's, **b**: a post office, **c**: a bank, **d**: a supermarket (trolley), **e**: a doctor's, **f**: a dentist's, **g**: a baker's, **h**: a grocer's, **i**: a cinema.

5.2 Example answers:
2 Yes. There's one in South Road, in front of the grocer's and one in North Road on the right of the cinema.
3 Yes, of course. It's in North Road, next to the traffic lights.
4 Yes. There's one in South Road, next to the supermarket, in front of the bank.
5 Yes, of course. It's in Smith Street, on the left of the traffic lights.
6 Yes, of course. There's one in Smith Street, next to the bank. There's another dentist's in Smith Street in front of the newsagent's.

Unit 25 Fluency practice Three regions in Britain

1 **1** The Highlands. **2** The Midlands. **3** The Midlands. **4** –.

Unit 26 Help yourself with a dictionary

2.2 bread – noun, in – preposition, speak – verb, make – verb, out – preposition, quickly – adverb.

2.3 get – got, sing – sang, wake – woke, drink – drank, hit – hit.

Unit 27 Test yourself

1 **1** Could you tell me the time, please?
2 Could you help me with this homework, please?
3 Could I use your dictionary, please?
4 Could I watch your new video tonight, please?
5 Could you lend me some money, please?

2 **1** Would you like an umbrella?
2 Would you like a hot drink?
3 Would you like to go to the cinema with me?
4 Would you like an ice-cream?
5 Would you like to use/play with my computer?

3 1 b 2 b 3 b 4 b 5 c

4

```
 1  I M P O R T
 2  M A D E
 3  I R O N
 4  R U B B E R
 5  F L O U R
 6  W A G E
 7  C O T T O N
 8 E X P O R T
 9  S U G A R
10 W I R E S
11 F O R E I G N E R
```

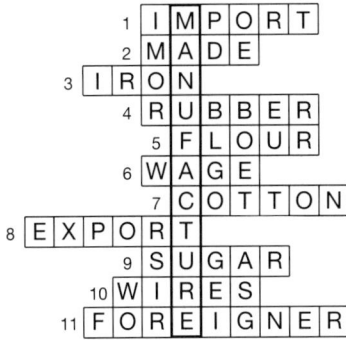

5.2   Address: Flat 26, Hendon House, Hill Road, Trenton.

A picture dictionary (5)

Label the pictures: Paper is made from wood. Books are made from paper. Cars are made from metal. Bread is made from flour. Clothes are made from cotton. Sweets are made from sugar. Nouns: iron, wheat, sugar, wages, rubber, cotton, leather. Adjectives: flat, dangerous, expensive, delicious, noisy.

Theme F

Unit 28   Topic   Blackout!

1

```
                  9
                  N      11
        1     4   E      E
      G     E     G 10   V
      E   3 L   6 7 A A  E
      N 2 R E 5 B L 8 T T R
      E L E C T R I C I T Y
      R I P T R O G A V R O
      A F E R O K H N E A N
      T T L I U E T A   C E
      O   C B   S D     T
      R   L     E A
          E
```

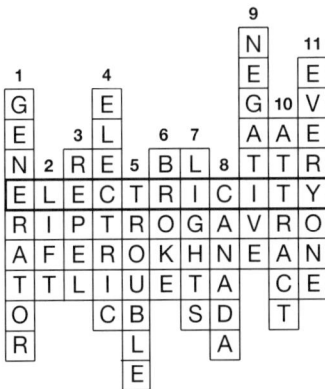

Unit 29   Language focus

1   The night was cold and dark. The bandits *were sitting* around the fire. They *were looking* into the flames and they *were thinking* about the next day. The wind *was blowing* gently. Somewhere in the distance, a wolf *was crying*. One bandit *was singing* softly. Another bandit *was cleaning* his gun. Suddenly, the leader of the bandits shouted:

'Pancho! Tell us a story.'

Pancho *was sleeping* but he woke up. He *was leaning* against a tree. He stood up and walked to the fire. He sat down next to where the leader *was sitting*. Everyone looked at him. He looked into their eyes and he told the following story. [repeated]

2   Example answers: **1a** She was eating a cake **1b** … when she found an insect. **2a** They were sleeping **2b** … when the tree came down. **3a** They were playing football **3b** … when the boy broke his leg. **4a** The burglar was climbing through a window **4b** … when the dog bit him. **5a** She was walking down the street … **5b** … when she met Steven. **6a** He was digging in the garden **6b** … when he found a Roman coin.

3   Examples: **a** Please close the gate, **b** Please put rubbish in here, **c** Press (for lift), **d** Please do not touch, **e** Please do not walk on the grass, **f** Please do not park here.

4   Example:
  2 Yes of course. You go straight down Wilson Road and take the first turning on the right. Cross the road and go down John Street. Turn left into North Road. The cinema is there on the corner.
  3 Yes, of course. You turn right here. That's Smith Street. Go straight on past the traffic lights. That's South Road. The supermarket is on the left, in front of the grocer's.
  4 Yes, go straight down here. Turn first right. That's Brown Lane. Turn left in South Road. Go straight down South Road. The post office is on the right in Smith Street, next to the traffic lights.
  5 Yes, of course. Go straight down South Road. The baker's is on the right, between Market Place and the traffic lights.
  6 Yes, go straight down the road, past the traffic lights. That's South Road. The grocer's is at the end, on the right, in front of the supermarket.

Unit 30   Fluency practice   Invent something!

1   Example answer: If the woman pulls the handle, the screen rises. The cat sees the mouse, and the mouse starts running. The wheel turns and pulls up some string. The string pulls up the spoon and lifts sugar from the bowl. The sugar drops into the drink.

Unit 32   Revision   Puzzle page – in the town

1   Some things that use electricity: a football stadium with large lights, street lights, traffic lights, an ice-cream machine, a computer, a lift, a clock, an electric bell, cars, a telephone, a television camera, a walkman, a microphone, an electric guitar, a TV camera.

2   The bicycle has only got one wheel. The dog has got two heads. The wings on the aeroplane are back to front. One person in the pop group doesn't have a guitar. There is a dinosaur in the park.

3   He is riding a bicycle. She is washing a car. He is in a park. He is reading a newspaper. They are in a park. They are playing football.

4   They were working in the factory. He was painting a shop door. She was writing a letter. They were eating. She was swimming.

A picture dictionary (6)

Label the picture: cables, transformer, underground cable, light, socket, plug, television. Nouns: hair, blackout, underground (UK)/subway (USA), prison, lift (UK)/elevator (USA), generator, comb. Verbs: turn, break down, land, break, fight, repel, jump, burn, attract.

Supplementary worksheets

This section includes 18 supplementary worksheets which you may photocopy for your classes. There are two types of worksheets.

LANGUAGE WORKSHEETS

The *Language worksheets* are intended to give extra support to those students who need further practice with the grammar areas presented in the *Language focus* Units. There are two worksheets for each *Language focus* Unit: one for each area of grammar covered. The worksheets have the same number as the *Language focus* Unit. For example, Worksheets 19.1 and 19.2 give extra practice in the two language areas presented in Unit 19. The worksheets can be done by students working alone, in pairs/groups, or for homework.

The *Language worksheets* are:

Ws. 2.1: Present simple and adjectives
Ws. 2.2: Present simple questions and pronouns
Ws. 2.3: Present continuous and comparatives
Ws. 4.1: 'special verbs' (verb '–ing')
Ws. 4.2: Adverbs
Ws. 9.1: 'was' and 'were'
Ws. 9.2: Past simple regular verbs
Ws. 14.1: Past simple irregular verbs
Ws. 14.2: Past simple questions and negatives
Ws. 19.1: 'going to'
Ws. 19.2: 'have to'
Ws. 24.1: 'could' and 'would' in requests and offers
Ws. 24.2: Asking the way (1)
Ws. 29.1: Past continuous
Ws. 29.2: Asking the way (2)

SAY IT CLEARLY! WORKSHEETS

The *Say it clearly! worksheets* give extra practice in pronunciation. They focus on the sounds and words which appear frequently in the *Topic* and *Language focus* Units and which appear in the *Say it clearly!* exercises in the Workbook. You can use these worksheets with the whole class, with individual students, or with a small group. You will need the Class Cassette and a cassette player.

The *Say it clearly! worksheets* are:

SIC Ws. 1: '–ing', '–ly/ily', /e/ and /ɑː/.
'–ed': /t/, /d/, /ɪd/.
SIC Ws. 2: /ɔː/ (saw), /eɪ/ (made) and /æ/ (had).
/iː/ (eat), /e/ (weather), and /h/.
SIC Ws. 3: /ə/ and /ʃ/, /ʌ/ and /ʊ/, /s/ and /tʃ/.

On the cassette, the recordings for each worksheet appear directly after the recordings for the relevant Units. For example, the recording for first half of the *Say it clearly!* worksheet 1 comes after the Unit 3 recording; the recording for the second part after the recording for Unit 4, and so on.

Language worksheet 2.1 *Present simple and adjectives*

Summary

You can use the **Present simple** to talk about facts and something that happens often. Remember the 's' with 'he', 'she' and 'it'!

I have homework every night. We eat lunch at school.
He come**s** to school on the bus but she walk**s** to school.

With the verbs 'have (got)', 'can' and 'be' you can put 'not' after the verb.

Peter hasn't got a car. He can't drive. He isn't old enough.

With other verbs, you use 'does not' or 'do not':

Andrew doesn't live in Engand. He lives in Italy.
Elephants don't eat meat. They eat fruit, leaves and grass.

Adjectives describe a noun. They do not change.
In English they go *before* the noun.

London is a big city. There are many interesting things there.

See also page 89 in your Workbook.

BRAZIL

Sao Paulo   Rio de Janeiro

1   Adjectives in sentences

Put the adjective in the correct place.

1 There are a lot of / books in the library. *interesting*   (interesting)

2 Be careful! There is a snake in the box. *dangerous*

3 Can I have a drink please? *cold*

4 There are two films at the cinema. *new*

5 Venice is a city. *beautiful*

6 Walk carefully on the floor! *wet*

7 That's a cat! *nice*

8 Pluto is a planet. *small*

2   Facts and figures

Write the correct form of the verb in the sentences.

come   live   boil   be   work   start   fall

1 There *are* seven continents.

2 Water .... at 100°C.

3 Fifty-five million people .... in Great Britain.

4 In Great Britain, some children .... school at 4 years old.

5 The word 'sputnik' .... from Russian.

6 Every day, 100 tons of stones .... from space to Earth.

3   In Brazil

Write the correct form of the verb.

Brazil .... (be) a very big country. It ....

(be) in South America. About 150 million people ....

(live) there. They .... (speak) Portuguese. Most of

Brazil .... (have) a tropical climate.

In Rio de Janeiro, for example, it is unusual if the temperature

.... (fall) below 18°C or .... (rise)

above 30°C. Many beautiful plants and animals ....

(live) in Brazil and agriculture .... (be) very important.

Brazil is the world's largest exporter of coffee. It also

.... (sell) sugar, cocoa, wood, fruit and many

other things.

4   All about you

Answer the questions with complete sentences.

1 Are you a teacher?

   No, I'm not a teacher. I'm a student.

2 Do you live in China?

3 Are you 65 years old?

4 Can you drive a car?

5 Have you got an elephant at home?

6 Do you go to school in a helicopter?

7 Do you drink cola for breakfast?

Language worksheet 2.2 *Present simple questions and pronouns*

Summary

You can make **questions** with 'be', 'have got' and 'can' like this:

You are English.   You can play tennis.   You have got a dog.

Are you from London?   Can you play basketball?   Have you got a cat?

Other verbs use 'does' (for 'he', 'she' and 'it') or 'do' (for 'I', 'you', 'we', and 'they'):

You live in Spain.   She likes swimming.   They walk to school at 7.30.

Do you live in Madrid?   Does he like football?   Do they start school at 8am?

You can add question words.

Where do polar bears live?   What do snakes eat?   When does your cat sleep?

Possessive pronouns. Can you complete the sentences?

I go to this school and this is *my* classroom.   *This dog* eats a lot and this is .... food.
You live in this road and this is .... house.   *We* go to school by bus. Here are .... tickets.
He likes English and this is .... book.   *They* write to me often and this is .... letter.
She has a walkman and this is .... cassette.

See also pages 89–90 in your Workbook.

1 Match the answers to the questions

1 Where is the River Amazon?   **a** More than one million
2 Who is on the British money?   **b** Because it's too hot
3 What is the capital of China?   outside.
4 Why do people live   **c** Fish.
   underground in Coober?   **d** Beijing.
5 How many legs does a crab have?   **e** Queen Elizabeth.
6 What does a penguin eat?   **f** Six.
7 How many kinds of insects are there? **g** In Brazil.

2 What are the questions?

Read about hummingbirds. Write the questions that the text answers.

1 Where ...?   4 What ...?
2 Where ...?   5 Why ...?
3 How big ...?   6 Why ...?

Hummingbirds are very beautiful. They live in North and South America[1]. They are not very big. The smallest hummingbird comes from Cuba and it is only 6 cm long[2]. The largest hummingbird is 21 cm long[3]. They drink nectar and eat small insects[4]. They move their wings fast so that they can stay in the same place in the air[5]. They have a long beak so they can drink from flowers[6].

3 Thanks for your letter

Read George's letter. Write a pronoun in the spaces.

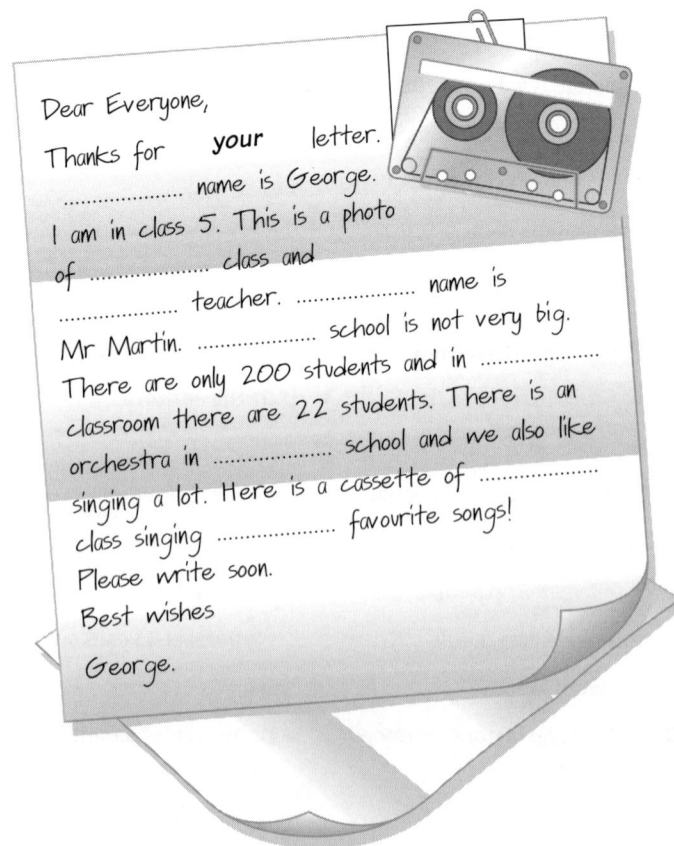

Dear Everyone,
Thanks for **your** letter.
.... name is George.
I am in class 5. This is a photo
of .... class and
.... teacher. .... name is
Mr Martin. .... school is not very big.
There are only 200 students and in ....
classroom there are 22 students. There is an
orchestra in .... school and we also like
singing a lot. Here is a cassette of ....
class singing .... favourite songs!
Please write soon.
Best wishes

George.

PHOTOCOPIABLE
© Cambridge University Press 1996

Language worksheet 2.3 *Present continuous and comparatives*

Summary

You use the **Present continuous** to talk about something that is happening *now*.

You are reading this.   I am looking at this paper.

You can also use it to talk about plans.

What are you doing tomorrow?   I'm going to the cinema.

You can **compare** things by putting '-er' and '-est' at the end of short adjectives. You use 'more' and 'the most' to make comparisons with long adjectives.

big   Mexico City is bigger than London. It is the biggest city in the world.
expensive   Gold is more expensive than iron. It is one of the most expensive metals.

Adjectives that end in 'y' change to 'i'.

sunny   It's sunnier today than yesterday.

'Good' and 'bad' are different.

good ——→ better ——→ the best   bad ——→ worse ——→ the worst

See also pages 90–91 in your Workbook.

1 A football game

Look at the TV pictures. Write what is happening.

1 ....   2 ....   3 ....   4 ....

5 ....   6 ....   7 ....   8 It's a goal!

2 What's happening?

Look around you now. What is happening at this moment? Write five sentences.

My friend is reading a book.   The teacher is talking to Anna.

3 Your plans

Think about tomorrow, next week, next month and next year. What plans have you got? Write about them.

Tomorrow, I'm meeting my friend at the cinema.

Next summer, we're going to the seaside.

4 Two houses

Look at these two houses. How many differences can you write about? You can use these words:

old   small   ugly   short   modern   big   beautiful   expensive
tall   cheaper

Mrs Brown's house

£ 250,000

Mrs White's house

£ 2,000

Mrs Brown's house is bigger than Mrs White's house.

Language worksheet 4.1 *'Special verbs'*

Summary

Some verbs in English are '**special**'. The verb *after* them usually has '–ing' at the end. Most of these verbs are about likes and dislikes:

love   hate   like   don't like   don't mind   enjoy

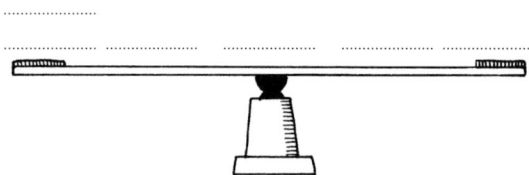

or about starting and stopping:

start   stop   continue   finish   begin

I like playing the guitar.
I enjoy going to school.
I started playing football when I was three years old.

See also page 91 in your Workbook.

1   From left to right

Look. We can put verbs in a logical order.

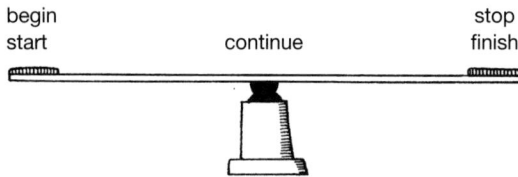

begin   stop
start   continue   finish

Now put these verbs in a logical order.

love   hate   like   don't like   don't mind   enjoy

2   All about you

Write your answers to the questions. Use full sentences.

I love playing the piano.

AN INTERVIEW WITH ....
....

1 What do you love doing in your free time?
....

2 What do you hate doing?
....

3 When did you start going to school?
....

4 What do you enjoy doing at school?
....

5 What don't you like doing at school?
....

3   In the park

Look at the picture. Write a sentence about each person. Use these verbs.

love   like   don't mind   don't like   hate

They love playing football.

PHOTOCOPIABLE   © Cambridge University Press 1996

Language worksheet 4.2 *Adverbs*

Summary

Adverbs describe a verb. They usually come *after* the verb. For most adverbs, you add '–ly' to the adjective, or '–ily' if the adjective ends with 'y'.

quiet ⟶ quietly   She is talking very quietly.   I can't hear her.

angry ⟶ angrily   The man shouted very angrily at the children.

Some adverbs are different!

good ⟶ well   fast ⟶ fast   hard ⟶ hard

She paints very well.   I can run very fast.   He works very hard.

See also page 91 in your Workbook.

1   A letter from an English student

Put the adverbs in the correct place. Read the letter carefully! Use *all* the words.

clearly   hard   quickly   carefully   quickly   slowly   well

Dear Serena

How are you?
I'm learning English at school. Everybody in my class enjoys the lessons very much and they work very ....
Our teacher speaks ...., so it is easy for us to understand. The people on the cassette speak very ...., but sometimes I think they talk very .... We get lots of homework and I always do it .... because I want to learn .... I want to speak English ....! Are you learning English?
I hope so, because this letter is in English!
Best wishes,

Elisabeta

2   Groups of adverbs

Look at these adjectives. Write the adverbs in the correct circle.

quiet   happy   heavily   dangerous   wonderful   bad   loud
slow   fast   good   sleepy   hard

'–ily'   '–ly'   Adverbs that
                                   are different

Look at pages 32 and 33 in your Student's Book. Can you add some more adverbs into the circles?

3   How are they speaking?

Match the adverbs to the pictures.

The person is talking …

sleepily   angrily   happily   slowly   fast   loudly

a   Good morning!

b   HellomynameisLindaSmith.

c   Hello, boys and girls!

d   What are you doing?

e   Hello – my – name – is – Jack – Brown.

f   Can you hear me?

Language worksheet 9.1 'Was' and 'were'

Summary

'**Was**' and '**were**' are past forms of 'be'. Can you complete the table?

I	was				
You	....	at home yesterday.	We	....	at home yesterday.
He	....	not very well last night.	You	....	not very well last night.
She	....	12 years old in 1995.	They	....	12 years old in 1995.
It	....				

See also page 92 in your Workbook.

1 At the time of the dinosaurs

Read more about the dinosaurs. Write 'was', 'wasn't', 'were', or 'weren't' for each space.

AT THE TIME OF DINOSAURS

TWO HUNDRED MILLION YEARS AGO, the world ...(1)... a very different place. There ...(2)... only one continent then, called 'Pangaea', and the climate ...(3)... very different from now. It ...(4)... very, very hot. There ...(5)... any people on Earth. At that time, there ...(6)... many different types of dinosaurs.

Some dinosaurs ...(7)... very big, but other dinosaurs ...(8)... very small. One of the smallest dinosaurs ...(9)... the Compsognathus. It ...(10)... only 50 cm long and it ...(11)... very heavy – only 4 kg. One of the biggest dinosaurs ...(12)... the Apatosaurus. It ...(13)... very big and very, very heavy – more than 30,000 kg! Its head ...(14)... long and thin and it moved very slowly.

There ...(15)... also many dangerous dinosaurs. The Tyrannosaurus Rex ...(16)... the biggest meat-eating animal of all time. It ...(17)... about 10 metres long and it ...(18)... very friendly!

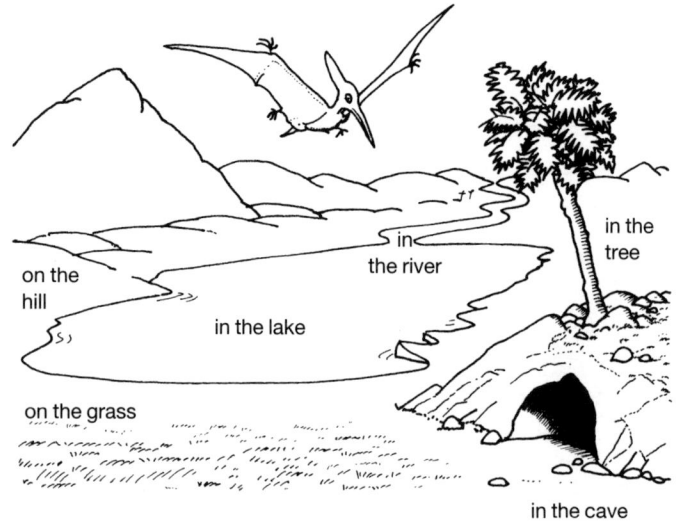

in
the river

on the
hill

in the
tree

in the lake

on the grass

in the cave

Now, take turns to ask questions.

Was Dr Zoom in the river?

Yes, they were!

No, she wasn't. Were the dinosaurs in the lake?

2 Play a game with a friend! Time traveller

Imagine that you have travelled back 150 million years with Dr Zoom, and her assistant, Jim. Suddenly a giant pterodactyl appeared. Where was everybody? First, write a different name in each place in the picture. Don't let your friend see!

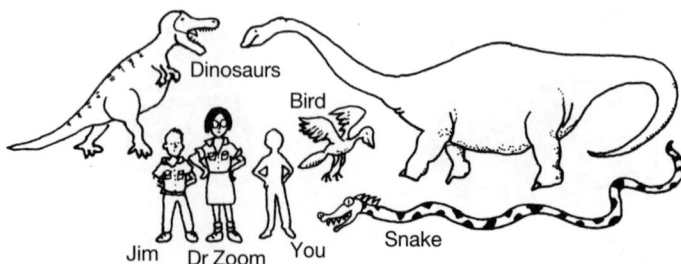

Dinosaurs

Bird

Jim   Dr Zoom   You   Snake

The winner is the first person to find three correct names and places. Mark your partner's answers in the box – ✓ if you are right, ✗ if you are wrong.

	cave	lake	tree	grass	river	hill
Dr Zoom						
Jim						
the dinosaurs						
the bird						
the snake						
your friend						

PHOTOCOPIABLE

© Cambridge University Press 1996

Language worksheet 9.2 *Past simple regular verbs*

Summary

> Many verbs in English end with '–ed'. We call these verbs **'regular' verbs**. We use '–ed' for all persons.
>
> I listened to the radio last night.
> My sister and I talked to my grandmother on the telephone yesterday.
> She started swimming when she was nine years old.
>
> See also page 92 in your Workbook.

1 A puzzle

Write the Past tense of the verbs in the puzzle.

1

2

3

4

5 Dinosaurs l................. millions of years ago.
6 An apatosaurus m..................... very slowly.
7 Many dinosaurs w..................... plant eaters.
8

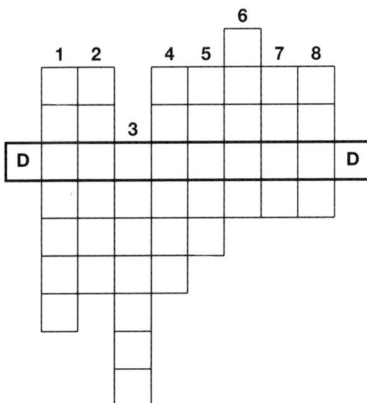

2 A true story!

Read the story and put the verbs in the correct form.

IN THE MOUNTAINS

Some years ago, two men .... (want) to go walking in a national park in Canada. When they .... (arrive) at the park, they .... (talk) to the people in the office there. The people in the office said it was very dangerous in the mountains. 'There are many bears here', they said. 'Cook all your food a long way from your tent and put your food in a bag in a tree.'

The two men .... (walk) in the mountains for many hours. It was a beautiful, warm day. They .... (stop) and .... (cook) some food and then .... (walk) again, higher and higher into the mountains. It .... (start) to become very cold so they .... (stop) and put up their tent. They .... (climb) inside and went to sleep.

About two o'clock in the morning, there was a strange noise. Scrrrrrrr! The men .... (open) their eyes. It was a noise ... like a bear! Then, something .... (push) on the walls of the tent! Scrrrrrrr, down the walls of the tent! The men were very frightened. They .... (wait) quietly. Then the thing pushed the wall of the tent in again. Scrrrrrrr! Down the walls of the tent, again.

Scrrrrrrr! Then, nothing. They .... (wait) and .... (wait) but the noise stopped. Tired, the men went to sleep again.

In the morning, the men .... (open) their tent slowly. They

.... (look) outside and there, in front of them, they saw ... snow on the ground!

What do you think the noise was?

© Cambridge University Press 1996　　**PHOTOCOPIABLE**

Language worksheet 14.1 *Past simple irregular verbs*

Summary

Many verbs in English end with '-ed' in the Past.

I walk to school every day.   I walk**ed** to school yesterday.

Some verbs are '**irregular**'. They don't end with '-ed'.

I come home from school by bus.   I **came** home by bus yesterday.

The Past form is the same for all persons.
Complete the list with the Past forms of the verbs.

become ⟶ *became* begin ⟶ .... buy ⟶ .... come ⟶ .... drink
⟶ .... eat ⟶ .... find ⟶ .... get ⟶ .... go ⟶ ___
have ⟶ .... make ⟶ .... put ⟶ .... see ⟶ .... speak
⟶ .... wear ⟶ ....

See also page 92 in your Workbook.

1 What's the verb?

1.1 Write the verb and the Past tense under each picture.

find, found   write ....

....

....

....

1.2 Write the Past tense of the verbs in the correct spaces.

come   be   eat   drink   write   see   buy   find

Dear Simon,

Thanks for your letter. I .... it on the table when I
.... home from school. It .... great to hear
from you. Thanks for the photos of our camping holiday. I
looked at them while I .... a piece of cake and
.... a glass or milk. I really laughed! I ....
a letter to you last week, but I can't find it! Yesterday, I
.... a book in a shop for you and I .... it.
We can use it on our next camping holiday. It's called
'Better Campfire Cooking'. I hope you like it!

Write soon

David

2 Some more irregular verbs

2.1 Make the pyramids match. Put the blocks in the correct place.

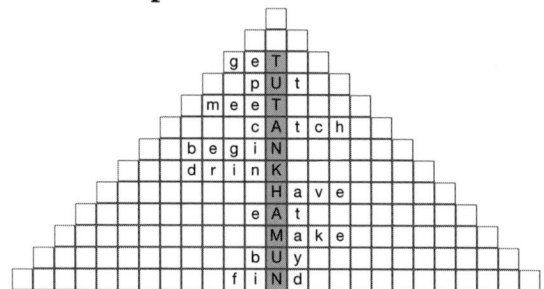

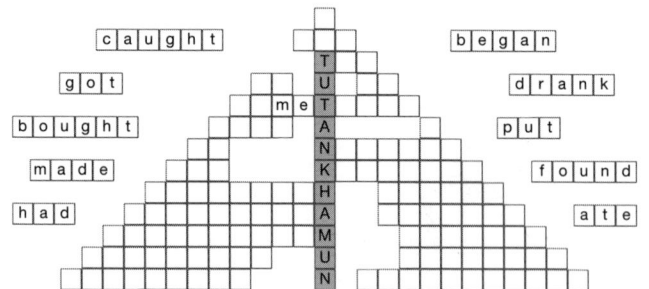

```
                g e T
                p U t
            m e e T
                c A t c h
            b e g i N
            d r i n K
                H a v e
                e A t
                M a k e
                b U y
                f i N d
```

```
    c a u g h t              b e g a n

    g o t                    d r a n k
            m e T
                U
    b o u g h t    T        p u t
                A
    m a d e        N        f o u n d
                K
    h a d          H        a t e
                A
                M
                U
                N
```

2.2 Write the verbs in the text.

Archaeologists first .... (come) to Egypt about 300 years
ago to study the pyramids. About 4,500 years ago the Egyptians
built more than 20 pyramids and they .... (put) many
things inside. Archaeologists .... (find) gold, Egyptian
writing and pictures in the pyramids. We know that Egyptians
.... (eat) many different things. There .... (be) a lot
of fish in the River Nile and they .... (have) gardens for
vegetables. They .... (go) to many different countries and
.... (buy) metals and perfumes there.

PHOTOCOPIABLE   © Cambridge University Press 1996

Language worksheet 14.2 *Past simple questions and negatives*

Summary

You can make a **question in the Past tense** with 'did' and the infinitive form of the verb. You use 'did' for all persons. You can make a **negative** sentence with 'did not' or 'didn't' and the infinitive form of the verb. You can also put a question word at the beginning of a question.

a Did you see the News last night?
No, I didn't watch television yesterday.
c Where did you go last night?

b Did they have cars 10,000 years ago?
No, they didn't have the wheel!
d How did they travel?

See also page 92 in your Workbook.

1 Make a question

Fill in the gaps to answer the question.

1 .... they win the football match yesterday?

No, they lost!

2 .... get up early this morning?

No. I got up very late.

3 .... finish Unit 15 last week?

No, we didn't. We finished Unit 14.

4 .... find many old things in Egypt?

Yes, she found some pots and jewellery.

5 .... go to the cinema on Saturday?

No. He went to the swimming pool.

6 .... tell Jack about the party?

No, I didn't see him yesterday.

2 Write a question

Write a question for the answer.

1 ....

No. I went to bed early

2 ....

No. Peter helped me with my homework

3 ....

No. She came to school on the bus.

4 ....

Yes. I brought the red umbrella.

5 ....

Yes. They started to use telescopes 3,000 years ago.

3 A history test

Match the questions and the answers.

1 When did the first people live in America?
2 Did they go by ship?
3 Where did people first use money?
4 Who did the Romans fight?
5 Why did the Egyptians build the pyramids?

a They fought against all their neighbours.
b People used metal coins and money 4,800 years ago in the Middle East.
c People started to live there about 28,000 years ago.
d They built them for the kings.
e No, they walked across a bridge of land from Asia.

4 That's wrong!

The facts in these sentences are wrong. Correct them! Use full sentences.

The French had the first newspaper. (The Chinese)

The French didn't have the first newspaper!
The Chinese had the first newspaper.

1 The Japanese built a wall across their country. (The Chinese)

....

....

2 The Olympic Games began in France. (Greece)

....

3 The Spanish built many roads in Britain. (The Romans)

....

4 The Russians went to the moon first. (The Americans)

....

© Cambridge University Press 1996

PHOTOCOPIABLE

Language worksheet 19.1 'Going to'

Summary

You can use '**going to**' in two ways.

To talk about *future plans*:

I'm going to watch the film tonight.

To talk about things that are certain to happen:

Look at that cloud! It's going to rain.

Negatives and questions are easy.

Are you going to do your homework?
It isn't going to rain. It's going to snow!

See also pages 92–93 in your Workbook.

1 Questions and answers

Match the questions with the answers.

1 What are you going to do after school?
2 Which Unit are we going to do next week?
3 Where is that plane going to land?
4 When is the bus going to leave?
5 Why are they going to build a new road here?

a Because they are going to build a new factory here.
b I don't know! Ask the driver.
c We are going to do Unit 20.
d I am going to play the guitar at home.
e I think it's going to land in Paris.

2 A week in the life of Sue

Look at Sue's diary. Write her answers to Pete's questions.

OCTOBER	
15 Monday	
16 Tuesday	Swimming lesson, 3pm—5pm
17 Wednesday	Revise for test!
18 Thursday	Open evening at school.
19 Friday	
20 Saturday	
21 Sunday	

PETE: Hi, Sue. How are you?

SUE: Fine, thanks.

PETE: It's my birthday on Tuesday. Can you come to my
        party after school?

SUE: ....

PETE: Oh dear. Well, we're going to see a film on
        Wednesday evening. Can you come?

SUE: ....

PETE: You're very busy. What about Thursday evening?

SUE: ....

PETE: Are you free on Friday?

SUE: ....

PETE: Oh no! I'm going to visit my grandparents on
        Friday. I'm going to stay there until Sunday
        evening.

SUE: Ring me next week!

3 What do you say?

Read the sentences. Write your reply.

The sky is very black.   → It's going to rain.

She's driving too fast.   → [   ]

They never do
their homework.   → [   ]

There is a lot of smoke
coming out of the volcano.   → [   ]

He's carrying too
many books.   → [   ]

It's ten to nine and she's in bed.
School starts at 9 o'clock.   → [   ]

PHOTOCOPIABLE

© Cambridge University Press 1996

Language worksheet 19.2 *'Have to'*

Summary

You can use '**have to/has to**' to describe something that it is necessary to do.

Children have to go to school.

You make negatives with 'don't' or 'doesn't'.

I don't have to work today. It's Saturday.
She doesn't have to do any homework in the holidays.

You make questions with 'do' or 'does':

Do you have to clean your bedroom every day?
When does she have to go home?

The past of 'have to' is 'had to'.

When I was young, I had to walk 4 kilometres to school.

See also page 93 in your Workbook.

1 Who are they?

1.1 Match the description with the people.

1 They have to listen to teachers.   a cavepeople.
2 They have to milk the cows.   b miners.
3 They have to fly to many different countries. c students.
4 They have to go underground.   d farmers.
5 They had to kill wild animals for food.   e pilots.

1.2 What do they have to do?

Write about these people.

police officers   doctors   lorry drivers   scientists   waiters
writers   film directors   journalists

....
....
....
....
....
....
....
....

1.3 What do you have to do? Write about yourself

....
....
....

2 In the town

Look at the picture. Write about each person.

He has to
deliver the
letters.

3 Two hundred years ago

Two hundred years ago in England, life was very different.
Look at the picture and write about what people had to do.

Two hundred years ago people had to ... They ...

....
....

Language worksheet 24.1 *'Could' and 'Would'*

Summary

You use '**could**' when you ask someone to do something.

Could you open the door for me please?

You use 'would' when you offer something to someone.

Would you like a sandwich? ('Would you like' + noun)
Would you like to play football with us? ('Would you like to' + verb)

See also page 93 in your Workbook.

1 What are they saying?

Match the sentences to the pictures.

a Could you dry the dishes, please?
b Could you post this letter for me?
c Could you lend me some money?
d Could I use your telephone, please?
e Could you open the door for me, please?

2 What do you say?

Write what you can say in these situations.

a You missed your bus. You ask someone to take you to school.

   Could you ....

b You want your penfriend to send you a photograph.

   ....

c You are very hungry. Your friend is eating some sandwiches.

   ....

d You didn't bring your dictionary to the English lesson.

   ....

3 Make an offer

Read the replies. Write the offers.

1 ....

   Yes, please. I love swimming.

2 ....

   No thanks. I saw that film last week.

3 ....

   Oh thanks. A cup of hot chocolate, please.

4 ....

   Well, yes please, but I don't know much about computers.

5 ....

   No thanks. I don't like that kind of music much.

6 ....

   Yes please! Is it your birthday?

PHOTOCOPIABLE

© Cambridge University Press 1996

Language worksheet 24.2 *Asking the way*

Summary

You can **ask the way** like this:

Excuse me. Could you tell me where ... is? Excuse me. Where can I find ...?

Write the correct preposition under each picture.

on the right of   next to   on the left of   behind   in front of

See also page 95 in your Workbook.

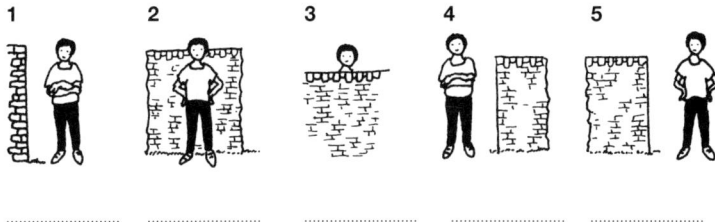

1	2	3	4	5
....	....	....	....	....

1 Where can we get these things?

Make lists of the things you can buy in each shop. Use your dictionary!

plasters apples postcards bread toothpaste milk stamps soap envelopes potatoes newspapers a birthday cake oranges magazines shampoo sugar peas biscuits

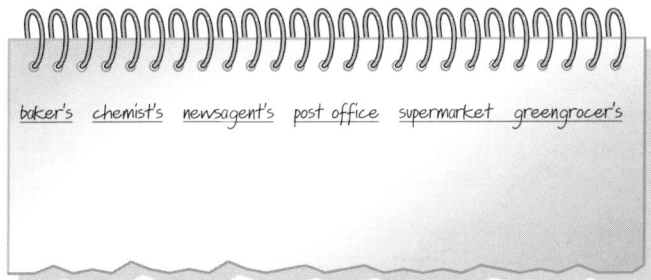

baker's   chemist's   newsagent's   post office   supermarket   greengrocer's

2 Where is it?

Look at the map and read the dialogues. Mark the shops on the map.

1
Excuse me, where can we find a supermarket?
There's a big one in Broad Street, opposite the cinema.

3
Excuse me, we're looking for a newsagent's.
Oh, yes. There's one in Silver Street, next to the bank.

5
Excuse me, do you know where we can buy some stamps?
Go to the Post Office. It's in Broad Street opposite the swimming pool.

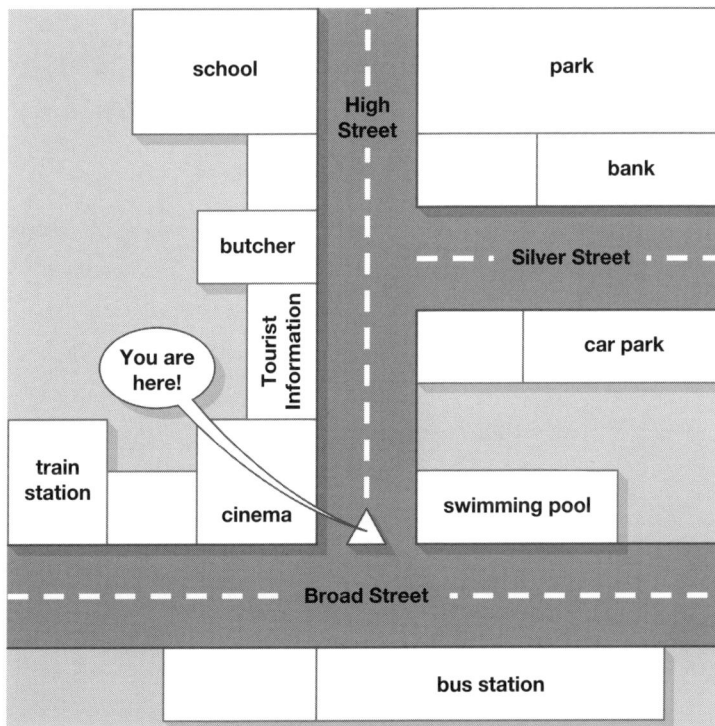

2
Excuse me, where can we find a chemist's?
There's one in the High Street, next to the butcher's.

4
Excuse me, we're looking for a greengrocer's.
Yes, there's one here in the High Street, opposite the Tourist Information.

6
Excuse me, where can we find a baker's?
Here! Next to the cinema.

Map labels: school, park, High Street, bank, butcher, Silver Street, Tourist Information, car park, You are here!, train station, cinema, swimming pool, Broad Street, bus station

3 Now you try it!

Read the answers and write the questions.

1 ....

It's in Broad Street, opposite the Post Office.

2 ....

Yes, it's in Broad Street, next to the baker's.

3 ....

Yes, there's a big one in Silver Street, opposite the bank.

4 ....

Yes, it's in the High Street, next to the butcher's.

5 ....

There's one in Broad Street, next to the Post Office.

© Cambridge University Press 1996

PHOTOCOPIABLE

Language worksheet 29.1 *Past continuous*

Summary

> You can use the **Past continuous** to describe the background for another action.
>
> They were sleeping when the noise woke them up.
> I was listening to my new cassette when my friend came.
> You walked into that wall because you weren't looking where you were going!
>
> See also page 93 in your Workbook.

1 What were they doing?

Look at the pictures. What were these people doing when the blackout happened? Match each sentence to one of the pictures.

1
> I was driving my car.

2
> I was doing some exercises.

3
> I was having a bath.

4
> I was getting dressed.

5
> I was repairing my bicycle.

What are the other people saying? Write a sentence for each person.

....

....

....

....

2 Use your imagination! Write a story!

First, write some notes.

Choose a time: early in the morning   at lunchtime   in the afternoon   in the evening   at night …

Choose a place: in a town   in the countryside   on the beach in a space rocket   in a school   on a boat …

Choose some characters: a man   a woman   a boy   a girl a dog   a cat …

What was happening?   What were they doing?   Brainstorm your ideas.
the wind was blowing   the sun was shining   people were singing they were playing a game   they were talking   they were making something   they were watching TV   they were having a party …

And then … what happened?
The lights went out.   There was an explosion.   The telephone rang.   An elephant walked into the room …

Now, use your notes to write a short story.

It was early in the morning, on the first day of the year. The town was very quiet. A man and a woman were walking with their dog. They were talking about the party. Somewhere, a bird was singing. It was very cold, but the sun was coming up. Suddenly, a big black car stopped next to them. 'Hey, you!', a voice said. 'Come here!' ....

....

....

....

....

PHOTOCOPIABLE

© Cambridge University Press 1996

Language worksheet 29.2 *Asking the way (2)*

Summary

Match the drawings to the directions.

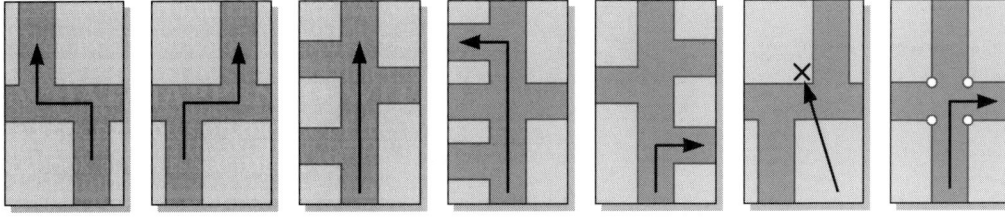

a ☐ Turn left and then right.
b ☐ Go straight on.
c ☐ Take the first turning on the right.
d ☐ Turn right and then left.

e ☐ Turn right at the traffic lights.
f ☐ It's on the corner.
g ☐ Take the third turning on the left.

See also page 95 in your Workbook.

1 Where am I going?

Look at the map. Read the directions. Where am I going?

a *I'm at place 1.*
Go straight on and take the second on the right. Then take the first turning on the right again. It's in Old Street.

....

b *I'm at place 3.*
Go straight on and turn left. That's New Street. Take the third turning on the left. It's there, on the right.

....

c *I'm at place 5.*
Go straight on and turn left at the traffic lights. Turn right again. It's opposite the newsagent's.

....

2 Can you tell me the way to ...

Write directions to the following places.

a We are at place 4. Can you tell me the way to the nearest chemist's?

....

b We are at place 2. Can you tell us where the Tourist Information is?

....

c We are at place 6. Can you tell me where the Sports Centre is?

....

....

d We are at place 1. Can you tell us where the nearest supermarket is?

....

....

e We are at place 3. Can you tell us how to get to the swimming pool?

....

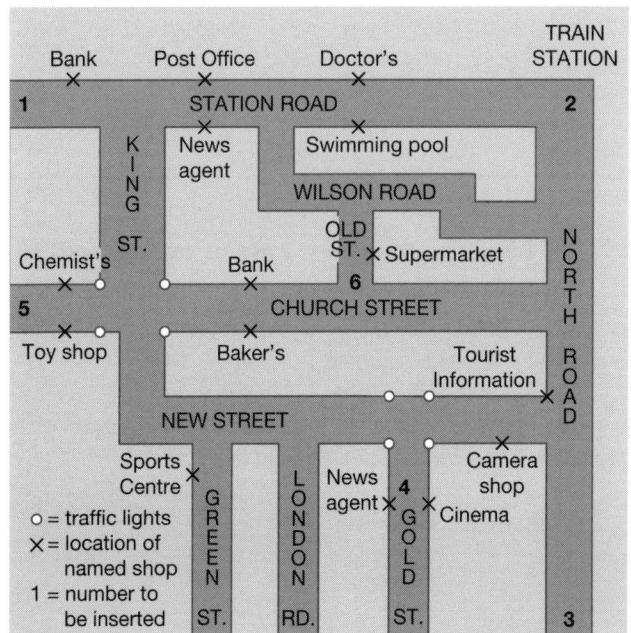

© Cambridge University Press 1996

PHOTOCOPIABLE

Say it clearly! Worksheet 1

THEME A

1 Sounds practised in Unit 3 /ɪŋ/

1.1 📼 **Listen. Say 'ing' clearly.**

Swimming, cycling, running and walking are all good for you.
Eating and sleeping are good for you, too!
What are you doing?
I am sitting here.
I am saying these words.
I am learning English.

2 Sounds practised in Unit 4 /liː/, /ɪliː/

2.1 📼 **Listen. What word do you hear – an adjective or an adverb? Put a tick [✓].**

1	dangerous ☐	dangerously ☐	5	easy ☐	easily ☐
2	slow ☐	slowly ☐	6	angry ☐	angrily ☐
3	quiet ☐	quietly ☐	7	noisy ☐	noisily ☐
4	happy ☐	happily ☐	8	beautiful ☐	beautifully ☐

2.2 📼 **Say the adjectives and the adverbs.**

slow	slowly	He speaks very slowly.
quiet	quietly	They are working quietly in the library.
happy	happily	I go happily to school every day.
easy	easily	I can do this exercise easily.

THEME B

3 Sounds practised in Unit 8 /e/, /ɑː/

3.1 📼 **Listen and say the words. Smile and show your teeth!**

/e/ pet let get very merry net went men better bed head
He went to get his pet a better bed.
Have a very merry Christmas!

Open your mouth wide and say /ɑː/.
/ɑː/ dark part hard barn park postcard class pass large plant
There's a large plant in the barn.
I've got a postcard of the park.

3.2 📼 **Listen. Underline the word you hear.**

| 1 pet part | 2 head hard | 3 peck park |
| 4 deck dark | 5 Ben barn | 6 pet park |

4 Sounds practised in Unit 9 '-ed': /t/, /ɪd/, /d/

4.1 📼 **Listen to the three ways of saying '-ed' in English. Say each word.**

/t/ looked asked liked
/ɪd/ visited wanted studied
/d/ stayed changed played
I asked my friend yesterday if she wanted to play football.
I visited my friend's house and I stayed the night.

4.2 📼 **Put these verbs in the correct list.**

Listen and check your answers.

landed discovered watched climbed happened washed talked dropped crashed disappeared lived died

/t/ watched ....

/ɪd/ landed ....

/d/ discovered ....

PHOTOCOPIABLE © Cambridge University Press 1996

Say it clearly! Worksheet 2

THEME C

1 Sounds practised in Unit 13

/ɔː/

1.1 🔊 **Listen. Say the words. They all have the same vowel sound. Open your mouth!**

door   four   saw   poor   more   before   or   floor

1.2 🔊 **Listen and say the words. Underline the word that has a different vowel sound. For example:**

four   <u>fire</u>   more

1 bought   poor   word   **3** or   are   paw   **5** paws   doors   eyes
2 saw   door   far   **4** ear   more   before   **6** for   or   fly

2 Sounds practised in Unit 14

made /eɪ/, had /æ/

2.1 **'Made' has a long 'a' sound. 'Mad' has a short 'a' sound.**

🔊 Listen and say the words.

Long: made   came   cake   late   wait   hate
Short: mad   bad   band   happy   fat   hat

2.2 🔊 **Say the words. Put them in the correct list.**

bad   bake   bat   lake   mat   name   plate   rat   sad   snake   cat   take

Check with your neighbour. Then listen and check your answers.

Long: ....

Short: ....

THEME D

3 Sounds practised in Unit 18

eat /iː/, weather /e/

3.1 🔊 **Listen. Say the words.**

/iː/ eat   heat   leaf   meal   meat
/e/ weather   dead   leather   head
/eə/ bear

3.2 Put the words in the circles.

beach   feather   health   heat   pear   please   repeat   weak   wear

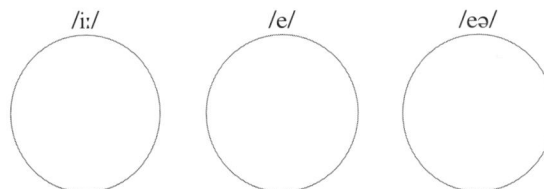

/iː/   /e/   /eə/

( )   ( )   ( )

🔊 **Listen and check your answers.**

4 Sounds practised in Unit 19

/h/

4.1 🔊 **Listen and repeat.**

Breathe out and say /h/.

old   hold   at   hat   it   hit   eat   heat   ear   here

I hear with my ears.   She left her hat at the hospital.
I hit it. It hit me.   We have heads and hands and hearts.

4.2 🔊 **Listen. Underline what you hear.**

1 eat   heat   **4** old   hold
2 it   hit   **5** at   hat
3 ear   hear   **6** and   hand

Say it clearly! Worksheet 3

THEME E

1 Sounds practised in Unit 23   /ə/

1.1 🔲 **Listen and say the words.**

September   October   November   December   computer   sugar
paper   rubber

1.2 🔲 **Read and say the sentences. How many**   2 He calculates the numbers on a computer. ☐
examples of /ə/ can you find? Write the number   3 Where were you last December? ☐
in the box.   4 There is a lot of butter and sugar in this cake. ☐

1 His birthday's on November the fourth. ☐

2 Sshh!   /ʃ/

2.1 🔲 **Listen and repeat. Say /ʃ/ clearly.**   **2.2** 🔲 **Listen. What word can you hear? Tick (✓)**
A dictionary helps you learn English.   **the box.**

Is television good for education?   1 chair ☐ share ☐   4 ship ☐ chip ☐

English is useful for international communication.   2 shoe ☐ chew ☐   5 sheep ☐ cheap ☐

                                                         3 sure ☐ chore ☐   6 shoes ☐ choose ☐

3 Sounds practised in Unit 24   bus /ʌ/, put /ʊ/

3.1 🔲 **/ʌ/ Listen. Open your mouth and say the words!**

bus   but   enough   jump   under   up   cut some

/ʊ/ Listen. Close your mouth more to say these words.

put   foot   sugar   would   book   look   pull

3.2 Say the sentences and write /ʌ/ or /ʊ/ under the   He cut his foot when he jumped off the bus
words.   []   []   []   []

That's enough sugar!   Would you like some sugar in your drink?
   []   []   []   []   []

THEME F

4 Sounds practised in Unit 28   /s/

🔲 **Say 's' clearly! Read the words and sentences aloud.**

Science   subject   school   Science is my favourite subject at
                                 school.

sand   seaside   summer   I like playing in the sand at the seaside
                                 in summer.

stars   space   shine   The stars in space shine at night.

5 Sounds practised in Unit 29   /tʃ/

🔲 **Listen. Say 'ch' with a /tʃ/ sound.**   Not all 'ch' words have a 'tsh' sound. Say these words.

touch   watch   Don't touch my watch!   character   Christmas   machine   school   echo   chemist
lunch   beach   Let's have lunch at the beach! archaeologist
much   chocolate   Don't eat too much chocolate!

PHOTOCOPIABLE   © Cambridge University Press 1996

Classroom language

This section lists some useful classroom phrases which you can adapt as required.

Brainstorming

Our next topic is …
What do you know about …?
Write down some points/information about …
Let's share some ideas about …
Let's start by putting the topic in the circle.
What can you think of?
Can anyone think of anything else?
Can anyone add anything to that?
Think quietly for a moment or two.
Write down as many ideas as you can in two minutes.
Who wants to say something first?
Let's compare ideas.

Checking answers

Check your answers with your partner.
Give your writing/exercise to your neighbour to check.
The answers are on the board. Check them when you have finished this exercise.
Let's go through your answers now.
There is an answer sheet here. Please pass it round and check your answers.
Work in small groups and check your answers together. I'll come round and help you.
If you have any problems put your hand up/ask me at the end of the lesson.
Did anyone get a different answer?
There are many different possible answers to this question. Let's see how many we can get.
Does everyone understand this exercise?

Discipline

Let's be quiet now, please!
Come on, come on, settle down now, please.
Ssshhh, please.
There's a lot of noise in here today!
Lets get down to some work now, please.
I think we can all work better when it's quieter.
The pairwork is not going very well. Why do you think this is?
Perhaps we can discuss why there is so much noise today.
We've got a problem. Our groupwork isn't working. Why is that? Any ideas?
What can we do about it?
Any ideas?

Discussions

Who would like to start?

What would you like to say, X?
Take turns to speak.
Listen to the other students' ideas, too.
Can you speak a little more loudly, please?
Did everyone hear what X said?
Can anyone add anything to that?
Does everyone agree with that?
Who disagrees with that?
Don't worry if you make a mistake. We just want to know your ideas.
Use a word/phrase in (mother tongue) if you don't know what to say.
Say it in (mother tongue).

Error correction

Good/Well done/?Excellent/ That's not bad. Can anyone think of another way to say that?
OK. Do you want to try again?
It's not easy to pronounce that word, is it? Listen to the cassette again.
I think it's probably better to write/say …

Evaluation

What do you think about pairwork/groupwork?
How do you think you can do it better next time?
What do you think was the easiest part of the Unit/exercise?
What do you think would be a better way to do the task next time?

Encouragement

That's a good point.
Well done, that was quite a difficult exercise/word to pronounce/spell.
Yes, excellent!
That was difficult. Well done!

Feedback

I think there are a lot of good ideas.
Do you think it would be a good idea to leave this part out/say more about/move this word …?
How about/what about saying something about …?
What about adding …?

Games

Before you start to play, read the rules.
Would you like to check/translate the rules first?

Do you know what you have to do?
Choose a referee to settle the arguments.
Have you got dice and counters?
Do you think 10 minutes is enough time to play the game?
Don't forget to take it in turns!

Groupwork

Can you get into groups of three or four, please?
Would you like to work in a different group this time?
Find the group you were working with in the last lesson.
If you want to, you can work in groups for this task.

Homework

There are two exercises on … in your Workbook. Choose one for homework.
Finish this exercise for homework, please.
Please do Exercise … for homework.
Please do your homework for Thursday.
Shall we go through this homework in the lesson on Friday?
Exercises x and x in the Workbook give more practice with this vocabulary/grammar.
On Friday we are doing Unit x. Please read it through first.

Listening

Listen to the cassette.
Can you hear the cassette?
Would you like to hear it again?
Read the text first and then we'll listen to the cassette.
Would you like to listen to the cassette before/while/after you read the text?
You can keep your books open while you listen to the cassette.
Do you want to close your books while you listen to the cassette?

Monitoring and guiding

How are you getting on with this …?
Are there any problems with this …?
Is it as easy/difficult as you thought?
Are you helping each other?
Would you like me to help you/suggest anything?
Shall I look at your work now or later?
Do you need more time to finish this?
What kind of mistakes do you think you are making here?

Mother tongue

If you don't know the word in English say it in …
I'll put the English word on the board.
You can write down some ideas in our language first and then we'll translate them.
When shall we use (mother tongue)?
Think about when you use (our language). When you do pairwork, or groupwork, or in an activity? Could you use English instead?

Pairwork

Work with your neighbour.
For this exercise you can work in pairs.
Work with a different partner this time.
Practise the dialogue together.
Check your answers with your neighbour.
Work together for five minutes.
Does everyone know what they have to do?
Has everyone got a partner?

Planning

We have 30 minutes to spare on Thursday. What would you like to do?
On …, we are going to make … . You will need some …
If you have any suggestions or requests, put them in the Suggestion Box.
What shall we try to finish this week?
When shall we collect the homework?

Pronunciation

Shall we say this sound/word together?
Is there a sound like this in our language?
Say it clearly!

Songs

Does anyone know this song/tune?
Let's listen to the song on the cassette first.
Look at the words in your book at the same time.
Do you know any other words for this song?
Can anyone play this on a guitar/violin, etc.?
This half of the class sing the verses, and this half sing the chorus.
If you don't know the words yet, hum like this (mmmmmm).
You can clap to the music first if you like.

Starting the lesson

In this lesson we are going to look at/finish Unit …
Does anyone want to ask anything about the lesson yesterday?
Has everyone got their Workbooks and Student's Books?
If you haven't got your books, share with your partner.
Please turn to Unit … Look at the pictures for a moment. What do you think the Unit is about?

Timing

We're going to work on … now. How long do you think you need?
Let's work on this for 10 minutes and see how far you get.
Tell me when you have finished.
Do you need some more time to finish this?
When you have finished, move to the *Time to spare?* or to the *Language Record*, please.
See how much you can do in 10 minutes.
There are five minutes left. Let's see if we can finish this.